§ Contesting Deregulation §

MAKING SENSE OF HISTORY

Studies in Historical Cultures
General Editor: Stefan Berger
Founding Editor: Jörn Rüsen

Bridging the gap between historical theory and the study of historical memory, this series crosses the boundaries between both academic disciplines and cultural, social, political and historical contexts. In an age of rapid globalization, which tends to manifest itself on an economic and political level, locating the cultural practices involved in generating its underlying historical sense is an increasingly urgent task.

For a full volume listing please see back matter.

CONTESTING DEREGULATION

Debates, Practices and Developments in the West since the 1970s

Edited by Knud Andresen and Stefan Müller

berghahn
NEW YORK · OXFORD
www.berghahnbooks.com

Published in 2017 by
Berghahn Books
www.berghahnbooks.com

Library of Congress Cataloging-in-Publication Data
Names: Andresen, Knud, 1965- editor. | Müller, Stefan, 1966- editor.
Title: Contesting deregulation : debates, practices and developments in
  The West since the 1970s / edited by Knud Andresen and Stefan Müller.
Description: New York : Berghahn Books, 2017. | Series: Making sense of
  history ; volume 31 | Includes bibliographical references and index.
Identifiers: LCCN 2017034069 (print) | LCCN 2017034547 (ebook) | ISBN
  9781785336218 (ebook) | ISBN 9781785336201 (hardback : alk. paper)
Subjects: LCSH: Trade regulation--Case studies. | Deregulation--Case
  studies. | International trade--Case studies.
Classification: LCC HD3612 (ebook) | LCC HD3612 .C66 2017 (print) | DDC
  338.9009182/1--dc23
LC record available at https://lccn.loc.gov/2017034069

British Library Cataloguing in Publication Data
A catalogue record for this book is available from the British Library

ISBN 978-1-78533-620-1 hardback
ISBN 978-1-78533-621-8 ebook

Contents

Tables

Acknowledgements

For the provision and realization of this book, we would like to thank the Hans Böckler Foundation in Düsseldorf, whose generous support enabled its publication. Our special thanks go to Ralf Richter and Nadine Raupach for their support, which also enabled the fine editorial work of James Patterson. Thanks also go to Anna Tartakovskij for reviewing the manuscript. Finally, we would like to thank Berghahn Books for our inclusion in their publication programme, and Stefan Berger for his support.

Contesting Deregulation

The 1970s as a Turning Point in Western History? Introductory Remarks

KNUD ANDRESEN AND STEFAN MÜLLER

Disputing the 1970s

The present-day reality of 'Western' industrialized societies[1] is defined by crisis phenomena. Since the beginning of the financial crisis in 2008, ever-more political crises have been born out of this one economic crisis, above all in the southern countries of the European Union. Yet irrespective of current events and estimations of their short- or even long-term nature, many diagnoses have long painted a pessimistic picture for the Western industrialized societies. Increasing social inequality regarding the distribution of wealth and growing unemployment is exacerbating social tensions, which are combining with problems of democratic legitimation. In 2004, Colin Crouch coined the term 'post-democracy' with this in mind.[2] According to Crouch, no longer is it the citizens who come to political and economic decisions through elections and democratic negotiations, but rather these decisions are being made by experts and multinational companies, who time and again refer to the 'market' as playing the deciding role – with one result being the 'commercialization of citizenship'. The sociologist Wolfgang Streeck has also presented a rather bleak interpretation of the last forty years. The 'final crisis of capitalism' has been held at bay by ever-newer monetary measures – initially by means of inflation during the 1970s, and then debt policy and the expansion of private credit markets, which ultimately led to the crisis in 2008. The greatest danger in doing this is that the new financial market capitalism no longer requires democracy and is able to exist independently.[3] Apparently, according to Crouch, Streeck and many others, neoliberalism now reigns triumphant with its credo being the trickle-down theory: if the wealthy achieve greater gains through tax cuts and reduced fees, then they will generate a general state of prosperity through investments and patronage. The state now only provides the required framework. Competition seems to have permeated all areas of life, including the individual's perception. The German sociologist Ulrich Bröckling, in following Michel Foucault, spoke pronouncedly of an 'entrepreneurial self' as the dominant form of subjectification.[4] The delusion of making individual decisions in a comparable manner to a company has permeated all areas of life. This is the subjective side of the societal changes of social regulation.

The market attempts to harness every social impulse and to turn it into a commodity; to this extent, capitalism no longer merely represents an economic structure but rather a way of life. As such it proves itself to be so flexible that it can also make use of oppositional pronouncements in their varying forms. In the 1980s, Jürgen Habermas spoke of a 'colonization' of living environments.[5] Even when Habermas was concerned with a normative approach, this pointed to the fact that new markets were being accessed in almost all areas of life, including those more intimate as well as family practices and even the large market of consultancy firms.[6]

Whether or not the subjective results of 'neoliberalism' as mentioned at the beginning are to be considered as purely negative is not yet clear. To a certain degree, the idea of denationalization also barely seems appropriate when considering the disappearance of state regulations. International political relations, for example, have become stronger and more effective since the 1970s, in comparison to national state competition. In Europe, the process of unification within the EU has not quite led to an abandonment of sovereignty, but it has however resulted in the reduction of national state regulations, and as such a decrease in inter-state dynamics of conflict.[7] To how great an extent the world economy, as well as the political regulation of it, has become transnational can be observed, according to Akira Iriye, in the financial crisis of 2008. This did not result in a global split or inter-state tensions, but rather in collectively conceived solutions, such as the Chinese support for the leading industrial nations affected by the crisis. The financial crisis did not annul the national regulatory authorities; they rather proved their value in a specific way. To a certain extent, a 'feeling of collective humanity' helped to marginalize post-1945 national resentments.[8] This transnational development is by no means complete, and the fact that inter-state conflicts are not a thing of the past can be seen presently in the Ukraine.

However, present-day political and sociological diagnoses are inscribed with a specific historical narrative. Whether explicitly formulated or taken as an unspoken basis, these analyses assume that the 1970s were a zenith of advancement both economically and in terms of the welfare state, since when we have found ourselves in a long-lasting state of decline. Hyperbolically, the former age appears as a refuge of the welfare state, or, as Eric Hobsbawm called it, 'the golden age of capitalism'.[9] Hence the majority of Western governments after 1945 aimed at diluting the class conflict and relieving social tensions, whereby the difference between the countries tended to be greater than between the respective political parties.[10] The state had a strong regulating and intervening function, and ensured the provision of basic services such as electricity, mobility and telecommunications through monopolies.[11]

These years were associated with an economic boom, in which rising income resulted from a growth in industrial productivity, which in turn led to consumer society becoming a mass phenomenon. The political, social and economic crises of the past, including their consequences of civil war, war and revolution from the time of the 'European Civil War', were consigned to obscurity, and the capitalistic crisis scenarios, mentioned not least by the political left, seemed to no longer apply.[12] Without doubt the neglect and loss of this fear distinguishes the time after 1989 from the decades before.[13] In this respect, history since the 1970s is also a history of neglect, only that the defining landmarks are still to be pinpointed.

The fact that many authors search for a fissure of some nature at the beginning of the 1970s is obvious at first glance, whereby we are concerned with the objective side of the historical narrative and contemporary self-perception. At first there was the initial oil crisis of 1973 and the more confident air of the Arab states. This was a crisis, which is discussed by some historians as spanning seemingly contrasting systems, due to the fact that it created the same problems in the industrialized and capitalist Western states as it did in the communist states.[14] Linked to this was the end of the Bretton Woods system with its exchange rates more closely tied to the gold standard, which nevertheless merely managed to alleviate the crisis of the dollar as the global reserve currency, ongoing to this day, rather than resolve it.[15] Then we have the bleak warnings from the Club of Rome as to the exhaustion of natural resources,[16] and finally the contemporaries themselves are predicting the end of the work-orientated society, as we know it, postulating entry into the 'post-industrial society', as Daniel Bell formulated it.[17] Indeed, such diagnoses and their terms were able to chronicle the end of an era, just as Lyotard's 'postmodernists' could, yet they were unable to characterize the burgeoning new era.[18]

Today it is above all the term – or rather often the buzzword – 'neoliberalism' with which the period since the 1970s is summed up, and the fundamental practice of which has been deregulation. This refers, first and foremost, to political decisions, the result of which has primarily been the privatization of state enterprises in Western countries since the 1980s, and with this the transferral of the provision of basic services onto the free market.[19] At that point in time, these policies were still associated with the political protagonists of the period, either critically with the term Thatcherism or with rather more positive connotations in the case of Reaganomics.[20] In this way we are able to ascertain that even the critically intended terms have themselves been assimilated into the abstracting logic of globalization. The changes since the (late) 1970s are no longer described with terms correlating to the protagonists of the age, but are instead ascribed to an anonymous process of globalization. At this juncture we do not wish to follow the discussion as to what extent globalization can be seen as a far older process of global trade relationships.[21] The following will be used to discuss the latest advance of globalization, which is defined among other things by improved telecommunications, quicker logistics systems and international work-related migration, with a focus not only on emigration. In this context, we also wish to deal with overcoming narrow national state horizons as a mental process.

Yet irrespective of this shift in analysis and discourse to an anonymous process, the desire for deregulation came from a nucleus, social in nature and far removed from economic interests. Critics on both the left and the right saw the state as too powerful. To loosen its grasp and to remodel it from an interventional and regulatory state into a merely controlling state seemed to enable new individual liberties. This was not a case of denationalization, but instead a concentration of state activities to support the processes of social change with an increase in the juridification of everyday life.

Questions and Objectives of this Volume

With this collection of works and by means of several case studies, we wish to pick up on a part of this period in history since the 1970s, which can also be characterized as the triumphant advance of 'neoliberalism'. Our interest lies in the shifted national and international modes of social regulation between the new paradigms of competition and denationalization. We ask whether and with what influence 'neoliberal' ideas have come to define forms of social regulation since the 1970s; and we ask whether this is related to older traditions, to which a breakthrough was only achieved at the end of the '*Trente Glorieuses*' or whether these are, in fact, completely new forms of social control. [22]

In their examination of the discourse and practices of regulation and deregulation, the essays in this volume concern themselves with a wide contemporary historical debate as to the character of the 1970s. Can the decade be, above all, characterized by its diverse cultural shifts, which were evident in new social movements, changing values and the individualization of lifestyles, and ultimately, with the onset of economic crisis, the loss of optimism about the future?[23] Or does this decade, above all, mark the beginning of a new epoch, whose technical foundation lay in computer technology, which not only enabled rationalization within industrial production but also an immense acceleration in channels of communication and social regulation? What remains beyond dispute is that an economic backlash was observed following the years of the boom. The end of the Bretton Woods system altered global economic relationships. Niall Ferguson writes of a 'shock of the global' in relation to the 1970s, yet he also points to the fact that it was, in part, rather more a perceived crisis than a real crisis.[24]

Then there was the decline of certain traditional industries in the 1970s, with grave rises in unemployment accompanied by the emergence of new service industries, which not only were but remain precarious in nature. In addition, it is rightly pointed out that the European working practice of a lengthy professional life with a guaranteed pension constitutes the exception rather than the rule when adopting a global perspective.[25] In this way, the German contemporary historians Anselm Doering-Manteuffel and Lutz Raphael speak of a *Strukturbruch* ('structural rupture') or 'discontinuation of traditional structures', which began to become apparent in the 1970s. The industrial world of work lost its dominant character in the Western states; but it was less a beginning of deindustrialization and more a fundamental change by means of the microchip production process. Doering-Manteuffel and Raphael diagnosed a 'digital stock market capitalism', which replaced the industrial nature of post-war capitalism up to this point, seeing as the 'social concept of neoliberalism' negates 'Keynes' and 'consensus'.[26] In doing this, many authors name 1973 as a turning point, or use the year as a fixed point, in order to reconcile these various fissures.[27] In contrast, other authors observe slower processes during the 1970s. Hartmut Kaelble believes it is more a matter of a 'soft turning point' in terms of Europe.[28] For Thomas Borstelmann, the 1970s – in reference to the United States – represent not simply a negative decade (or as he quotes from a Doonesbury cartoon, 'a kidney stone of a decade'), but equally a decade of transition, in which the state withdrew and gave large chucks of social regulation over to the financial market, while at the same time new freedoms arose for minorities such as homosexuals, who had until then been excluded.[29]

Seen as such, the 1970s are an ambivalent decade. The end of the postwar boom and the return of mass unemployment, a growing awareness of the finite nature of natural resources, the beginnings of a second Cold War towards the end of the decade and also the triumph of conservative politics in the United States and the United Kingdom, shroud these ten years in a dark and, where politics is concerned, conservative fog. At the same time, the 1970s could also rightly be considered a decade of the 'left'.[30] As a decade of economic crisis, the 1970s appears very close to us again today, yet as a time of political upheaval with a worldwide desire for democratization and participation it is rather somewhat removed.

This collection of chapters both questions and discusses these varying views of the 1970s from a variety of differing perspectives. Thematically, the focus of our collection lies with the questions of which political ideas legitimized policy making and economic developments within this decade, and what kinds of social practices were connected to this. From a contemporary historical perspective we are above all interested in the question of whether the 1970s can be understood as the beginning of long-term change, and should at the same time inquire as to the permanence and stability of social and political structures. By assigning the beginning of state deregulation to the 1970s, do we begin to understand the decade, or should we not, for the sake of differentiation, also state the existence of contradictory developments?[31] In doing so, we primarily focus on political discourse, which was accompanied by a market-orientated structuring of almost all areas of society – from education to public services, as well as lifestyle choices. Morten Reitmayer makes the point that the rise of neoliberalism represents not so much a new form of class warfare but rather a sense of orientating oneself within a 'politically ideal dimension', which allows for the prevalence of a worldview dogmatically arranged by market-based regulation.[32] The mentioning of a politically ideal dimension also means that a market-based worldview was part of a process of negotiation with other ideas and concepts, never being able to fully exert its dominance over powers of social resistance.[33]

If we are to observe the prehistory of the modern day from this perspective, we have no need to tell the entire history of neoliberalism, nor its theoretical arguments (a great deal of literature is available on this subject in particular);[34] but, with the aid of individual case studies, we would rather discern what we can of those ideas of regulation and their processes of change from local and respective in-depth regional studies in areas specific to this sector and field of politics.

Continuities after 1945?

A further aspect in the rise of neoliberalism is its positioning within the late 1970s and the 1980s. The emphasis on single decades that goes along with this can sometimes loom large here, and this seems increasingly to be the case with sociological diagnoses of the present, which tend to paint history in a rather mild light. However, are Fordian regulation and neoliberal deregulation in fact as contradictory as they seem? Do state activity and governmental action change to such a degree that the 1970s are to be understood as the beginning of a new epoch? Adopting a globalized perspective, Patrick Neveling (Chapter 1) sees the 1970s not as a decade of fracture but rather a phase of consolidation. He examines the development of special economic areas – propagated by the United Nations as a model of economic development – that have been established by underdeveloped countries and regions since the 1940s in order to offer cheap locations for production. Thus Neveling considers the resulting expansion as part of the global mobility of capital, which had first taken place prior to the 1970s. To follow Neveling, changes in industrial production in the Western industrial nations then took place in parallel to a relocation of precarious activity in other regions of the world. The capitalistic method of production, with its need for accumulation, therefore puts into perspective the fissure of the 1970s. Neveling has argued that global capitalism is coined with 'untimely coincidences of modes of production and structural contingencies'.[35]

Continuity may also be positioned within specific economic cultures and mentalities, even if the results may initially appear contradictory. Alexander Ebner (Chapter 2) takes a closer look at the term 'social market economy', which is central to the Federal Republic of Germany. To follow on from the starting point of the 'varieties of capitalism' it can be considered as the defining Federal German model of a corporate form of capitalist regulation. Ebner goes into the history and the thinking behind this model, and comes to the conclusion that, despite deregulation and privatization, the fundamental elements of a social market economy continue to define economic and sociopolitical thinking in Germany. The specifically German model therefore exhibits a form of stability that was able to withstand the caesurae observed during the 1970s.

If we assume that deregulation and (neo)liberal competition are not phenomena of the 1970s, and nor do they have their beginnings there, then we must not only consider the pre-history of this decade but also its 'post'-history. Chapter 3, by Marcus Böick, is devoted to the employees of the *Treuhandanstalt* or 'Trust Agency', which carried out the privatization of the state-owned companies in the former German Democratic Republic (GDR) industries after 1990. The 1990s marked an end point, at least for ideological transformations. Certainly the collapse of state socialism in Eastern Europe was without historical precedent, due to its speed and its profound political, economic and social nature, radically cutting off the industrial and economic developments of the 1960s and 1970s.[36] A state economy was completely privatized. Yet Böick also shows that regulations of the welfare state were no longer even discussed by the protagonists of privatization. There was barely any political control, with the transformation of the GDR economy left exclusively in the hands of financial experts. The former GDR economists, who were taken on board in the Trust Agency, as well as the managers dispatched from West Germany were then only able to conceive of economic regeneration in the capitalist sense as shock therapy. In this situation, neoliberalism seemed to triumph economically, and it is possible that it was not until the 1990s that the neoliberal social and regulatory model reached its zenith.

The story of state deregulation since the 1970s becomes fragmented when taking into account one of the cornerstones of any state – the law. Out of a growing number of both individual and collective legal claims emerge commitments, which are to be regulated. To a great extent these were and are to be found in the field of labour law, which due to the increased participation (co-determination) lost out to state regulation. Even if employment is becoming more precarious and legal formalities are decentralized, the state still acts in a central role.[37] However legal rulings have increased rather than declined in the field of consumer protection, and the same is true of state-run measures to combat discrimination.

Larry Frohman (Chapter 4) refers to another issue by examining legal rulings in the field of data protection. With a view to international comparison, yet above all based on Federal German examples, he is unable to detect any deregulation in the field of legislation. The German Federal Data Protection Act of 1977, and a series of regulations expanding thereon, resulted in a wave of regulation on new media. Even when the possibilities of private internet use were not yet foreseeable, it was still deemed necessary to regulate the application of computer technology on private information, of which there was at that time already an immense amount. Federal German case law concerned itself with the protection of the individual from state access and the 'right to informational self-determination', which was granted by the highest German court in 1983. Frohman points out that the juridification of several areas – data protection being a shining example, as it constituted virgin territory – did not involve a withdrawal of the state but in fact its expansion. Therefore, Frohman speaks pronouncedly of a wave of regulation in the era of deregulation. In doing so, he points to the fact that with the juristic focus on individual human rights, legal regulation was actually expanded rather than reduced. Any sense of 'denationalization' is therefore not the case here.

Enrico Beltramini (Chapter 5) also addresses this aspect about the regulation of work relationships in the context of anti-discrimination measures. He explores the field of state regulation and examines the efforts of the

American administration in the 1960s to force an opening in the ethnically segregated worlds of work, in collaboration with protagonists of civil society. As with Frohman, this addresses an area of state regulation that does not disappear but rather increases. Ethnical diversification within the world of work has been a success over the last forty years, yet what remains unaffected by this is that human relationships cannot be administrated. Frohman and Beltramini's examples help to underline that state action since the 1970s cannot simply be understood under the umbrella of deregulation. The juridification of different parts of society, in particular the far-reaching field of liability law, has a significant effect on social conditions. In view of this, one can sum up a certain aporia of neoliberalism: while the withdrawal of the state continues to serve as a paradigm, at the same time calls remain for it to carry out a protective function, which necessitates state intervention and regulation.

Conceptual Transition in (State) Regulation

If the chapters by Neveling and Ebner support the continuity argument on an economic level and relativize the fissure of the 1970s, then the contributions by Frohman and Beltramini challenge the deregulation argument. There is, however, no doubt that a conceptual shift can also be observed since the 1970s. One of the most important changes is the transition from the Keynesian to the monetarist steering models. Giovanni Bernardini (Chapter 6) shows us a contrasting picture of the 1970s as the dawn of (neo) liberal ideas of reform. He discusses the role of the German minister of finance and later federal chancellor, Helmut Schmidt. Despite the fact that Keynesian models of regulation were still represented within his social democratic party, Schmidt had a low opinion of such political approaches. He was far more eager to exchange ideas with the leading Western politicians and, with the G6 summit from 1976 onwards, he established a place for discussing problems among the leading Western industrial nations, which explicitly distanced themselves from other countries' desires of co-determination. Schmidt attempted to develop solutions, which went far beyond the model of social democracy. Just as most parties had previously, during the post-war boom, endorsed an intervening state, the move away from Keynesian regulation and towards monetarism was equally no domain of the conservative politician.

In his chapter, Bernardini traces the shifts in social paradigms with the aid of leading politicians. There is reason to believe that within capitalist regulations, monetarism was seen as an escape from the on-setting crisis/ crises of the early 1970s. The social democratic politician Schmidt tended to argue 'unideologically' and 'pragmatically'. Even if the case study only adopts specific perspectives, it shows general tendencies nevertheless. During the 1970s, the amount of criticism aimed at state intervention grew within elite political circles, and this criticism spread evermore internationally. The case remains though that, as Ebner shows, specific economic cultural traditions from the respective countries remained defining elements in terms of discourse and self-perception.

The initially gradual nature of change to ideological foundations and suppositions can be witnessed in the changes within international institutions. The economic caesurae of 1973 did not immediately cross over into the world of either national or international political policy making. The next two chapters, by focusing on the European Community, show how political rationale and practices gradually shifted in the central regulatory sectors. Hannah Lierse (Chapter 7) examines a phenomenon in her historical-political narrative about the ambitions of the European Community to develop a common tax policy, the greatest stumbling block to which is that tax policy concerns a core area of the sovereignty of nation states. However, a plan conceived by the European Commission in 1975 envisaged a unitary tax policy that aimed at creating harmony and state intervention. After the plan failed, it was only in 1997 that a non-binding 'code of conduct' for national levels of taxation appeared, which was supposed to explicitly promote competitive taxation among the member states of the European Community. Due to the rise in taxes on consumption, in contrast to direct payments from businesses, a downward spiral of tax gains set in. Competitive taxation among the member states of the European Community – with reductions in customs barriers – thus promoted a funding gap in state finances.

In the field of educational policy, political-ideological reasoning shifted from a widespread concept of education as an opportunity for emancipation to ideas of competition. Simone Paoli (Chapter 8) addresses the issue of European attempts to coordinate education policy. In the decade of structural intervention, emancipation was still considered a positive thing, and the goal of academic and professional development was an increase in social mobility and equal opportunities. Thanks to an initiative of several delegates of the European parliament, the rationale behind European education policy was redefined in the 1980s. The focus was now on maintaining the capacity to compete with global competitors such as Japan and the United States, as well as the economic use of education. In this way, the cultural-historical supposition that a European identity among students should be strengthened by the ERASMUS student exchange programme, is, in fact more of an indirect by-product than the programme's primary aim. The emphasis was on securing Europe's capacity to compete.

Anna Wellner (Chapter 9) comes to similar conclusions in her examination of the shift in educational innovations. Modernization saw university education adopt new forms, yet also lose its critical and emancipatory aspirations. This should be considered paradigmatic, because deregulation mostly means that the previous forms are allocated new content. In her case studies, Wellner discusses changes in the education system, with the help of the Reform University in Bremen, Germany and the Michigan State University in Lansing, USA. The starting point for this is the criticism of curricula in the 1960s by the student movement and the project learning scheme established shortly thereafter as an emancipatory didactic form, which aimed to mediate a greater practical orientation. However, the ideas behind the inclusion of this new form of mediation in the curriculum migrated somewhat. The high expectations of the reform were not met and soon this form of mediation was being propagated as a building block for careers and economic use. Here it is evident that forms can remain yet their content may develop in a completely different direction. The results of our case studies in the educational sector correlate with the observation of Luc Boltanski and Éve Chiapallo, who present in detail the integration of criticism towards capitalism around 1968, which they term 'artists' critique', within management discourse of the present day. Boltanski and Chiapallo coined the phrase 'New Spirit of Capitalism' as a key term for a new modus operandi in European business culture.[38]

Transitions in Enterprise Regulation

Although Keynesianism lost backing within the world of politics, this did not result in the reduction of state regulation of institutions or within the sphere of economic competition. On the contrary, there are areas in which state regulation tended to play an increasing rather than decreasing role. This was particularly true in the field of risk technology, which required significant financial sums for research and testing. Nuclear technology was one such particular area, in which there was also special military and political interest. Simone Selva (Chapter 10) carries out a detailed examination of the American financial aid contributions towards the development of the Italian nuclear power industry during the time of the first oil crisis of 1973. In opposition to older theories, Selva argues that the aim of American support was to secure the economic hegemony of the United States in Europe. In doing so the US aimed, on the one hand, at securing a trade relationship in a sector that, due to the volume of investment, research and state security interests, required a high level of state regulation, while on the other hand, in addition to American efforts to secure a long-term alternative to the oil supply, they also wanted to prevent the ascension of the Italian left wing by ensuring economic stability.

In addition to the question of risk technology, which is only one aspect, Selva also touches on international or transnational issues. Just as Lierse and Paoli point out the gradual nature of change in supranational institutions, this type of timescale can also be found at the level of multinational business. International relationships between countries require corresponding regulation and contractual safeguards, not only in spite of but also directly because of globalization. This should provide for the juridification of economic developments and their tailoring to distinctive national characteristics. Multinational companies have served as negative symbols of globalization since the 1960s, the regulation of which Francesco Petrini looks at in Chapter 11. In particular, it was international trade union federations that attempted to bring such a form of regulation onto the agenda in order to manage the exchange between employees and companies' boards of directors. However, a 'code of conduct', as such, for multinational companies did not result from these declarations of intent, even if the UN, the OECD and the European Community had discussed the question intensely. The international organizations had too little power to enforce such a thing, and even the trade unions were unable to create universally binding regulations for the exchange within international companies.

The economic challenges and highly volatile markets led to changes in regulation at a company level, within the periods that are of interest to us. From the 1960s onwards one could observe the transition of business patriarchs to managers within the executive echelons of business. In larger and also globally operating business, the steering model also changed. Instead of a hierarchical structure, functional organization became more widespread, with executive management requiring more and more external expertise. This led, for example, to the rise of business consultants, who became important service providers for companies. Christian Marx (Chapter 12) addresses the topic of transnational cooperation of businesses. The two producers of synthetic fibres, Vereinigte Glanzstoff-Fabriken AG (VGF) in Germany and the Dutch company Algemene Kunstzijde Unie (AKU), planned to merge their companies at the end of the 1960s. Marx is interested in the influence of the corporate advisor, McKinsey. In 1969, the assertive management rejected his recommendation for the restructuring of the company from a functional to a departmentalized structure, with more decentralized responsibility. In the face of the enduring sales crisis in the chemical industry, McKinsey's suggestions were extensively implemented in 1975. This no longer only affected the structure of the company but also altered its general approach. The market orientation of companies involved an increase in the role of external advisors and comprehensive market analysis. The exogenous 'shock of the global' worked more as a catalyst and less as a fissure regarding the transformations in management methods.

The rapidly growing finance sector was one reason for the transformation of the economic elite's steering models. In this collection of works we discuss this point with the aid of the social economy in the UK. It was only at the end of the 1980s that the housing market here was extensively privatized; yet as early as the 1970s, due to technological innovations, political-ideological changes also began to show in the cooperative building societies.

Matthew Hollow (Chapter 13) conducts an examination of the largest building society in Britain – the Halifax. The 1980s was the decade in which it became integrated into the financial sector and gave up its special status as a common interest company, ultimately floating on the stock market in 1997. Hollow examines the organizational changes and the management culture of the 1970s. In addition to an immense expansion in construction activity with new organizational structures, changes were also apparent in the recruitment sector, with the hiring of external professionals and the systemization of careers in management. The newly implemented computer technology also enabled more rapid reactions to financial transactions. The changes of the 1980s had their roots in the decade before, however the global crisis played a more minor role in the lead up to this.

Conclusions – Unity of the Post-war Period

In-depth studies with the aid of certain examples do not tell the big story, yet they are necessary in order to understand and arrange the processes and courses of events. In the case of this study, it is also apparent that the 1970s cannot solely be understood as a decade of transition. Varying lines of development are evident, which suggest the assumption of a very drawn-out process of change, of varying distributions of power and varying national directions. The European Budgetary Treaty of 1975 was still conceived in the spirit of the intervening state, while members of the governing parties were already thinking beyond Keynesianism. Equally, the onset of privatization was not in the 1980s; it emerged far earlier as a central vision of affected businesses, such as the Halifax. Then in 1990, during the transformation of the GDR economy, the suggestion of any state-led regulatory intervention had vanished from the horizon. This and the other individual studies force us to look for the many small signposts of change. They also challenge the view of each decade being a defined period, which dominates the study of contemporary history. The studies found here do not endorse a view of either short or long decades. Our argumentation is far more that at least the 1970s and 1980s be examined as one unified period of time, which has, above all, the global political shifts of 1989–91 to thank for its conclusion. Taking into account Patrick Neveling's globalized perspective, it is equally valid to argue that the post-war period since 1945 be considered in its entirety. Whatever conclusions further research might arrive at, and whatever reflections we might have with the aid of increased temporal distance to the 1970s, at least it is already clear that the move to neoliberalism was not eruptive in nature. Yet many questions remain unanswered in the study of international relations and national policy. *Contesting Deregulation* should contribute to answering some of these.

Within this collection of works we aim to argue for differentiation with regards to content and of expanded periodization. Therefore it is of no great surprise, but must be highlighted nonetheless, that, in the debate surrounding neoliberalism, there must be greater differentiation between the varying areas of society. Many core areas of capitalism remain highly regulated, whereas such areas that have been expanded in the previous decades in the name of social progress – and have drawn criticism since at least the 1980s (labour protection and affirmative action, data protection and liability law) – are still controlled and regulated by the state. That, which is now appearing to the individual as the phenomena of unsafe big data, is still awaiting regulation. It is a highly disputed topic, and economic and political (security) concerns undoubtedly collide with privacy rights of the individual; yet the fact that regulation is indispensable remains undisputed. At the same time, one can observe the continual decrease in business taxes since the 1980s, and other measures aimed at relieving the transfer of capital to the advantage of capital assets. Even the sale of state ownership (privatization) was pushed in the hope that the free market would benefit from competition; it is also beyond doubt that the economization of several areas of life, as well as the raised expectations of efficiency in organizing our individual lives, are both visible developments.

These forms of deregulation are, however, by no means a trend that has infiltrated, bit by bit, all areas of society since the 1970s, in the way a wave symmetrically expands from its point of eminence. This collection of works discusses accordingly the contradictory movements and the forever-contentious implementation of purely market-based structures. In terms of criticism of the societal disavowal, which has generated a new sense of economic liberalism for several decades now, we assert that the liberalization and globalization of world trade and politics has been organized to a high degree; liberalization had and has to be implemented by a state policy of deregulation. The debate surrounding the transatlantic trade and investment partnership (TTIP) is the latest example of this. The organization of policy on a nation-state level has admittedly suffered restrictions; however we cannot yet speak of denationalization. The state continues to regulate the general parameters and succumbs to political demands, even if intermediary institutions and bodies such as the EU are playing a growing role. Even Brexit marked a potential disturbance of this trend.

Secondly, in this collection of works we argue against decadism, so widespread in the field of contemporary history, and call for the consideration of longer periods of change. The chapters show that case studies on individual subjects and aspects enable a deeper understanding of our history. It is not the 'shock of the global' alone that governed trade; and nor can we assume that a deep caesura or even a fissure in the 1970s constituted a worldwide phenomenon. It is far more the case that one can observe a drawn-out process, in which social regulation changed. Although this did not pave the way for denationalization, the state still determined the regulatory framework and drew upon approval of its regulation and means of conflict management. In addition to necessary examinations of the changes within the context of the large crises of the 1970s, we call for the second post-war period of the previous century to be considered as a unitary period. This began in 1945 and ended abruptly with the global political collapse of the socialist states in 1989–91. Obviously the system collapse sped up the trends of liberalization and deregulation, which became prevalent in the post-war periods. If our assumptions are correct, it was only after the political caesura of 1989–91 (for the West a completely 'exogenous' crisis) that the 1970s were, in fact, considered a decade of rapid development, because slow developments had been sped up by the caesura.

Stefan Müller is research fellow at the Archiv der sozialen Demokratie (AdsD) der Friedrich-Ebert-Stiftung. His research interests are labour history, contemporary transnational history, oral history and the history of cartography. Recent publications are 'Globalgeschichte einer Mercator-Kritik: Arno Peters und die Idee der "gerechten" Weltkarte', in *Gerhard Mercator: Wissenschaft und Wissenstransfer*, edited by Ute Schneider and Stefan Brakensiek, Darmstadt 2015, pp. 246–64; 'DGB und Ostpolitik 1969–1989: Gewerkschaften als parastaatliche Akteure im Entspannungsprozess', in *Teilungen überwinden: Europäische und Internationale Geschichte im 19. und 20. Jahrhundert*, edited by Michaela Bachem-Rehm, Claudia Hiepel and Henning Türk, Munich 2014, pp. 223–34; and 'West German Trade Unions and the Policy of Détente (1969–1989)', *Moving the Social* 52 (2014): 109–37. An edited volume on representation of labour is forthcoming in 2017.

Knud Andresen is research fellow at the Forschungsstelle für Zeitgeschichte in Hamburg. His main research interests are labour history, New Left, history of the youth, biography, and oral history. His recent publications are: *Gebremste Radikalisierung: die IG Metall und ihre Jugend 1968 bis in die*

1980er Jahre, Göttingen 2016; 'Apartheid und Anti-Apartheid: Südafrika und Westeuropa' [Apartheid and Anti-Apartheid: South Africa and Western Europe], edited with Detlef Siegfried, *Zeithistorische Forschungen* [*Studies in Contemporary History*] Issue 2 (2016); and *A European Youth Revolt: European Perspectives on Youth Protest and Social Movements in the 1980s*, edited with Bart van der Steen, Basingstoke 2016.

Notes

   1. By this we mean the West European and North American societies. We are aware of the problems of the implied bias, yet we tie this in with the social and contemporary historical debates about the 1970s.
   2. Colin Crouch, *Post-democracy* (Cambridge, 2004).
   3. Wolfgang Streeck, *Buying Time: The Postponed Crisis of Democratic Capitalism* (London and New York, 2014).
   4. *Ulrich Bröckling, Das unternehmerische Selbst: Soziologie einer Subjektivierungsform (Frankfurt am Main, 2007). See also Ulrich Bröckling, 'Gendering the Enterprising Self: Subjectification Programs and Gender Differences in Guides to Success', in Distinktion: Scandinavian Journal for Social Theory 6(2) (2005), 7–25; Jonathan Crary, 24/7: Late Capitalism and the Ends of Sleep (London and New York, 2014).*
   5. Jürgen Habermas, *Theorie des kommunikativen Handelns*, 2 vol. (Frankfurt am Main, 1981; engl. 1984/1987).
   6. Richard Sennett, *The Corrosion of Character: The Personal Consequences of Work in the New Capitalism* (New York, 1998).
   7. See most recently on European unification: Wilfried Loth, *Building Europe: A History of European Unification* (Berlin and Boston, MA, 2015).
   8. Akira Iriye, 'Die Entstehung einer transnationalen Welt', in *Geschichte der Welt: 1945 bis heute – die globalisierte Welt*, ed. Akira Iriye and Jürgen Osterhammel (Munich, 2013), 813f.
   9. Eric Hobsbawm, *The Age of Extremes: The Short Twentieth Century, 1914–1991* (New York, 1994).
   10. See in particular the political-economical approach to 'the varieties of capitalism', which distinguishes between the liberal and coordinated market economy. Peter A. Hall and David Soskice, *Varieties of Capitalism: The Institutional Foundations of Comparative Advantage* (Oxford, 2001); for a criticism of this model as being too static, see Wolfgang Streeck and Kathleen Thelen, *Beyond Continuity: Institutional Change in Advanced Political Economies* (Oxford, 2005).
   11. An instructive volume about legal regulation of economy from the nineteenth century until today: Günther Schulz, Mathias Schmoeckel and William Hausmann (eds), *Regulation between Legal Norms and Economic Reality. Intentions, Effects, and Adaption: The German and American Experiences* (Tübingen, 2014).
   12. Here we share the position with Traverso, to have the European Civil War beginning in 1914, and not, as the German historian Nolte (to whom the term is accredited) suggests, beginning with the October Revolution of 1917. Enzo Traverso, *À Feu et à sang: De la guerre civile européenne, 1914–1945* (Paris, 2007); Ernst Nolte, *Der europäische Bürgerkrieg 1917–1945: Nationalsozialismus und Bolschewismus* (Frankfurt am Main, 1987).
   13. See Tony Judt, 'Introduction: The World We Have Lost', in Tony Judt, *Reappraisals: Reflections on the Forgotten Twentieth Century* (London, 2008), 1–22.

14. See Ivan T. Berend, *From the Soviet Bloc to the European Union: The Economic and Social Transformation of Central and Eastern Europe since 1973* (Cambridge, 2009). The oil crisis comes increasing into focus from the field of historical science; see Frank Bösch and Rüdiger Graf (eds), *The Energy Crises of the 1970s: Anticipations and Reactions in the Industrialized World*, *Historical Social Research* 39(4) (2014).

15. Barry Eichengreen, *Exorbitant Privilege: The Rise and Fall of the Dollar and the Future of the International Monetary System* (New York, 2010).

16. Donella H. Meadows, Dennis L. Meadows, Jørgen Randers and William W. Behrens III, *The Limits to Growth: A Report for the Club of Rome's Project on the Predicament of Mankind* (New York, 1972).

17. Daniel Bell, *The Coming of Post-Industrial Society: A Venture in Social Forecasting* (New York, 1973).

18. Jean-Francois Lyotard, *La condition postmoderne: Rapport sur le savoir* (Paris, 1979); English: *The Postmodern Condition: A Report on Knowledge* (University of Minnesota, 1984).

19. Case studies on the United States, Great Britain, Germany and Poland in: Norbert Frei and Dietmar Süß (eds), *Privatisierung: Idee und Praxis seit den 1970er Jahren* (Göttingen, 2012).

20. The term Thatcherism was introduced by the recently deceased Stuart Hall: Stuart Hall, *The Politics of Thatcherism* (London, 1983). The term Reaganomics supposedly originates from the radio journalist Paul Harvey ('Beloved Radio Broadcaster Paul Harvey Dies at 90', in *Washington Post*, 1 March 2009).

21. For the view of world historians that globalization has been going on for several centuries if not millennia, see Andre Gunder Frank, *ReOrient: Global Economy in the Asian Age* (Berkeley, CA, 1998); Jerry H. Bentley, 'Asia in World History', *Education About Asia* 4, 5–9.

22. Jean Fourastié, *Les Trente Glorieuses, ou la révolution invisible de 1946 à 1975* (Paris, 1979).

23. This line of argumentation comes from Andreas Wirsching (ed.), 'Forum: The 1970s and 1980s as a Turning Point in European History?', with contributions from Göran Therborn, Geoff Eley, Hartmut Kaelble and Philippe Chassaigne, *Journal of Modern European History* 9(1) (2011), 7–26.

24. Niall Ferguson, 'Introduction. Crisis, what Crisis? The 1970s and the Shock of the Global', in *The Shock of the Global: The 1970s in Perspective*, ed. Niall Ferguson, Charles S. Maier, Erez Manela and Daniel J. Sargent (Cambridge, MA, 2010), 1–21.

25. Marcel van der Linden, *Workers of the World: Essays toward a Global Labor History* (Leiden, 2008).

26. Anselm Doering-Manteuffel and Lutz Raphael, *Nach dem Boom: Perspektiven auf die Zeitgeschichte seit 1970* (Göttingen, 2008), 53.

27. See also Charles S. Maier, 'Two Sorts of Crisis? The "Long" 1970s in the West and the East', in *Koordinaten deutscher Geschichte in der Epoche des Ost-West-Konflikts*, ed. Hans Günther Hockerts (Munich, 2004), 49–62.

28. Hartmut Kaelble, 'The 1970s in Europe: A Period of Disillusionment or Promise?' (German Historical Institute London, The 2009 Annual Lecture, 2010), 18.

29. Thomas Borstelmann, *1970s: A New Global History from Civil Rights to Economic Inequality* (Princeton, NJ, 2012); for the USA, see also Bruce J. Schulman, *The Seventies: The Great Shift in American Culture, Society, and Politics* (Cambridge, MA, 2002).

30. For the USA, see Edward D. Berkowitz, *Something Happened: A Political and Cultural Overview of the Seventies* (New York, 2006); and Schulmann, *The Seventies*. For Germany, see Bernd Faulenbach, *Das sozialdemokratische Jahrzehnt: Von der Reformeuphorie zur neuen Unübersichtlichkeit. Die SPD 1969–1982* (Bonn, 2011). See also Duco Hellema, 'Die langen 1970er Jahre – eine globale Perspektive', in *Radikalismus und politische Reformen: Beiträge zur*

deutschen und niederländischen Geschichte in den 1970er Jahren, ed. Duco Hellema, Friso Wielenga and Markus Wilp (Münster, New York, Munich and Berlin, 2012), 15–32.

31. See also the differing findings in Konrad H. Jarausch (ed.), *Das Ende der Zuversicht? Die siebziger Jahre als Geschichte* (Göttingen, 2008).

32. Morten Reitmayer, 'Deutsche Konkurrenzkulturen nach dem Boom', in *Konkurrenz in der Geschichte: Praktiken – Werte – Institutionalisierungen*, ed. Ralph Jessen (Frankfurt and New York, 2014), 262.

33. See Peter Hall and Michèle Lamont (eds), *Social Resilience in the Neoliberal Era* (Cambridge, 2013).

34. Daniel Stedman Jones, *Masters of the Universe: Hayek, Friedman and the Birth of Neoliberal Politics* (Princeton, NJ, 2012); Nicholas Wapshott, *Keynes Hayek, The Clash that Defined Modern Economics* (New York, 2011); idem., *The Road from Mont Pèlerin: The Making of the Neoliberal Thought Collective*, ed. Philip Mirowski and Dieter Plehwe (Cambridge, MA, 2009).

35. Patrick Neveling, 'Structural Contingencies and Untimely Coincidences in the Making of Neoliberal India: The Kandla Free Trade Zone, 1965–91', in *Indian Sociology* 48 (2014), 18.

36. Philipp Ther, *The New Order on the Old Continent: A History of Neoliberal Europe* (Princeton, NJ, 2016).

37. See as overview: Brian Bercusson, *European Labour Law* (Cambridge, 2009).

38. Luc Boltanski and Éve Chiapallo, *The New Spirit of Capitalism* (London and New York, 2005).

Bibliography

Bell, Daniel, *The Coming of Post-Industrial Society: A Venture in Social Forecasting* (New York, 1973).

Bentley, Jerry H., 'Asia in World History', *Education About Asia* 4: 5–9.

Bercusson, Brian, *European Labour Law* (Cambridge, 2009).

Berend, Ivan T., *From the Soviet Bloc to the European Union: The Economic and Social Transformation of Central and Eastern Europe since 1973* (Cambridge, 2009).

Berkowitz, Edward D., *Something Happened: A Political and Cultural Overview of the Seventies* (New York, 2006).

Boltanski, Luc, and Éve Chiapallo, *The New Spirit of Capitalism* (London and New York, 2005).

Borstelmann, Thomas, *1970s: A New Global History from Civil Rights to Economic Inequality* (Princeton, NJ, 2012).

Bösch, Frank, and Rüdiger Graf (eds), *The Energy Crises of the 1970s: Anticipations and Reactions in the Industrialized World* (Mannheim, 2014).

Bröckling, Ulrich, 'Gendering the Enterprising Self: Subjectification Programs and Gender Differences in Guides to Success', *Distinktion: Scandinavian Journal for Social Theory* 6(2) (2005): 7–25.

———. *Das unternehmerische Selbst: Soziologie einer Subjektivierungsform* (Frankfurt am Main, 2007).

Crary, Jonathan, 24/7: *Late Capitalism and the Ends of Sleep* (London and New York, 2014).

Crouch, Colin, *Post-democracy* (Cambridge, 2004).

Doering-Manteuffel, Anselm, and Lutz Raphael, *Nach dem Boom: Perspektiven auf die Zeitgesichte seit 1970* (Göttingen, 2008).

Eichengreen, Barry, *Exorbitant Privilege: The Rise and Fall of the Dollar and the Future of the International Monetary System* (New York, 2010).

Faulenbach, Bernd, *Das sozialdemokratische Jahrzehnt: Von der Reformeuphorie zur neuen Unübersichtlichkeit. Die SPD 1969–1982* (Bonn, 2011).

Ferguson, Niall, 'Introduction. Crisis, what Crisis? The 1970s and the Shock of the Global', in *The Shock of the Global: The 1970s in Perspective*, ed. Niall Ferguson et al. (Cambridge, MA, 2010), 1–21.

Fourastié, Jean, *Les Trente Glorieuses, ou la révolution invisible de 1946 à 1975* (Paris, 1979).

Frank, Andre Gunder, *ReOrient: Global Economy in the Asian Age* (Berkeley, CA, 1998).

Frei, Norbert, and Dietmar Süß (eds), *Privatisierung: Idee und Praxis seit den 1970er Jahren* (Göttingen, 2012).

Habermas, Jürgen, *Theorie des kommunikativen Handelns, 2 vol.* (Frankfurt am Main, 1981; engl. 1984/1987).

Hall, Peter A., and David Soskice, *Varieties of Capitalism: The Institutional Foundations of Comparative Advantage* (Oxford, 2001).

Hall, Stuart, *The Politics of Thatcherism* (London, 1983).

Hall, Peter, and Michèle Lamont (eds), *Social Resilience in the Neoliberal Era* (Cambridge, 2013).

Hellema, Duco, 'Die langen 1970er Jahre – eine globale Perspektive', in *Radikalismus und politische Reformen: Beiträge zur deutschen und niederländischen Geschichte in den 1970er Jahren*, ed. Duco Hellema, Friso Wielenga and Markus Wilp (Münster, New York, Munich and Berlin, 2012), 15–32.

Hobsbawm, Eric, *The Age of Extremes: The Short Twentieth Century, 1914–1991* (New York, 1994).

Iriye, Akira, 'Die Entstehung einer transnationalen Welt', in *Geschichte der Welt: 1945 bis heute – die globalisierte Welt*, ed. Akira Iriye and Jürgen Osterhammel (Munich, 2013), 671–825.

Jarausch, Konrad H. (ed.), *Das Ende der Zuversicht? Die siebziger Jahre als Geschichte* (Göttingen, 2008).

Jones, Daniel Stedman, *Masters of the Universe: Hayek, Friedman and the Birth of Neoliberal Politics* (Princeton, NJ, 2012).

Judt, Tony, 'Introduction: The World We Have Lost', in Tony Judt, *Reappraisals: Reflections on the Forgotten Twentieth Century* (London, 2008), 1–22.

Kaelble, Hartmut, 'The 1970s in Europe: A Period of Disillusionment or Promise?' (German Historical Institute London, The 2009 Annual Lecture, 2010).

Linden, Marcel van der, *Workers of the World: Essays toward a Global Labor History* (Leiden, 2008).

Loth, Wilfried, *Building Europe: A History of European Unification* (Berlin and Boston, MA, 2015).

Lyotard, Jean-Francois, *La condition postmoderne: Rapport sur le savoir* (Paris, 1979); English: *The Postmodern Condition: A Report on Knowledge* (University of Minnesota, 1984).

Maier, Charles S., 'Two Sorts of Crisis? The "Long" 1970s in the West and the East', in *Koordinaten deutscher Geschichte in der Epoche des Ost-West-Konflikts*, ed. Hans Günther Hockerts (Munich, 2004), 49–62.

Meadows, Donella H., et al., *The Limits to Growth: A Report for the Club of Rome's Project on the Predicament of Mankind* (New York, 1972).

Neveling, Patrick, 'Structural Contingencies and Untimely Coincidences in the Making of Neoliberal India: The Kandla Free Trade Zone, 1965–91', *Indian Sociology* 48 (2014): 17–43.

Nolte, Ernst, *Der europäische Bürgerkrieg 1917–1945: Nationalsozialismus und Bolschewismus* (Frankfurt am Main, 1987).

Reitmayer, Morten, 'Deutsche Konkurrenzkulturen nach dem Boom', in *Konkurrenz in der Geschichte: Praktiken – Werte – Institutionalisierungen*, ed. Ralph Jessen (Frankfurt and New York, 2014), 261–88.

Schulman, Bruce J., *The Seventies: The Great Shift in American Culture, Society, and Politics* (Cambridge, MA, 2002).

Schulz, Günther, Mathias Schmoeckel and William Hausmann (eds), *Regulation between Legal Norms and Economic Reality. Intentions, Effects, and Adaption: The German and American Experiences* (Tübingen, 2014).

Sennett, Richard, *The Corrosion of Character: The Personal Consequences of Work in the New Capitalism* (New York, 1998).

Streeck, Wolfgang, *Buying Time: The Postponed Crisis of Democratic Capitalism* (London and New York, 2014).

Streeck, Wolfgang, and Kathleen Thelen, *Beyond Continuity: Institutional Change in Advanced Political Economies* (Oxford, 2005).

Ther, Philipp, *The New Order on the Old Continent: A History of Neoliberal Europe* (Princeton, NJ, 2016).

Traverso, Enzo, *À Feu et à sang: De la guerre civile européenne, 1914–1945* (Paris, 2007).

Wapshott, Nicholas, *The Road from Mont Pèlerin: The Making of the Neoliberal Thought Collective*, ed. Philip Mirowski and Dieter Plehwe (Cambridge, MA, 2009).

———. *Keynes Hayek: The Clash that Defined Modern Economics* (New York, 2011).

Wirsching, Andreas (ed.), 'Forum: The 1970s and 1980s as a Turning Point in European History?', with contributions from Göran Therborn, Geoff Eley, Hartmut Kaelble and Philippe Chassaigne, *Journal of Modern European History* 9(1) (2011), 7–26.

Part I

CONTINUITIES, OR: THE LONG SECOND HALF OF THE TWENTIETH CENTURY

The Global Spread of Export Processing Zones, and the 1970s as a Decade of Consolidation

PATRICK NEVELING

Introduction

Much work by historians of the recent past focuses on the 1970s. Often, the decade is presented as one of radical rupture.[1] In this respect, historians have aligned themselves with social scientists who have identified a change in the predominant global regime of capitalist accumulation – from Fordism to neoliberalism, for example.[2] Increasingly, however, such clear-cut periodization of global history is being met with scepticism. For example, labour regimes for West German workers may have changed profoundly in the said period, but such a radical rupture does not apply to the experiences of the so-called *Gastarbeiter* – migrant workers who had been recruited during the 1950s and 1960s boom years.[3] This meets earlier criticisms by social scientists who pointed to the diversity of patterns of capitalist accumulation to show that there was no radical rupture in the early 1970s, or that this rupture was partial at best.[4] In what follows, I introduce a third perspective, which identifies the 1970s as a period of consolidation.

An analysis of the global spread of export processing zones (EPZs) and special economic zones provides the empirical foundation for identifying the 1970s as a period of consolidation. My research shows how EPZs have spread since the foundation of the first such zone in Puerto Rico in 1947,

just after the Second World War.[5] Since then, EPZs have come to be a
crucial feature of what is often called the neoliberal era. Known under a
range of denominations, including free trade zones, foreign trade zones and
special economic zones, EPZs have been set up mainly by so-called underdeveloped countries and regions. Their purpose is to attract manufacturing
relocations in sectors such as garments and light consumer electronics, in
which cheap labour is paramount for generating profit and where transport
costs matter less than for bulkier items. In the early years, such relocations
were from industrially advanced countries to underdeveloped countries.
EPZs sought to attract investors with exceptional tax and customs holidays,
state spending for industrial infrastructure, cheap, docile and non-unionized labour, and other factors facilitating accumulation that were increasingly hard to find in industrially advanced countries with Keynesian and
Fordist regimes.

In sum, EPZs are emblematic of the high capital mobility and precarious working conditions that many social scientists and contemporary historians identify as core criteria for the radical rupture of the early 1970s. To
substantiate an alternative reading of world history that sees the 1970s as a
period of consolidation, I show how an increasing number of mainly postcolonial nation states have set up EPZs since 1945. This will reveal that many
of the above listed and further features substantiating the notion of radical
rupture were actually widespread much earlier. As the number of EPZs has
increased over the years, relocations from one zone to another have become
common practice, for example. In other words, industrial relocation on a
South–South basis was as common in the early 1970s as was South–South
economic cooperation.[6] Nevertheless, the 1970s mark a turning point in
the global spread of EPZs. This is because the very concept of an 'export
processing zone' was coined in that decade, in both economic development
practice and academic analysis.

In the academic world, Folker Fröbel, Otto Kreye and Jürgen Heinrichs
were among the first to identify increasing relocations of garments and light
consumer electronics production from industrially advanced countries to
EPZs in developing countries. Empirical research on this phenomenon provided important evidence for identifying a 'New International Division of
Labour' (NIDL) emerging in the 1970s.[7] One central finding was that relocations to EPZs caused 'structural unemployment in industrialised countries
and industrialisation in developing countries'.[8]

Surprisingly, however, historians of the recent past discussing 1970s
efforts in social forecasting have paid little attention to the NIDL concept or
to the global spread of EPZs. Instead, Daniel Bell's 1970s books announcing
a third industrial revolution and 'the coming of post-industrial societies' are
popular references.[9] In my view this is unfortunate, as many social scientists

have pointed out that Bell's analysis was limited to the Western, industrially advanced capitalist sphere, an issue only recently considered among historians.[10]

This chapter makes use of the example of EPZs to move forward the critical engagement with the 1970s in two ways. First it outlines why and in what ways the common explanatory focus on a so-called 'crisis of Keynesianism' fails to engage with the long-term causes of that crisis.[11] It then summarizes development leading to and resulting from the establishment of the world's first EPZ regime in Puerto Rico. While this section highlights that practices commonly associated with neoliberalism and the 1970s and after were common in manufacturing relocations from the US mainland to Puerto Rico in the late 1940s, the next section shows how the EPZ became a standardized model for development in the 1970s when a working group of the United Nations Industrial Development Organization (UNIDO), concerned with 'Exports Promotion' (EP), surveyed EPZ-like activities worldwide and established the term 'EPZ'.

My concluding remarks introduce an explanatory model for understanding capitalism as a global system with competing models of accumulation operating at a given time. EPZs were part and parcel of a larger political initiative against Keynesian policies that emerged in reaction to New Deal policies of the 1930s. The global spread of such zones is, then, empirical evidence for the fact that global capitalism cannot be portrayed as a succession of eras, each dominated by a single coherent mode of accumulation. Instead, neoliberal and Fordist/Keynesian models of accumulation have been competing since the 1930s.

The 1970s: Assessing and Contesting Historians' Notions of Radical Rupture

The missing global perspective on the 1970s pointed out above is evidenced in Doering-Manteuffel and Raphael's work, for example. Around 1975 a 'social transformation of revolutionary quality' took place because three sets of changes that had so far developed along independent trajectories now coincided. These were 'digitalisation', the rise of neoliberal ideology evidenced in monetarism as the leading global economic theory, and the promotion of an individualistic conception of human beings.[12] The evidence presented to substantiate the declaration of a radical rupture is based on Western Europe, however.[13] This analysis has another weakness, according to a recent critique by Graf and Priemel. Notions of radical rupture popular in the 1970s are taken at face value, particularly the populist sociology of Daniel Bell. Doering-Manteuffel and Raphael award centre stage to Bell's work on 'post-industrial society'. But his proclamation that the inventions of a techno-scientific elite triggered large-scale unemployment of manufacturing workers does not consider that manufacturing had been relocated elsewhere. In fact, even today, workers in China and elsewhere assemble the means of production for 'post-industrial' professions, which gives a very industrial dimension to post-industrial work.[14]

However, this critique only partly identifies the analytical shortcomings that go along with the identification of a radical rupture around 1975. Graf and Priemel have suggested that historians of the recent past should relegate the work of 1970s social scientists to the status of historical sources.[15] What remains hidden, then, is that even contemporary social scientists spoke out against Bell's clear-cut periodization of world history. The above-mentioned notion of a new international division of labour is an obvious contemporary counterpoint to the notion of post-industrial society.

There is thus a lot more at stake than the question of how to deal with historical sources. Clear-cut periodizations of world history have to do with a more general analytical problem. Modes of regulating capitalist accumulation, such as Fordism, Keynesianism, neoliberalism and post-Fordism, never go uncontested. Therefore, in any given period of world history there is always a plethora of ways of exploiting labourers. An important precondition for the stability of the Fordist/Keynesian tripartite agreement between state, capital and labour (that is, trade unions) throughout much of the post-war era was early Cold War anti-communist witch-hunts. Keynesians and neoliberals shared anti-communism, and one of the pre-eminent politicians of the neoliberal era was able to build his career on such witch-hunts. Ronald Reagan, whose 1980s US presidency is often mentioned as a turning point towards neoliberalism in global politics,[16] was a key figure in the prosecution of presumed communists in Hollywood in the 1950s and central to the anti-union policies of General Electric (GE) during the 1950s and 1960s, one of the first large-scale multinational corporations.[17] Anti-communist operations were not necessarily to the benefit of the Keynesian regime, although they were very much in line with the managerial ideas of Henry Ford, of course. General Electric paid Reagan for campaigning against trade unions on its factory shop floors all over the United States, and he was also host of a company-sponsored TV show that helped him to nationwide fame.[18] As has been pointed out elsewhere, GE's efforts should not be studied as the efforts of a single corporation, however large and powerful, but in light of a much wider campaign against the New Deal that was gaining momentum in the 1950s.[19]

Thus if we want to speak of a Keynesian consensus for the period before 1975 it is important to consider how this consensus was manufactured. It should now be evident that decimating opponents in the trade union movement and elsewhere achieved comparative political stability for the Keynesian/Fordist pattern of accumulation, possibly at the cost of opening the door for neoliberal ideology.

It is surprising how the rise of neoliberalism is so often attributed to the 1970s when in that same decade Foucault pointed out, in his ground-breaking analysis of the intellectual origins and trajectory of neoliberalism in his 1978–79 lectures at the Collège de France, that New Deal policies were already under attack in the United States and Great Britain during the Second World War. Central figures in these attacks were emigrants of the Freiburg School, such as Friedrich Hayek and Wilhelm Röpke. Their analytical strategy was to depict state intervention and employment programmes as the road to Nazism.[20] The intellectual trajectory of neoliberalism and the role of individuals and institutions are well studied in the legacy of Foucault. There is thus sufficient work at hand for the history of ideas to dismiss, on empirical grounds, claims that the 1970s was a decade of radical rupture.

Yet, there is little empirical work on the way neoliberal policies were spread and implemented on a global scale. The following is a contribution to filling this gap. The global spread of EPZs will serve to show that the neoliberal thinkers' and businessmen's intellectual crusade for neoliberalism was well reflected in corporate policies and economic actions after the Second World War.

The Emergence of a Prototypical EPZ Regime in Puerto Rico in the 1940s

The global spread of EPZs did not happen only because, for corporations, the zones were highly attractive destinations for manufacturing relocations. From the beginning, EPZs were also hotspots for experiments and innovation in labour relations, the organization of production processes, and regional and national economic policies.

EPZs were at the forefront of radical changes in the production networks of old and new light consumer electronics, for example. Companies such as the Radio Corporation of America (RCA) and other branches of General Electric established production outlets in EPZs on the Mexican side of the US–Mexican border and in the Shannon Free Zone in Ireland throughout the 1960s.[21] From the beginning of the 1970s, EPZs attracted South–South connections. Companies from newly industrialized countries (NICs) such as South Korea set up shop in the Mexican zones, while Japanese companies outsourced production to the Masan Free Zone in South Korea and the Kaoshiung EPZ in Taiwan.[22]

From the early days, marketing agencies promoted relocations from industrialised to developing countries and regions. Many Northern corporations producing garments, textiles, light consumer electronics or other commodities that allowed for mobility set up shop in the US South after the Second World War because labour was cheaper and unions were weak.[23] But such relocations were not limited to the US mainland. At the same time, the United States dependency Puerto Rico radically altered its economic development policies. While these had been firmly based on a New Deal version for this Caribbean colony in the 1930s and throughout the war, the island's ruling Partido Popular set up the first EPZ-style development regime in 1947.

This regime, a 'Puerto Rican lure' in the words of the *Wall Street Journal*,[24] offered mainland investors customs- and tax-free production for several years, alongside other government subsidies such as cheap leases for industrial plots, low rents for state-owned factories and a cheap and docile labour force. The Boston-based consulting corporation Arthur D. Little Inc. (ADL) was hired to promote relocations, and an Office of Information for Puerto Rico in Washington sent out a monthly letter to 14,000 people and institutions and 35,000 brochures to manufacturers, bankers, business writers, and so on in 1946 alone, promoting 'Puerto Rico's potential as a site for textile apparel and other industries'.[25]

One of the first investors to set up shop in Puerto Rico was Royal W. Little. It is insightful to follow Little's biography if we want to grasp how the establishment and marketing of the Puerto Rican EPZ contributed to ongoing changes in the landscape of US industrial manufacturing. This brief and indicative summary of the making and unmaking of operations of one of the larger US textile companies in the 1940s and 1950s reveals that patterns often asserted to be genuinely post-1970s were in fact common business practice much earlier.

Royal Little was the nephew of the ADL owner, whose marketing agency had helped in planning, and was later in charge of promoting, the Puerto Rican EPZ. Until 1939, Little had made good profits by manufacturing parachutes and other equipment for the US Army. When he lost those contracts, he set up a new company called Textron, Inc. The ambition was to establish the first vertically integrated synthetic fibre-based textile company. And indeed, after operations started in 1943, Textron expanded rapidly, buying up several spinning mills and other plants in New England. This was unusual, as the US South was the place to invest in those days. But although labour was cheaper in the South and unions were weak, acquisitions in New England meant that a state-imposed quota for raw materials allocated per plant could be obtained. Textron became a successful brand of nationwide renown, selling its produce to 'selected department stores' and spending around USD 1 million annually on advertising in magazines, on radio programmes and at the retail level.[26]

Once the war was over, demand fell and quota were less important. The South was now even more attractive and Textron turned away from its New England acquisitions. These had often been textile and garment manufacturers, such as Lonsdale and the Nashua Manufacturing Company (NMC), whose operations dated back to the early nineteenth century. NMC, for example, was subjected to what nowadays social scientists and historians might identify as prototypical neoliberal restructuring. Textron hired a consulting production engineering company that conducted time–motion studies for a period of twelve months. Based on this it was recommended to purchase modern machinery at USD 1 million and to lay off more than 35 per cent of NMC's four thousand workers. Little then took the consultants to see Emile Rieve, the general president of the Textile Workers' Union of America (CIO). He presented Rieve with two options: either operations would be closed down as NMC had much lower profitability than southern mills, or Rieve could accept the restructuring proposals and in this way save 65 per cent of NMC jobs. According to Little's autobiography, Rieve agreed but failed to convince NMC's workforce to do the same. Because Textron then moved on to close down the Nashua plant completely, except for the famous 'Indian Head' blankets brand, a US Senate subcommittee convened a hearing about the closures.[27]

This hearing did not only look at relocations to the US South. Significant shares of production had been moved to Puerto Rico where Textron had set up shop with the support of the 'Fomento Industrial'. This was a New Deal-founded development corporation that was now under the control of Teodoro Moscoso, son of a middle-class pharmacist from the southern city of Ponce. Fomento was selling off several plants owned by the local government to US investors. During New Deal days, these factories had been paid for with US Treasury Department rebates from excise taxes on rum and tobacco exports.[28] Instead of buying one of these plants, Little got Textron an even better deal. He convinced Moscoso that Fomento should put up USD 4 million for machinery, and Textron would enter into business with USD 1 million as working capital.[29] As the projected 100 per cent annual return on investment did not materialize for Textron, Puerto Rican operations were subsidized by Fomento in the early 1950s but nevertheless closed down in 1957.[30]

Little's family relations and Textron's company policies add important insights into the actual practice of early post-Second World War neoliberalism in light manufacturing industries to existing works, revealing how US businessmen supported neoliberal think tanks.[31] The case of Textron shows that present-day terms such as 'runaway shops', used to describe the operations of multinational corporations in EPZs and elsewhere since the 1970s, are well applicable to much earlier periods too.[32]

The Global Spread of EPZ Regimes in the 1950s and 1960s

Importantly, the entangled cases of Textron and Puerto Rico are not single cases but, on my reading, emblematic of a pattern of diffusion of the global EPZ regime. A Ford Foundation-funded biography of the above-introduced Fomento Industrial chairman, Teodoro Moscoso, speaks of ten thousand visits by foreign officials to Puerto Rico that various US ministries arranged after 1947.[33] This impressive number of inspections of the Puerto Rican success story might be genuine, because successive US administrations promoted the island's neoliberal export-oriented industrialization drive as blueprints for successful development policies throughout the Third World. At the onset of the Cold War, the Truman administration promoted capitalist-style development under the 'Point Four' programme, announced by Truman in early 1949 and implemented in 1950. 'Point Four' development assistance to Egypt and many other nations replicated Puerto Rican policies as best-practice example of how to achieve export-oriented growth.[34] Indeed, contemporary debates on tax evasion, runaway shops and super-exploitation in export processing zones have precursors in the 1950s, when there was widespread debate among economists and social scientists about the upsides and downsides of Puerto Rican export-oriented development policies based on tax and customs exemptions and strong local government support for investors.[35]

In the following decade, the Kennedy administration set up the 'Alliance for Progress' after the failures of the Cuban crisis. Again, tax exemptions and state-support for export-oriented industrialization policies ranked high on the list of US development-policy recommendations. Many Puerto Rican politicians and bureaucrats now became US envoys to Latin America in an effort to give the development policy success a human face, and Moscoso was appointed ambassador to Venezuela.[36]

Although Little's Textron left Puerto Rico in 1957, this did no harm to the fortunes of his uncle's company Arthur D. Little, Inc. and their consulting and marketing activities in Puerto Rico and elsewhere. In 1957, Richard Bolin took over as head of the ADL office in San Juan and stayed until 1962,[37] when he moved on and set up his own consulting corporation called 'International Parks'. Possibly subcontracting for ADL with this company, he obtained several consulting contracts with cities on the Mexican–US border. This was a few years prior to the large-scale 'Border Industrialization Programme' of the Mexican federal state that established what would later become known as the 'maquiladora' industry of bonded factories, with the usual EPZ incentives such as tax and customs exemptions, state-funded industrial estates and zones, oppressive anti-unionization policies, and so forth in several border cities. In a book-length study of the Mexican border region inspired by Fröbel, Heinrich and Kreye's NIDL paradigm, anthropologist María Patricia Fernández-Kelly defines this programme as 'the last in a series of systematic efforts' to industrialize that region dating back to the granting of free-trade privileges for bonded warehouses in the 1930s.[38]

While Bolin's work laid the foundations for the maquiladoras in Ciudad de Juarez, Taiwan built an EPZ as part of the Kaoshiung international container harbour, with successive funding from US AID, the World Bank and the United Nations Technical Assistance Programme from the early 1960s.[39] India designed a somewhat similar strategy as early as 1951, when first plans were made for a 'foreign trade zone' adjacent to the container port development in Kandla. Port and EPZ were to compete with Karachi, which since partition was part of Pakistan. To provide employment for refugees in a planned settlement called Gandhidham, development plans were drawn up for that remote region. The Kandla Foreign Trade Zone opened its gates just a few months before Kaoshiung EPZ, thus making this Asia's first EPZ.[40]

Elsewhere, it did not take fourteen years from EPZ planning to EPZ opening. The Shannon Free Zone became operational after a short planning phase in 1959 in an effort to keep the remote so-called 'mid-west' region of the Republic of Ireland afloat. Most stopovers on transatlantic flights were routed through Shannon after the Second World War but now that technological advances allowed planes to go all the way to European destinations, business was dwindling, and the airport duty-free regime that had been set up for the sale of alcoholic beverages, tobacco and other luxury commodities was extended to manufacturing. Brendan O'Reagan, customs comptroller at Shannon and owner and director of several public-private companies doing most of the airport business, had acquired knowledge of EPZ operations during visits to Puerto Rico and also to the Zona Libre in Colon Harbour, Panama, where an EPZ regime had been established in the 1950s.[41]

Despite all these activities across the globe, the labelling of the zones was rather open, ranging from export processing zone, free zone, Spanish-language terms such as 'zona libre' and 'zona franca', to foreign trade zone in India. Academic writings of the 1950s and 1960s, on Puerto Rico, for example, discussed tax and customs incentives, and also touched on the emergence of what sociologists nowadays call a transnational capitalist class of entrepreneurs, consultants and celebrities who were meeting in glamorous hotels such as the Caribe Hilton in San Juan.[42] But, ironically, it was left to a United Nations' organization that would otherwise be known for very different policies to come up with a coherent label for the export-oriented development regime that was established on that Caribbean island in 1947.

The growing political impact of the non-aligned movement in the 1960s led to the establishment of new UN agencies such as the United Nations Commission on Trade and Development (UNCTAD), headed by famous Latin American economist Rául Prebisch, the United Nations Development Programme (UNDP) and the United Nations Industrial Development Organization (UNIDO). Independent scholars have not written detailed histories of these organizations yet, and it is beyond the scope of this chapter to make even a minor effort in this direction. Evident from existing summaries is that the important debates about setting up these agencies took place in the UN Economic and Social Council (ECOSOC). ECOSOC resolution 751 (XXIX) of April 1960 established an Industrial Development Committee (IDC), whose fourth session, in 1964, unanimously voted for recommending the creation of an autonomous organization, UNIDO, to the UN General Assembly.[43]

The foundational work of the IDC-associated Centre for Industrial Development (CID) included surveying the world for models of industrialization. The covering letter to a questionnaire distributed to member states via the office of the UN Secretary General in September 1966 highlighted the potential of export industries to circumvent price fluctuations of primary commodity exports on the global market, as identified in ECOSOC resolution 1178 (XLI). Responses to the questionnaire reveal, for example, that Cyprus[44] and Malta[45] both had EPZ-like regimes in place from 1959 and even earlier. Other countries, such as the Philippines, were developing EPZs with US AID funding.[46] Also, one member of the CID made efforts to bring about a first global survey of EPZ activities in September 1966. Correspondence available on this in the UN archival record is limited to an exchange of letters with KEPZ, however.[47]

Responses to the CID questionnaire on general export-oriented policies figured prominently in the 1967 proceedings of the first session of UNIDO's general assembly, the 'Industrial Development Board' (IDB). A '[p]rogress report on steps taken by developing countries to develop and establish export-oriented industries' to the IDB included extended reference to EPZ-like regimes, and suggested UNIDO should recommend replicating them.[48] Accordingly, one of fifteen groups in UNIDO's initial institutional set-up operated under the heading 'Export Promotion' (EP) as part of the 'Industrial Policies and Programming Division'. This group conducted the first concise global survey on EPZ activities in 1970. In February that year the first letters to the administrations of known free zones, free trade ports, export processing zones and so forth were sent out. Throughout that year, correspondence was spread more widely as this global mailing activity also became the centrepiece of promoting UNIDO EP services to national development agencies and ministries.[49] A first technical assistance mission to Mauritius had been commissioned and conducted in 1969. This was regularly mentioned in marketing-style letters to ministries and development authorities, as the head of EP, William Tanaka, sought to acquire further technical assistance requests from member states.[50]

At the same time, correspondence for the survey established contacts with the US Department of Commerce, whose executive secretary of the Foreign Trade Zones Board would be a regular speaker at UNIDO workshops training 'Third World' officials how to set up export processing zones. Established EPZs in Shannon and Barranquilla, Colombia, hosted these workshops.[51] Tanaka had made contact with these zones' administrations during that global survey as well. The Shannon Free Airport Development Corporation (SFADCo) realized first that UNIDO's EP group was an ideal platform for establishing something bigger, and entered negotiations to become the central UNIDO outpost for EPZ promotion. SFADCo affiliate Peter Ryan followed Tanaka as head of UNIDO's EP and hired Shannon entrepreneur Tom Kelleher to write a handbook on Export Processing Zones. Published in 1976, one year before Fröbel, Heinrich and Kreye's NIDL book, that UNIDO handbook laid out in detail how to set up an EPZ, including templates for organizational structures from EPZs in Bataan in the Philippines, Masan in South Korea, and Shannon.[52] Since the first UNIDO international workshop for setting up EPZs held in Shannon in 1972, the label 'export processing zone' was standard for UNIDO, and applied in hundreds of technical assistance missions.

Concluding Remarks: Capitalism, Regulation, and Anti-Social Movements

In this chapter, I have established the case of the global spread of export processing zones (EPZs) to argue that the 1970s may well be regarded as a 'decade of consolidation', because the global division of labour in light industrial manufacturing had previously been in transition. The fact that EPZs became the most prominent economic development policy for attracting investment in light industrial manufacturing, ultimately dominating this in the 2000s, had surely not been evident when Puerto Rico set up an EPZ-like regime in 1947. From a US perspective, it may not even have been intended that EPZs took centre stage in a political project called 'development' that sought to convince newly independent nation states of the benefits of alliances with the capitalist block during the era of decolonization.[53] Crucially, however, the global spread of EPZs shows that it would be wrong to assume that a global Keynesian or Fordist consensus, or practice, ever existed, as Giovanni Arrighi does when he identifies development as a 'global new deal'.[54] My findings instead underline a much broader analytical stance: capitalism here has been analysed on a global scale. This reveals that an analysis of capitalism as driven by a singular pattern of accumulation, Keynesianism or neoliberalism for example, unnecessarily narrows our perspective.

Instead, from a global perspective on the spread of EPZs, there is strong evidence that the 1970s should be regarded as a period of consolidation. This is not to say that nothing changed during that decade. The regime established in Puerto Rico in 1947, which subsequently spread across the world, received a standard label of 'export processing zone' that came about via the work of one group within the newly established UN agency, UNIDO. Workshops, a handbook and hundreds of technical assistance missions (often conducted by Irish consultants affiliated to or directly employed by the Shannon Free Airport Development Corporation) then spread the label 'export processing zone', and even more so the pattern of regulating capitalist accumulation. Other terminologies spread as well: for example, the road where the administration headquarters of the Kingston (Jamaica) Free Trade Zone are located is called 'Shannon Drive'. The fact that Jamaica's first EPZ, established in 1976, is called 'Free Zone' indicates that the label 'EPZ' did not instantly become standard throughout the world. Importantly for my argument, however, standardization has worked to the extent that since the 1970s thorough academic studies such as Fröbel, Heinrich and Kreye's book, as well as policy guidelines published by the World Bank, do use 'EPZ'.

The example I have given in this chapter does not, of course, qualify as an outright contradiction of the important works on the 1970s by historians of the recent past. No matter whether that decade is seen as one of radical rupture or one of continuity, the empirical substance of works on changes in industrially advanced Western countries should not be disputed. What is important, however, is to use the notion of the 1970s as a decade of consolidation to ask how the 1970s looked for those people who took the jobs of manufacturing workers in industrially advanced countries, as corporations increasingly shifted production to EPZs.

For the small island nation state Mauritius, I have argued elsewhere that the 1970s saw the percentage of women in the labour force rising as EPZ production spread. Again though, a historical analysis of labour relations reveals that gendered exploitation is not a unique feature of EPZs, and only emerged in a supposedly 1970s radical rupture towards flexible accumulation. This has regularly been stated in anthropological studies labelling female EPZ workers as 'neophyte', because zone factories were the first industrial ventures to help women in developing countries to enter the labour market.[55] In Mauritius, however, the colonial sugar industry already had significant female labour and gendered exploitation, and there is strong evidence that in many other former plantation colonies setting up EPZs, we find a continuation of the gendered exploitation that existed in the colonial era, in part sustained by local 'myth[s] of the male breadwinner', which continue to deny the wage labour contribution of women to households in Puerto Rico and elsewhere.[56]

Similarly, most newly established EPZ companies were actually joint ventures of foreign investors and those Mauritian corporations that had controlled the colonial economy in sugar production and beyond.[57] In Mauritius then, we find further patterns of consolidation in the 1970s when the transition from colonial to postcolonial exploitation of workers by the very same capitalists came full circle.

The above arguments and empirical evidence show that in order to identify radical ruptures in national and world history there is a need for detailed and comparative global research, and an analysis that reconsiders capitalism from the perspective of world history as a history of contradictions and a constant balancing of the demands of competing (anti-)social movements. For a particular mode of regulating capitalism is always contested, even from within the ranks of national and international bourgeoisies, which organize in anti-social movements and quarrel over the best way to exploit workers and consolidate a particular pattern of regulating capitalist exploitation. A strong focus on inequality and related issues – such as exploitation, accumulation and class division – may therefore help us to show how radical rupture for some (e.g. German workers losing their job in the 1970s) is continuity for others (e.g. Mauritian workers experiencing a continuity of colonial labour regimes in postcolonial EPZs). Building on the case of the global spread of EPZs discussed in this chapter, a global historical analysis interested in the entanglements of exploitation will, most likely, reveal how in many other sectors – international finance and the tourism industry, to name two – the 1970s was a period of consolidation, as one among several contested options for capitalist accumulation became dominant.

Patrick Neveling works at the Department of Development Studies, School of Oriental and African Studies/University of London. He has lead-edited special issues for *Sociologus*, *Etnográfica* and *Contributions to Indian Sociology*, and co-edited a book on *Tradition Within and Beyond the Framework of Invention* (Halle University Press). His work addresses the historical-political economy of capitalism, with a special focus on the global spread of export processing zones/special economic zones and on the small island state of Mauritius, and he is currently finishing a book on a global historical anthropology of special economic zones.

Notes

Research for this publication was supported by the Swiss National Science Foundation (Grant Nos: 126642 and 140848). The author would like to thank the staff members at the General Archives of Puerto Rico and at the archives of the United Nations Industrial Development Organization for their kind support.

1. Anselm Doering-Manteuffel and Lutz Raphael, *Nach dem Boom: Perspektiven auf die Zeitgeschichte seit 1970*, 2nd rev. edn (Göttingen, 2010); Niall Ferguson, *The Shock of the Global: The 1970s in Perspective* (Cambridge, MA, 2010).

2. See, for example, David Harvey, *The Condition of Postmodernity: An Enquiry into the Origins of Cultural Change* (Oxford and Cambridge, MA, 1990).

3. See Knud Andresen, Ursula Bitzegeio and Jürgen Mittag (eds), *Nach dem Strukturbruch?: Kontinuität und Wandel von Arbeitsbeziehungen und Arbeitswelt(en) seit den 1970er-Jahren* (Bonn, 2011).

4. See, for example, Georg Baca, 'Legends of Fordism: Between Myth, History, and Foregone Conclusions', in *The Retreat of the Social: The Rise and Rise of Reductionism*, ed. Bruce Kapferer (New York and Oxford, 2005), 31–46; June Nash, 'Post-Industrialism, Post-Fordism, and the Crisis in World Capitalism', in *Meanings of Work: Considerations for the Twenty-First Century*, ed. Frederik C. Gamst (Albany, NY, 1995), 189–211.

5. E.g. Patrick Neveling, 'Export Processing Zones and Global Class Formation', in *Anthropologies of Class: Power, Practice, and Inequality*, ed. James Carrier and Don Kalb (Cambridge, 2014), 171–96; idem, 'Export Processing Zones, Special Economic Zones and the Long March of Capitalist Development Policies during the Cold War', in *Negotiating Independence: New Directions in the History of Decolonisation and the Cold War*, ed. Leslie James and Elisabeth Leake (London, 2015), 63–84.

6. Recent reports by international organizations indicate the global spread of EPZs. While assessments differ regarding the upsides and downsides of EPZ development, there is consensus on global employment figures counting close to 70 million workers in EPZs worldwide for the late 2000s. For 2007, an in-focus group on EPZs set up by the International Labour Office counted more than 3,500 EPZs in more than 130 countries, employing more than 60 million workers. This count includes the widest possible spectrum of zones, as it not only considers 'classic' manufacturing zones but also offshore-banking centres, free ports and so on. See Jean-Pierre Singa Boyenge, 'ILO Database on Export Processing Zones (Revised)', *ILO Working Papers* 251 (2007), http://www.ilo.org/public/english/dialogue/sector/themes/ epz/epz-db.pdf. A 2008 investor and donor guide published by the International Finance Corporation/The World Bank applies different criteria and uses the denomination 'special economic zones' (although the denomination 'EPZ' often slips into the text and is used synonymously). See Gokhan Akinci, James Crittle, and FIAS/The World Bank Group, *Special Economic Zones: Performance, Lessons Learned, and Implications for Zone Development* (Washington DC, 2008). The count is 266 zones for 'industrialized countries' and 2,301 zones for 'developing and transition countries' (ibid., 13, 18). Direct zone employment is estimated at 68.4 million for 2008 (ibid., 34).

7. See Folker Fröbel, Jürgen Heinrichs and Otto Kreye, *Die neue internationale Arbeitsteilung: strukturelle Arbeitslosigkeit in den Industrieländern und die Industrialisierung der Entwicklungsländer* (Reinbek bei Hamburg, 1977).

8. This is the subtitle of the English-language publication of their work. See Folker Fröbel, Jürgen Heinrichs and Otto Kreye, *The New International Division of Labour: Structural Unemployment in Industrialised Countries and Industrialisation in Developing Countries* (Cambridge, 1981).

9. For example, Doering-Manteuffel and Raphael, *Nach dem Boom.*

10. For the social sciences see Nash, 'Post-Industrialism'. For summaries of this critique, see Patrick Neveling, 'Einleitende Überlegungen: Wissen um Veränderung: Entwicklung, Geschichte, sozialer Wandel (Engl.: Introductory Remarks: The Production of Knowledge about Change: Development, History, Social Transformation)', *Sociologus* 60(1) (2010), 1–14. Also idem, 'Flexible Capitalism and Transactional Orders in Colonial and Postcolonial Mauritius: A Post-Occidentalist View', in *Flexible Capitalism: Exchange and Ambiguity at Work*, ed. Jens Kjaerulf (Oxford, 2015). Reference to the territorial limitations of Bell's analysis is made by historians Rüdiger Graf and Kim Christian Priemel, 'Zeitgeschichte in der Welt der Sozialwissenschaften: Legitimität und Originalität einer Disziplin', *Vierteljahreshefte für Zeitgeschichte* 59(4) (2011): 485.

11. For this focus, see Doering-Manteuffel and Raphael, *Nach dem Boom*; and Harvey, *The Condition*.

12. Doering-Manteuffel and Raphael, *Nach dem Boom*, 31.

13. Ibid., 38.

14. Graf and Priemel, 'Zeitgeschichte', 485.

15. Ibid., 479.

16. See Doering-Manteuffel and Raphael, *Nach dem Boom*, 29–36.

17. For an analysis of workers' support for anti-communist propaganda, see June C. Nash, *From Tank Town to High Tech: The Clash of Community and Industrial Cycles* (New York, 1989).

18. Kim Phillips-Fein, *Invisible Hands: The Businessmen's Crusade against the New Deal* (New York and London, 2009), 111–14.

19. Ibid. For an early assessment of this campaign from a social science perspective, see M. Patricia Marchak, *The Integrated Circus: The New Right and the Restructuring of Global Markets* (Montreal and Buffalo, NY, 1991), 111–15.

20. Michel Foucault, Michel Senellart and Collège de France, *The Birth of Biopolitics: Lectures at the Collège de France, 1978–79* (Basingstoke and New York, 2008), 101–11.

21. For RCA, see Jefferson Cowie, *Capital Moves: RCA's Seventy-Year Quest for Cheap Labor* (Ithaca, NY, 1999). For Shannon, see Neveling, 'EPZs and Global Class Formation'.

22. S. Watanabe, 'Constraints on Labour-Intensive Export Industries in Mexico', *International Labour Review* 109 (1974): 23–45. Seung-Kyung Kim, *Class Struggle or Family Struggle? The Lives of Women Factory Workers in South Korea* (Cambridge, 1997).

23. See Baca, 'Legends'.

24. M.M. Diefenderrer (Staff Correspondent of the *Wall Street Journal*), 'Puerto Rican Lure', *Wall Street Journal*, 7 June 1946.

25. See Office of Information for Puerto Rico/Washington. 'Annual Report' San Juan. 1946, Tarea 96-20, Puerto Rico General Archives (Documents Section), Oficina del Gobernador.

26. Royal Little, *How to Lose $100,000,000 and Other Valuable Advice*, 1st edn (Boston, 1979), 74.

27. Ibid.

28. See Neveling, 'EPZs and Global Class Formation'.

29. Ibid see also Little, *How to Lose*, 82–83.

30. Julio Rivera, 'Reabrirá en Ponce Fábrica de Textron', *El Mundo*, 27 September 1957.

31. See Phillips-Fein, *Invisible*.

32. This has, of course, been well captured for the US South in Baca, 'Legends'.

33. A.W. Maldonado, *Teodoro Moscoso and Puerto Rico's Operation Bootstrap* (Gainesville, FL, 1997).

34. Neveling, 'EPZs and Global Class Formation'.

35. For the repercussions of this debate in academic journals, see an exchange between two economic sociologists/development economists: Gordon K. Lewis, 'Puerto Rico: A Case Study of Change in an Underdeveloped Area', *The Journal of Politics* 17(4) (1955): 614–50. David F. Ross, 'Gordon Lewis on Puerto Rico's Development Program', *The Journal of Politics* 19(1) (1957): 86–100.

36. Leigh Miller, 'Oral History Interview with Teodoro Moscoso for the John F. Kennedy Library', Boston, 18 May 1964, Moscoso, Teodoro JFK Interview #1, #2, #3, John F. Kennedy Presidential Library and Archives.

37. Arthur D. Little Inc. 'New Puerto Rican Office is Opened', Boston, Massachusetts. Winter 1957, Series 7, Box 5, MC 579, History Earl Stevenson, MIT Archives, Arthur D. Little, Inc.

38. María Patricia Fernández-Kelly, *For We Are Sold, I and My People: Women and Industry in Mexico's Frontier*, SUNY series in the anthropology of work (Albany, NY, 1983), 23–26.

39. See W.B. Leonard (Acting Commissioner for Technical Assistance), 'Letter Concerning: China – Request of the Government of the Republic of China for Four Experts under WCRF', New York, 19 May 1965, S-0175-0308, United Nations Archives and Records Managment.

40. For a summary of the Kandla story, see Patrick Neveling, 'Structural Contingencies and Untimely Coincidences in the Making of Neoliberal India: The Kandla Foreign Trade Zone, 1965–1991', *Contributions to Indian Sociology* 48(1) (2014): 17–43.

41. For a summary of the Shannon story, see Neveling, 'EPZs and Global Class Formation'.

42. See Ross, 'Gordon Lewis', 88.

43. Youry Lambert, *The United Nations Industrial Development Organization: UNIDO and Problems of International Economic Cooperation* (Westport, CT, 1993), 7–21.

44. Cyprus Ministry of Foreign Affairs/Ministry of Commerce & Industry. 'Letter to the Secretary-General of the United Nations', New York, 5 December 1966, S-0450-0555, UN Archives and Records Management, Economic Affairs.

45. Permanent Mission of Malta to the United Nations. 'Answers to Questionnaire to the Secretary-General of the United Nations, New York', New York, 22 November 1966, S-0450-0555, UN Archives and Records Management, Economic Affairs.

46. Rizalino R. Pablo (Executive Director Republic of the Philippines National Economic Council). 'Letter to the Secretary-General of the United Nations, New York', 16 November 1966, S-0450-0555, UN Archives and Records Management, New York, Economic Affairs.

47. Cf. Council for International Economic Cooperation and Development S.Y. Dao (Secretary General, Executive Yuan); 'Letter to Dr W.M. Svoboda, Room 3277, United Nations, New York', New York, 18 October 1966, S-0450-0555, UN Archives and Records Management, Economic Affairs.

48. Executive Director of the United Nations Industrial Development Organization. 'Progress Report on Steps Taken by Developing Countries to Develop and Establish Export-Oriented Industries', Vienna, 1967, ID/B/8, English, United Nations Industrial Development Organization Archive.

49. For the correspondence, see United Nations Industrial Development Organization Archives, Folder TS 221/2 (21).

50. For example, William H. Tanaka. 'Letter to Teodore Q. Pena, Commissioner and Executive Officer, Foreign Trade Zone Authority, Port Area, Manila', Vienna, 16 April 1970, Folder TS 221/2 (21), United Nations Industrial Development Organization Archive.

51. See United Nations Industrial Development Organization. 'Training Workshop in Industrial Free Zones as Incentives to Promote Export-Oriented Industries, Shannon, 1972. Programme of Work', Vienna, 1972, 003166, United Nations Industrial Development

Organization Archives, Industrial Development Abstracts; and United Nations Industrial Development Organization. 'Regional Expert Working Group Meeting on Industrial Free Zones, Barranquilla, 1974', Vienna, 1974, 005642, United Nations Industrial Development Organization Archives, Industrial Development Abstracts.

52. Tom Kelleher, 'Handbook on Export Processing Zones', Vienna, 1976, 007125, United Nations Industrial Development Organization Archives, Industrial Development Abstracts, Appendix 5.

53. There would be a lot more to say about the role of EPZs in the era of decolonization and the Cold War, cf. Neveling, 'EPZs/Cold War'.

54. Giovanni Arrighi, 'The Global Market', *Journal of World Systems Research* 2 (1997): 247.

55. E.g. Aiwha Ong, 'The Gender and Labor Politics of Postmodernity', *Annual Review of Anthropology* 20 (1991): 290–91.

56. Helen Icken Safa, *The Myth of the Male Breadwinner: Women and Industrialization in the Caribbean* (Boulder, CO, 1995).

57. See Patrick Neveling, 'Manifestationen der Globalisierung. Kapital, Staat und Arbeit in Mauritius, 1825–2005' (DPhil, Martin Luther University, Halle-Wittenberg, 2012).

Bibliography

Akinci, Gokhan, James Crittle and FIAS/The World Bank Group, *Special Economic Zones: Performance, Lessons Learned, and Implications for Zone Development* (Washington DC, 2008).

Andresen, Knud, Ursula Bitzegeio and Jürgen Mittag (eds), *Nach dem Strukturbruch?: Kontinuität und Wandel von Arbeitsbeziehungen und Arbeitswelt(en) seit den 1970er-Jahren* (Bonn, 2011).

Arrighi, Giovanni, 'The Global Market', *Journal of World Systems Research* V(2) (1997): 217–251.

Baca, Georg, 'Legends of Fordism: Between Myth, History, and Foregone Conclusions', in *The Retreat of the Social: The Rise and Rise of Reductionism*, ed. Bruce Kapferer (New York and Oxford, 2005), 31–46.

Cowie, Jefferson, *Capital Moves: RCA's Seventy-Year Quest for Cheap Labor* (Ithaca, NY, 1999).

Doering-Manteuffel, Anselm, and Lutz Raphael, *Nach dem Boom: Perspektiven auf die Zeitgeschichte seit 1970*, 2nd rev. edn (Göttingen, 2010).

Ferguson, Niall, *The Shock of the Global: The 1970s in Perspective* (Cambridge, MA, 2010).

Fernández-Kelly, María Patricia, *For We Are Sold, I and My People: Women and Industry in Mexico's Frontier* (Albany, NY, 1983).

Foucault, Michel, Michel Senellart and Collège de France, *The Birth of Biopolitics: Lectures at the Collège de France, 1978–79* (Basingstoke and New York, 2008).

Fröbel, Folker, Jürgen Heinrichs and Otto Kreye, *Die neue internationale Arbeitsteilung: strukturelle Arbeitslosigkeit in den Industrieländern und die Industrialisierung der Entwicklungsländer* (Reinbek bei Hamburg, 1977). English translation: *The New International Division of Labour: Structural Unemployment in Industrialised Countries and Industrialisation in Developing Countries* (Cambridge, 1981).

Graf, Rüdiger, and Kim Christian Priemel, 'Zeitgeschichte in der Welt der Sozialwissenschaften: Legitimität und Originalität einer Disziplin', *Vierteljahreshefte für Zeitgeschichte* 59(4) (2011): 479–508.

Harvey, David, *The Condition of Postmodernity: An Enquiry into the Origins of Cultural Change* (Oxford and Cambridge, MA, 1990).

Kim, Seung-Kyung, *Class Struggle or Family Struggle? The Lives of Women Factory Workers in South Korea* (Cambridge, 1997).

Lambert, Youry, *The United Nations Industrial Development Organization: UNIDO and Problems of International Economic Cooperation* (Westport, CT, 1993).

Lewis, Gordon K., 'Puerto Rico: A Case Study of Change in an Underdeveloped Area', in *The Journal of Politics* 17(4) (1955): 614–50.

Little, Royal, *How to Lose $100,000,000 and Other Valuable Advice*, 1st edn (Boston, 1979).

Maldonado, A.W., *Teodoro Moscoso and Puerto Rico's Operation Bootstrap* (Gainesville, FL, 1997).

Marchak, M. Patricia, *The Integrated Circus: The New Right and the Restructuring of Global Markets* (Montreal and Buffalo, NY, 1991).

Nash, June C., *From Tank Town to High Tech: The Clash of Community and Industrial Cycles* (New York, 1989).

———, 'Post-Industrialism, Post-Fordism, and the Crisis in World Capitalism', in *Meanings of Work: Considerations for the Twenty-First Century*, ed. Frederik C. Gamst (Albany, NY, 1995), 189–211.

Neveling, Patrick, 'Einleitende Überlegungen: Wissen um Veränderung: Entwicklung, Geschichte, sozialer Wandel' [Introductory Remarks: The Production of Knowledge about Change: Development, History, Social Transformation], *Sociologus* 60(1) (2010): 1–14.

———, 'Manifestationen der Globalisierung: Kapital, Staat und Arbeit in Mauritius, 1825–2005' (DPhil, Martin Luther University, Halle-Wittenberg, 2012).

———, 'Structural Contingencies and Untimely Coincidences in the Making of Neoliberal India: The Kandla Foreign Trade Zone, 1965–1991', *Contributions to Indian Sociology* 48(1) (2014): 17–43.

———, 'Export Processing Zones and Global Class Formation', in *Anthropologies of Class: Power, Practice, and Inequality*, ed. James Carrier and Don Kalb (Cambridge, 2015), 164–82.

———, 'Export Processing Zones, Special Economic Zones and the Long March of Capitalist Development Policies during the Cold War', in *Negotiating Independence: New Directions in the History of Decolonisation and the Cold War*, ed. Leslie James and Elisabeth Leake (London, 2015), 63–84.

———, 'Flexible Capitalism and Transactional Orders in Colonial and Postcolonial Mauritius: A Post-Occidentalist View', in *Flexible Capitalism: Exchange and Ambiguity at Work*, ed. Jens Kjaerulf (Oxford, 2015), 207–34.

Ong, Aiwha, 'The Gender and Labor Politics of Postmodernity', *Annual Review of Anthropology* 20 (1991): 279–309.

Phillips-Fein, Kim, *Invisible Hands: The Businessmen's Crusade against the New Deal* (New York and London, 2009).

Ross, David F., 'Gordon Lewis on Puerto Rico's Development Program', *The Journal of Politics* 19(1) (1957): 86–100.

Safa, Helen Icken, *The Myth of the Male Breadwinner: Women and Industrialization in the Caribbean* (Boulder, CO, 1995).

Singa Boyenge, Jean-Pierre, 'ILO Database on Export Processing Zones (Revised)', *ILO Working Papers* 251 (2007), http://www.ilo.org/public/english/dialogue/sector/themes/epz/epz-db.pdf.

Watanabe, S., 'Constraints on Labour-Intensive Export Industries in Mexico', *International Labour Review* 109 (1974): 23–45.

CHAPTER 2

Continuity and Change in Germany's Social Market Economy

A Matter of Economic Style?

ALEXANDER EBNER

Introduction

Recent discussions in the research strand of comparative capitalism have reconsidered the matter of institutional change in distinct varieties of capitalism by highlighting the aspect of ideas and discourses. The German variety of capitalism, and its politico-economic paradigm of the social market economy, provides a particularly relevant case in point. In outlining this case, the first section of this chapter discusses key components of the German variety of capitalism, in particular its system of production and related complementarities. The second section addresses the corresponding dynamics of continuity and change. It outlines policy-related efforts at institutional reform that have been shifting various institutional and structural components of the German model while confirming its basic rationale of combined market and non-market coordination. In examining the corresponding dimension of ideas and discourse, the third section explores the concept of the social market economy and its intellectual evolution in terms of the notion of economic style, as put forward most prominently by Alfred Müller-Armack.

Notes for this section begin on page 51.

Varieties of Capitalism and the Problem of Institutional Change

The comparative analysis of capitalist market economies perceives capitalism as a system of socio-economic interactions within an institutional order,
which takes different forms at different times and in different places. This
broad perspective of comparative capitalism usually proceeds by comparing
national institutional configurations that define comparative advantages for
firms and industries.[1] The 'varieties of capitalism' approach has emerged as
a potent line of reasoning in these endeavours. It undertakes a firm-centred
analysis of micro-behaviour in the exploration of national types of capitalist development, approached in terms of the institutional foundations of
competitive advantage, which determine firms' strategies. These include
the systems of finance, corporate governance, industrial relations, education
and training, and inter-firm relations. In this institutional context, firms face
coordination problems in their relationships with other firms and agents,
which are reflected in the level of transaction costs. Two 'ideal types' of capitalism are differentiated: liberal market economies with a dominant pattern
of market coordination through investment in transferable assets, and coordinated market economies with a dominant pattern of strategic coordination
through investment in specific assets.[2]

  In the related firm-centred perspective, liberal types of capitalist economies such as the United States share the market-oriented characteristics of
short-term company finance, deregulated labour markets, general education
and strong inter-company competition. In coordinated economies such as
Germany, firms' strategic behaviour is coordinated to a much larger extent
through non-market mechanisms, characterized by long-term company
finance, cooperative industrial relations, high levels of firm-specific vocational training and inter-firm cooperation in technology and standardization,
framed by industry associations. Liberal market economies exhibit advantages
in radical innovation, due to their flexible institutional setting that is more
conducive to entrepreneurial start-ups and their need for venture capital.
Coordinated market economies tend to specialize in incremental innovations
within stable organizational settings, based on endowments of skilled manual
workers, long-term capital investment and cooperative labour relations.
Crucially, these capitalist varieties specialize in industrial areas that complement their particular institutional advantages. As no single 'best model' is
achievable, and the gradual character of path-dependent institutional change
excludes isomorphic convergence, the diversity of capitalist models prevails.
However, the liberal model may prove superior in times of rapid technological change, whereas firms from coordinated economies operate best within
established technological paradigms.[3]

In this view, the systemic dynamism of institutional stability and change is fuelled by the impact of complementarities among the major institutional subsystems of the prevailing capitalist varieties. This scenario implies that each set of institutions depends on other sets in order to function effectively. In the words of Hall and Soskice, '[i]t suggests that nations with a particular type of coordination in one sphere of the economy should tend to develop complementary practices in other spheres as well'.[4] This phenomenon is caused by positive feedback effects: 'One set of institutions is said to be complementary to another when its presence raises the returns available from the other'.[5] A telling example of these complementarities in the post-war model of German capitalism is provided by the positive feedback mechanisms between the system of corporate governance that would allow for long-term financial relations, the firm-centred system of education and training with its long-term investments in human capital, and the cooperative system of industrial relations with its long-term outlook on economic performance.[6]

An important implication of this view of complementarities is that viable policy changes must be compatible with existing institutional patterns; that is, they must be 'incentive compatible' with the coordination mechanisms of the prevailing political-economic system. Critical reconsiderations of this viewpoint have underlined the wide scope for institutional 'hybridization', which changes the quality of complementarities by adding new institutional components. On a conceptual level, speaking of hybridization implies dealing with deviations from empirically grounded ideal types, and thus allows for an understanding of capitalist diversity in terms of institutional recombination and change.[7] In related terms, institutions do not represent optimal solutions to coordination problems, but rather temporary stable compromises in a setting of social conflicts that mirror the heterogeneity of the underlying interests. It follows that institutional change as a manifestation of social power asymmetries is subject to political considerations and influences, thus bringing the problems of institutional change closer to the domain of political economy.[8] Institutional change in varieties of capitalism, therefore, is to be perceived as a subtle political process that is covered by the temporary stability of formal institutional regimes. At this point, state–market relations, as well as the organizational pattern of interest groups, have a major role to play in shaping national pathways of change.[9] Similarly, the notions of path dependence and lock-in are said to characterize the evolution of the institutional setting of capitalist economies most adequately. In analytically comparing the options of incremental and abrupt processes of change, as well as its continuous and discontinuous results, both incremental and discontinuous change shape market liberalization as a major trend of the institutional transformation of advanced capitalist economies.[10]

Nevertheless, in discussing strategic efforts in the promotion of institutional change, the role of interests needs to be augmented by ideas and discourses. Such ideational institutionalism highlights the discursive dimension of institutions in shaping perceptions and understandings in the diverse orientations of policy-related affairs.[11] This leads to a perception of institutional change that accounts for both the involved structures and agents by invoking the role of ideas in terms of the cultural underpinnings of institutional change as reflected by the prevailing sets of norms and paradigms that both enable and constrain strategic action.[12] In related terms, the notion of discursive institutionalism sets out to explore the role of ideas and discourse in the politics of institutional change. Ideas are defined as the substantive content of discursive efforts in the interactive conveying of policies, providing a context of inter-subjective meaning.[13] In effect, these considerations of institutional change hint at the matter of ideas and discourses in understanding the dynamics of persistence and change in distinct varieties of capitalism. Indeed, in international comparison, different knowledge regimes in support of specific policy ideas may result in major differences concerning policy performance.[14] An example of these ideational variations and their actual policy impact is provided by the impact of distinct sets of ideas on monetary policy and currency affairs that have been most relevant in the setting of the German model of the social market economy.[15] In line with these aspects, the following section discusses the German variety of capitalism, followed by a reconsideration of its long-standing ideational framework that has been framing adaptive changes in its institutional setting.

Continuity and Change in the German Variety of Capitalism

The German economy has been Europe's export-oriented 'growth motor' throughout the post-war era, combining competitive openness with an extensive welfare state, framed by a favourable international economic environment with expanding trade and investment.[16] The corresponding production model has been based on flexible specialization; that is, a sectoral production model in industries such as machine tools and automobiles, with an adaptive flexibility to handle rapid shifts in demand based on a skilled workforce, cooperative industrial relations and high levels of social compensation.[17] In related terms, diversified quality production characterizes Germany's competitive advantages in the specialized production of high quality manufactured goods. Again, the adaptive flexibility of this production system and the integrated role of the workforce in industrial relations are decisive.[18]

Based on these conditions, the key complementarities in the German coordinated market economy evolved on the basis of systemic linkages between the following subsystems:[19]

- Corporate governance: permitting the flow of long-term financial resources with reputational monitoring as a non-market coordination mechanism in the financial sector.
- Industrial relations: permitting cooperative capital–labour relations with strategic bargaining and situational moderation in centralized wage setting as exercised by employers' associations and trade unions.
- Education and training: permitting sunk investment in firm- and industry-specific types of skills and human capital, organized in an encompassing framework that involves self-governing business associations.
- Inter-company relations: permitting the non-market diffusion of common standards and practices that support a cooperative mode of inter-firm technology transfer.

The corresponding pattern of managerial organization in large business firms has been held together by centralized stakeholder supervision, often coordinated by major banks. The basic rationale of this system of non-market coordination involves comprehensive institutional constraints favouring consensual patterns of activity.[20]

Historically, the German variety of capitalism emanated from the period of post-war reconstruction that led to sustained economic growth throughout the 1950s and 1960s. This was labelled the '*Wirtschaftswunder*' (economic miracle), and was dominated intellectually by a pragmatic type of ordoliberalism.[21] The steady decline of this growth performance led to an intermezzo of Keynesian regulation from the mid-1960s to the late 1970s, institutionalized in the format of the *Stabilitätsgesetz* from 1967 with its complex policy concerns for full employment, monetary stability, balanced foreign trade and steady economic growth. However, even this new type of economic policy was presented as a synthesis of ordoliberal ideas and a Keynesian approach.[22] Germany passed comparatively unscathed through the international stagflation phase of the 1970s by flexibly adapting its production regime, especially the mechanisms of wage coordination. Even the crisis of corporatist regulation in the late 1970s and the liberal-conservative power shift that came with the Kohl government in 1982 would not entail a political-economic break with non-market coordination.[23] Nevertheless, the economic challenges of structural change during the 1970s brought a reconsideration of policy ideas, now heralding supply-side strategies of privatization and deregulation that would become dominant in the 1980s.[24] During the 1990s, mass unemployment, growth stagnation and the fiscal burdens of reunification exerted further pressure for institutional reform, aggravated by the adverse impact of international macroeconomic policy conditions, in particular the Maastricht Treaty criteria.[25] Accordingly, the German model of the social market economy and its related policy paradigms have been subject to patterns of path dependence and institutional adaptation to changing internal and external conditions.

In this context, German policy discourse has been preoccupied with institutional changes intended to reinvent the system of the social market economy. In the ensuing 'clash of cultures of production regime', economic problems have been attributed to a lack of market dynamics in relational coordination. Thus, there have been efforts at liberalization that have seemingly been aimed at transplanting elements of liberal market economies into the setting of the German coordinated market economy.[26] The corresponding reconfiguration of the coordination environment of business firms pinpoints the key complementarities of the German variety of capitalism. This involves the drive for market-oriented corporate governance as well as flexibility in wage setting and labour regulations with an emphasis on the productivity of local firms, thus also reconfiguring the German brand of corporatism. Both 'social partners', involving employer associations and trade unions respectively, are experiencing decreasing organizational capacity, although institutional codetermination, which gives the unions a strong standing in supervisory boards and works councils of large firms, remains firmly in place.[27] Similar patterns of selective change apply to the financial system with its bank-based governance procedures in capital allocation, based on equity and monitoring interdependencies. Although it has opened up for capital markets, it still differs from market-based financial systems, as reflected in the marginal role of markets for corporate control. Also, the role of venture capital in Germany is still far from the one it plays in liberal market economies. The failure of Germany's '*Neuer Markt*' and its dissolution in 2004 indicate that institutional transplants from liberal varieties of capitalism may lose their momentum due to a mismatch with the complementary institutions of the German variety of capitalism.[28]

Institutional reform has also addressed social policy and unemployment. The importance of this area is accentuated by the fact that one-third of Germany's GDP is allocated to social policy, financing budgets for social transfers in areas such as unemployment benefits, health-care provision and old-age pensions. The combination of labour market policy and social policy has been a key issue since the 1970s, and it remained a fundamental concern during the 1990s, confronting fiscal pressures exercised by persistent unemployment and further aggravated by reunification and demographic change. Related liberalization efforts are well exemplified by the local differentiation of wage coordination and the activation approach in labour market policy, accompanied by the establishment of a secondary labour market with low-wage and part-time jobs intended to boost employment in a manner more typical of liberal varieties of capitalism, and thus deviating from the ideological norms of the German model.[29] This orientation became a priority after the failure of neo-corporatist labour market initiatives in the shape of the doomed efforts such as the '*Bündnis für Arbeit*', part of the red–green Schröder government's efforts to implement the reform proposals of the '*Agenda 2010*' programme, with its key components of labour market activation and social policies that intensified the dualism of the labour market with far-reaching social consequences.[30] In effect, market-oriented reforms have fuelled the differentiation of household incomes since the 1980s, with a further polarization during the 2000s.[31] In this setting, a particularly revealing issue is social attitudes about conflicts of interest between different wealth and income groups. In fact, conflict levels in Germany were moderate even during the 1980s, whereas the relative proportions of those noticing an intensification of social conflicts between capital and labour, or between the wealthy and the less well off, rose above 70 per cent in the 2000s.[32]

Nevertheless, despite political and social changes, any assessment of the corresponding reform efforts needs to account for the fact that the main institutional patterns of coordination in the German variety of capitalism persist.[33] In examining the corresponding dimension of ideas and discourses, which seems to have contributed to the prevailing combination of adaptive change and systemic continuity, the following section explores the concept of the social market economy as an integrative ideological factor in the development of the German variety of capitalism.

The Concept of the Social Market Economy as an Economic Style

The production regime of the German variety of capitalism is still largely shaped by the rationale of diversified quality production, as exemplified by industries such as automobiles and tool-making. Reform projects that favour a drive for adaptive flexibility without due consideration of systemic complementarities and interactions among the major institutional components are thus doomed to create unintended inefficiencies.[34] These aspects of industrial flexibility and social integration have been framed by the ideological setting of a neo-corporatist consensus democracy that provides the political backbone for the international competitiveness of the German variety of capitalism.[35] When it comes to understanding patterns of persistence and change, a key aspect of these institutional complementarities is outlined by the prevailing policy paradigms and ideas. In the German case, the corresponding ideas point to the ordoliberal credo that is associated with the competitive order of the market system, to be executed by a strong state with a level of policy competence able to reject the demands of special interest groups.[36] Both this policy orientation and its institutional framework coincide with the integrative ideas of the 'social market economy'. This approach was originally presented in the analytical terms of a distinct style of economic life, a well-established line of reasoning in the historical comparison of economic systems – with normative implications that would echo traditions of German *Socialpolitik*.[37]

Conceptually, the notion of economic style is in the tradition of the German Historical School and its diverse manifestations in economic sociology and political economy.[38] Arthur Spiethoff's related work built on Max Weber and Werner Sombart, among others, as his notion of economic style or *Wirtschaftsstil* is intended to provide analytical tools for grasping the nature of an economic formation by highlighting its most important characteristics. These involve attitudes and habits of economic action, the natural and technological basis of economic life, the social structure of economy and society, as well as their institutional underpinnings, accompanied by the dynamism of economic growth.[39] In this manner, Spiethoff's notion of economic style encompasses material and structural as well as institutional and cultural elements, without establishing a hierarchy of priorities, while it remains sensitive to the indeterminateness of historical processes.[40] In subsequent debates on these issues, Alfred Müller-Armack's approach to economic styles has proved to be most influential in the domain of comparative economic systems, also due to related elaborations on the concept of the social market economy. An assessment of Müller-Armack's approach needs to account for the major change that occurred in the intellectual atmosphere of German economics after the Second World War, shifting from historicist positions to ordoliberal thought. Pioneering contributions of ordoliberal theorists would focus on the relationship between economic, legal and social issues, as exemplified by Walter Eucken. The corresponding ordoliberal credo related the competitive order of market processes, primarily based on a market price system, with a set of well-established property rights and competition-promoting policies by a strong state, framed by institutional pillars such as religion-based communities.[41]

Paralleling these concerns, Müller-Armack's reasoning combined theoretical positions of ordoliberal theory with Weberian and Sombartian motifs, highlighting a culturally sensitive understanding of the role of religion and related worldviews in economic life.[42] The intellectual context of the German Historical School mattered most for that particular perspective, in accordance with Müller-Armack's general interest in the contours of economic development.[43] In reconsidering Weberian arguments on the genesis of modern capitalism, Müller-Armack used religious worldviews as a criterion for the historical-geographical identification of certain economic styles, as they shape economic, political and technological attitudes in a particular historical and spatial setting.[44] Economic styles should represent the 'unity of expression and attitude' of a certain people or nation in a particular historical period; that is, as a unity of the cultural expressions of economic and sociocultural life and its underlying worldviews. These styles of economic life would become subject to fragmentation over time, resulting in ever more complex style configurations.[45]

Based on these considerations, Müller-Armack formulated the concept of the social market economy as an economic style of reconciliation in the face of the economic, social and political fragmentation that shaped Germany after 1945. This fragmentation was supposed to be overcome by social regulation of market competition without giving way to contemporary programmes on socialist planning, which had become prevalent in both the Social Democratic and Christian Democratic camps during the late 1940s.[46] From the outset, an 'irenical formula' was to reconcile diverse worldviews and ideologies: an 'enlightened' Catholic social philosophy with its principles of social balance and subsidiarity was to be combined with the Protestant ethos of communal cooperation, socialist concerns for the social question and liberal principles of progress in liberty.[47] The resulting model of the social market economy was meant to represent a new economic style that would reach beyond the laissez-faire principles of liberal capitalism and the centralized planning efforts of state socialism. It was intended to emphasize a socially managed market mechanism with its flexible price system.[48] This would go together with the acknowledgement of market failure and the possible incongruence of market process and social justice. In effect, the competitive order was to be embedded in an institutional framework that provides for integration and reconciliation through common norms and values.[49] It is noteworthy that subsequently formulated policy conclusions on European integration since the 1950s also referred to the requirements of such an ethical-cultural style consensus.[50] Indeed, according to Müller-Armack, both the social market economy and European integration could be perceived as outstanding types of integrative ideas.[51]

This integrative character of the concept of the social market economy also informs its conceptual adaptiveness concerning the actual combinations of market competition and social concerns. While motives of a religious-cultural framing of economic and social affairs remained crucial in the conceptualization of the social market economy, later presentations of the subject would follow a much more secular mode of argumentation that confronted the market-distorting interventionism of structural policies and the expansion of the welfare state. A second phase of the social market economy was to focus on interrelations between economy and society, again combining the logic of market competition with social regulation through a strong state. This perspective would become prevalent during the 1970s, when the decline of the post-war age of full employment, monetary stability and fiscal consolidation seemed to herald a new set of legitimization problems of capitalist market economies.[52] In fact, however, this line of reasoning proved to be fairly compatible with major strands of social democracy, as put forward by Karl Schiller in the context of contemporary efforts at promoting a neo-corporatist steering model of the economy. Already in the aftermath of the Godesberg Programme of the SPD in 1959 with its market-embracing components, social democratic discourses on economic policy had largely accepted the basic formula of the social market economy with its reconciliatory motives.[53] Thus, the reform discussions of the 1970s did not alter the basic formula of the adaptive framework of the social market economy, and nor did the ecological concerns that would dominate the 1980s. The intellectual underpinnings of social democratic reform efforts under Chancellor Schröder in the late 1990s finally renewed the original agenda of the social market economy by focusing on the competitive activation of society that already existed on the individual level.[54] In this manner, the notion of the social market economy persists as an integrative idea in the German variety of capitalism.

Conclusion

The institutional integration and coherence of political–economic systems requires supportive configurations of ideas and discourses. This aspect informs the debate on the comparative institutional analysis of capitalist varieties as outlined above with regard to the German variety of capitalism and the concept of the social market economy. A particularly relevant point of departure in this endeavour is the reconsideration of the system of production and related complementarities that shape a particular variety of capitalism. The corresponding complementarities define a corridor of reform efforts and thus effectuate institutional changes. In the case of Germany, recent efforts at institutional reform have shifted the established patterns of market and non-market coordination towards a more market-oriented constellation, yet without giving up key positions of non-market coordination in economic and social affairs. Even though privatization and deregulation have stimulated an expansion of the private sector and its related logic of market competition, it is fair to state that key features of the German model persist. With regard to the underlying role of ideas and discourses, the concept of the social market economy stands out as an integrative factor in mediating continuity and change. Its intellectual profile fits the adaptive flexibility of the German variety of capitalism in general.

Alexander Ebner is professor of Political Economy and Economic Sociology at Goethe University Frankfurt. His major research interests address the comparative institutional analysis of modern capitalism as well as the history of economic thought. Most recent publications include the editorship of a special issue of *Regional Studies* on regional varieties of capitalism (2015). A monograph on the Schumpeterian view of entrepreneurship and capitalist development is forthcoming in 2017.

Notes

1. Gregory Jackson and Richard Deeg, 'From Comparing Capitalisms to the Politics of Institutional Change', *Review of International Political Economy* 15(4) (2008): 680–709.

2. Peter A. Hall and David Soskice, 'An Introduction to Varieties of Capitalism', in *Varieties of Capitalism: The Institutional Foundations of Comparative Advantage*, ed. Peter A. Hall and David Soskice (Oxford, 2001), 1–68.

3. Ibid., 38–41.

4. Ibid., 18.

5. Peter A. Hall and Daniel W. Gingerich, 'Varieties of Capitalism and Institutional Complementarities in the Political Economy: An Empirical Analysis', in *Debating Varieties of Capitalism*, ed. Bob Hancké (Oxford, 2009), 136.

6. Hall and Soskice, 'Introduction', 28.

7. Colin Crouch, *Capitalist Diversity and Change: Recombinant Governance and Institutional Entrepreneurs* (Oxford, 2005).

8. Bruno Amable, *The Diversity of Modern Capitalism* (Oxford, 2003), 10.

9. Bob Hancké, Martin Rhodes and Mark Thatcher, 'Introduction: Beyond Varieties of Capitalism', in *Beyond Varieties of Capitalism: Conflict, Contradictions, and Complementarities in the European Economy*, ed. Bob Hancké, Martin Rhodes and Mark Thatcher (Oxford, 2007), 3–38; Peter A. Hall and Kathleen Thelen, 'Institutional Change in Varieties of Capitalism', *Socio-Economic Review* 7(1) (2009): 7–34.

10. Wolfgang Streeck and Kathleen Thelen, 'Institutional Change in Advanced Political Economies', in *Beyond Continuity: Institutional Change in Advanced Political Economies*, ed. Wolfgang Streeck and Kathleen Thelen (Oxford, 2005), 8–9.

11. John L. Campbell and Ove K. Pedersen, 'Introduction: The Rise of Neoliberalism and Institutional Analysis', in *The Rise of Neoliberalism and Institutional Analysis*, ed. John L. Campbell and Ove K. Pedersen (Princeton, NJ, 2001), 6.

12. John L. Campbell, *Institutional Change and Globalization* (Princeton, NJ, 2004), 4–6.

13. Vivien A. Schmidt, 'Discursive Institutionalism: The Explanatory Power of Ideas and Discourse', *Annual Review of Political Science* 11(2) (2008): 303–26.

14. John L. Campbell and Ove K. Pedersen, *The National Origins of Policy Ideas: Knowledge Regimes in the United States, France, Germany, and Denmark* (Princeton, NJ, 2014).

15. Terence W. Hutchison, 'Notes on the Effects of Economic Ideas on Policy: The Example of the German Social Market Economy', *Zeitschrift für die gesamte Staatswissenschaft* 135(3) (1979): 426–41.

16. Barry Eichengreen, *The European Economy since 1945: Coordinated Capitalism and Beyond* (Princeton, NJ, 2007); Horst Siebert, *The German Economy: Beyond the Social Market* (Princeton, NJ, 2005).

17. Michael Piore and Charles Sabel, *The Second Industrial Divide: Possibilities for Prosperity* (New York, 1984).

18. Arndt Sorge and Wolfgang Streeck, 'Industrial Relations and Technical Change: The Case for an Extended Perspective', in *New Technology and Industrial Relations*, ed. Richard Hyman and Wolfgang Streeck (Oxford, 1988), 19–47.

19. Hall and Soskice, 'Introduction', 28.

20. Herbert Kitschelt and Wolfgang Streeck, 'From Stability to Stagnation: Germany at the Beginning of the Twenty-First Century', in *Germany: Beyond the Stable State*, ed. Herbert Kitschelt and Wolfgang Streeck (London, 2004), 1–35.

21. James C. Van Hook, *Rebuilding Germany: The Creation of the Social Market Economy 1945–1957* (Cambridge, 2004).

22. Werner Abelshauser, *Deutsche Wirtschaftsgeschichte seit 1945* (Munich, 2004), 410–13.

23. Peter A. Hall, 'The Evolution of Varieties of Capitalism in Europe', in *Beyond Varieties of Capitalism: Conflict, Contradictions, and Complementarities in the European Economy*, ed. Bob Hancké, Martin Rhodes and Mark Thatcher (Oxford, 2007), 60–63.

24. Monica Prasad, *The Politics of Free Markets: The Rise of Neoliberal Economic Policies in Britain, France, Germany, and the United States* (Chicago, 2006).

25. Sigurt Vitols, 'Das "deutsche Modell" in der politischen Ökonomie', in *Gibt es einen deutschen Kapitalismus? Tradition und globale Perspektiven der sozialen Marktwirtschaft*, ed. Volker Berghahn and Sigurt Vitols (Frankfurt am Main, 2006), 44–61; Wendy Carlin and David Soskice, 'German Economic Performance: Disentangling the Role of Supply-Side Reforms, Macroeconomic Policy and Coordinated Economy Institutions', *Socio-Economic Review* 7(1) (2009): 67–99.

26. Werner Abelshauser, *Kulturkampf: Der deutsche Weg in die neue Wirtschaft und die amerikanische Herausforderung* (Berlin, 2003); idem, 'Der "Rheinische Kapitalismus" im Kampf der Wirtschaftskulturen', in *Gibt es einen deutschen Kapitalismus? Tradition und globale Perspektiven der sozialen Marktwirtschaft*, ed. Volker Berghahn and Sigurt Vitols (Frankfurt am Main and New York, 2006), 186–99.

27. Wolfgang Streeck, *Re-Forming Capitalism: Institutional Change in the German Political Economy* (Oxford, 2009).

28. Sigurt Vitols and Lutz Engelhardt, 'National Institutions and High Tech Industries: A Varieties of Capitalism Perspective on the Failure of Germany's "Neuer Markt"', WZB Discussion Paper SP II 2005-03 (Berlin, 2005).

29. Hall, 'Evolution', 69–71.

30. Roland Czada, 'Die neue deutsche Wohlfahrtswelt: Sozialpolitik und Arbeitswelt im Wandel', in *Wohlfahrtsstaat – Transformation und Perspektiven*, ed. Susanne Lütz and Roland Czada (Wiesbaden, 2005), 127–54.

31. Hans-Ulrich Wehler, *Deutsche Gesellschaftsgeschichte. Bd.5: Bundesrepublik und DDR 1949–1990* (Bonn, 2009); Jens Becker and Jürgen Faik, 'Konflikt und Ungleichheit. Anmerkungen zur sozialen Verfasstheit der "Berliner Republik"', *Mittelweg* 36 (2010), 81–89.

32. See Wolfgang Glatzer, Jens Becker, Oliver Nüchter, Roland Bieräugel and Geraldine Hallein-Benze, *Reichtum im Urteil der Bevölkerung: Akzeptanzprobleme und Spannungspotentiale in Deutschland* (Opladen, 2009), 95.

33. David Soskice, 'Systemische Reform: Der Fall Deutschland', in *Gibt es einen deutschen Kapitalismus? Tradition und globale Perspektiven der sozialen Marktwirtschaft*, ed. Volker Berghahn and Sigurt Vitols (Frankfurt am Main, 2006), 215–24.

34. Hall and Gingerich, 'Varieties', 168–69.

35. Abelshauser, *Wirtschaftsgeschichte*, 51–52.

36. Christian Watrin, 'The Social Market Economy: The Main Ideas and their Influence on Economic Policy', in *The Social Market Economy: Theory and Ethics of the Economic Order*, ed. Peter Koslowski (Berlin, 1998), 13–28; Ralf Ptak, 'Neoliberalism in Germany: Revisiting the Ordoliberal Foundations of the Social Market Economy', in *The Road from Mont Pèlerin: The Making of the Neoliberal Thought Collective*, ed. Philip Mirowski and Dieter Plehwe (Chicago, 2009), 98–138.

37. Alexander Ebner, 'The Intellectual Foundations of the Social Market Economy: Theory, Policy and Implications for European Integration', *Journal of Economic Studies* 33(3) (2006): 206–23.

38. Alexander Ebner, 'Wirtschaftskulturforschung: Ein sozialökonomisches Forschungsprogramm', in *Theorie und Geschichte der Wirtschaft: Festschrift für Bertram Schefold*, ed. Volker Caspari (Marburg, 2009), 121–46.

39. Arthur Spiethoff, 'Die Allgemeine Volkswirtschaftslehre als geschichtliche Theorie: Die Wirtschaftsstile', *Schmollers Jahrbuch für Gesetzgebung, Verwaltung und Volkswirtschaft im Deutschen Reich* 56(2) (1932): 76.

40. Bertram Schefold, 'Theoretical Approaches to a Comparison of Economic Systems from a Historical Perspective', in *The Theory of Ethical Economy in the Historical School*, ed. Peter Koslowski (Heidelberg, 1995), 221–47.

41. Heinz Rieter and Mathias Schmolz, 'The Ideas of German Ordoliberalism 1938–45: Pointing the Way to a New Economic Order', *European Journal of the History of Economic Thought* 1(1) (1993): 87–114.

42. Peter Koslowski, 'The Social Market Economy: Social Equilibration of Capitalism and Consideration of the Totality of the Economic Order – Notes on Alfred Müller-Armack', in *The Social Market Economy: Theory and Ethics of the Economic Order*, ed. Peter Koslowski (Berlin, 1998), 73–95, 74n.

43. Bertram Schefold, 'Vom Interventionsstaat zur Sozialen Marktwirtschaft: Der Weg Alfred Müller-Armacks', in *Vademecum zu einem Klassiker der Ordnungspolitik*, ed. Bertram Schefold (Düsseldorf, 1999), 5–42, 16.

44. Alfred Müller-Armack, 'Genealogie der Wirtschaftsstile: Die geistesgeschichtlichen Ursprünge der Staats- und Wirtschaftsformen bis zum Ausgang des 18. Jahrhunderts' (Stuttgart, 1941), reproduced in idem, *Religion und Wirtschaft: Geistesgeschichtliche Hintergründe unserer europäischen Lebensform*, 3rd edition (Bern, 1981), 46–244, 48.

45. Ibid., 57.

46. Philip Manow, 'Ordoliberalismus als ökonomische Ordnungstheologie', *Leviathan* 29 (2001), 179 –98.

47. Alfred Müller-Armack, 'Soziale Irenik', *Weltwirtschaftliches Archiv* 64 (1950), reproduced in idem, *Religion und Wirtschaft: Geistesgeschichtliche Hintergründe unserer europäischen Lebensform*, 3rd edition (Bern, 1981), 559–78, 564.

48. Alfred Müller-Armack, 'Wirtschaftslenkung und Marktwirtschaft' (Hamburg, 1946), reproduced in idem, *Wirtschaftsordnung und Wirtschaftspolitik: Studien und Konzepte zur Sozialen Marktwirtschaft und zur Europäischen Integration* (Freiburg, 1966), 19–170, 109.

49. Alfred Müller-Armack, 'Stil und Ordnung der Sozialen Marktwirtschaft', in *Wirtschaftliche Entwicklung und soziale Ordnung*, ed. E. Lagler and J. Messner (Vienna, 1952), reproduced in Alfred Müller-Armack, *Wirtschaftsordnung und Wirtschaftspolitik: Studien und Konzepte zur Sozialen Marktwirtschaft und zur Europäischen Integration* (Freiburg, 1966), 231–42, 234.

50. Ebner, 'Intellectual Foundations'.

51. Alfred Müller-Armack, 'Das gesellschaftspolitische Leitbild der Sozialen Marktwirtschaft', *Wirtschaftspolitische Chronik* 3 (1962), reproduced in idem, *Wirtschaftsordnung und Wirtschaftspolitik: Studien und Konzepte zur Sozialen Marktwirtschaft und zur Europäischen Integration* (Freiburg, 1966), 293–315.

52. Ludwig Erhard and Alfred Müller-Armack, *Soziale Marktwirtschaft: Ordnung der Zukunft – Manifest '72* (Frankfurt am Main, 1972).

53. Andrea Rehling, 'Die konzertierte Aktion im Spannungsfeld der 1970er Jahre: Geburtsstunde des Modells Deutschland und Ende des modernen Korporatismus', in *'Nach dem Strukturbruch'? Kontinuität und Wandel von Arbeitsbeziehungen und Arbeitswelt(en) seit den 1970er Jahren*, ed. Knud Andresen, Ursula Bitzegeio and Jürgen Mittag (Bonn, 2011), 65–86.

54. Alexander Ebner, 'Die europäische Beschäftigungsstrategie in der Reform des Wohlfahrtsstaats: Aktive Arbeitsmarktpolitik, aktivierende Sozialpolitik und das Leitbild der Wettbewerbsfähigkeit', in *Keine Arbeit und so viel zu tun*, ed. Helge Peukert (Münster, 2007), 195–217.

Bibliography

Abelshauser, Werner, *Deutsche Wirtschaftsgeschichte seit 1945* (Munich, 2004).

———, *Kulturkampf: Der deutsche Weg in die neue Wirtschaft und die amerikanische Herausforderung* (Berlin, 2003).

———, 'Der "Rheinische Kapitalismus" im Kampf der Wirtschaftskulturen', in *Gibt es einen deutschen Kapitalismus? Tradition und globale Perspektiven der sozialen Marktwirtschaft*, ed. Volker Berghahn and Sigurt Vitols (Frankfurt am Main and New York, 2006), 186–99.

Amable, Bruno, *The Diversity of Modern Capitalism* (Oxford, 2003).

Becker, Jens, and Jürgen Faik, 'Konflikt und Ungleichheit: Anmerkungen zur sozialen Verfasstheit der "Berliner Republik"', *Mittelweg* 36 (2010): 81–89.

Campbell, John L., *Institutional Change and Globalization* (Princeton, NJ, 2004).

Campbell, John L., and Ove K. Pedersen, 'Introduction: The Rise of Neoliberalism and Institutional Analysis', in *The Rise of Neoliberalism and Institutional Analysis*, ed. John L. Campbell and Ove K. Pedersen (Princeton, NJ, 2001), 1–23.

———, *The National Origins of Policy Ideas: Knowledge Regimes in the United States, France, Germany, and Denmark* (Princeton, NJ, 2014).

Carlin, Wendy, and David Soskice, 'German Economic Performance: Disentangling the Role of Supply-Side Reforms, Macroeconomic Policy and Coordinated Economy Institutions', *Socio-Economic Review* 7(1) (2009): 67–99.

Crouch, Colin, *Capitalist Diversity and Change: Recombinant Governance and Institutional Entrepreneurs* (Oxford, 2005).

Czada, Roland, 'Die neue deutsche Wohlfahrtswelt: Sozialpolitik und Arbeitswelt im Wandel', in *Wohlfahrtsstaat – Transformation und Perspektiven*, ed. Susanne Lütz and Roland Czada (Wiesbaden, 2005), 127–54.

Ebner, Alexander, 'The Intellectual Foundations of the Social Market Economy: Theory, Policy and Implications for European Integration', *Journal of Economic Studies* 33(3) (2006): 206–23.

———, 'Die europäische Beschäftigungsstrategie in der Reform des Wohlfahrtsstaats: Aktive Arbeitsmarktpolitik, aktivierende Sozialpolitik und das Leitbild der Wettbewerbsfähigkeit', in *Keine Arbeit und so viel zu tun*, ed. Helge Peukert (Münster, 2007), 195–217.

———, 'Wirtschaftskulturforschung: Ein sozialökonomisches Forschungsprogramm', in *Theorie und Geschichte der Wirtschaft: Festschrift für Bertram Schefold*, ed. Volker Caspari (Marburg, 2009), 121–46.

Eichengreen, Barry, *The European Economy since 1945: Coordinated Capitalism and Beyond* (Princeton, NJ, 2007).

Erhard, Ludwig, and Alfred Müller-Armack, *Soziale Marktwirtschaft: Ordnung der Zukunft – Manifest '72* (Frankfurt am Main, 1972).

Glatzer, Wolfgang, et al., *Reichtum im Urteil der Bevölkerung: Akzeptanzprobleme und Spannungspotentiale in Deutschland* (Opladen, 2009).

Hall, Peter A., 'The Evolution of Varieties of Capitalism in Europe', in *Beyond Varieties of Capitalism: Conflict, Contradictions, and Complementarities in the European Economy*, ed. Bob Hancké, Martin Rhodes and Mark Thatcher (Oxford, 2007), 39–85.

Hall, Peter A., and Daniel W. Gingerich, 'Varieties of Capitalism and Institutional Complementarities in the Political Economy: An Empirical Analysis', in *Debating Varieties of Capitalism*, ed. Bob Hancké (Oxford, 2009), 135–79.

Hall, Peter A., and David Soskice, 'An Introduction to Varieties of Capitalism', in *Varieties of Capitalism: The Institutional Foundations of Comparative Advantage*, ed. Peter A. Hall and David Soskice (Oxford, 2001), 1–68.

Hall, Peter A., and Kathleen Thelen, 'Institutional Change in Varieties of Capitalism', *Socio-Economic Review* 7(1) (2009): 7–34.

Hancké, Bob, Martin Rhodes and Mark Thatcher, 'Introduction: Beyond Varieties of Capitalism', in *Beyond Varieties of Capitalism: Conflict, Contradictions, and Complementarities in the European Economy*, ed. Bob Hancké, Martin Rhodes and Mark Thatcher (Oxford, 2007), 3–38.

Hutchison, Terence W., 'Notes on the Effects of Economic Ideas on Policy: The Example of the German Social Market Economy', *Zeitschrift für die gesamte Staatswissenschaft* 135(3) (1979): 426–41.

Jackson, Gregory, and Richard Deeg, 'From Comparing Capitalisms to the Politics of Institutional Change', *Review of International Political Economy* 15(4) (2008): 680–709.

Kitschelt, Herbert, and Wolfgang Streeck, 'From Stability to Stagnation: Germany at the Beginning of the Twenty-First Century', in *Germany: Beyond the Stable State*, ed. Herbert Kitschelt and Wolfgang Streeck (London, 2004), 1–35.

Koslowski, Peter, 'The Social Market Economy: Social Equilibration of Capitalism and Consideration of the Totality of the Economic Order – Notes on Alfred Müller-Armack', in *The Social Market Economy: Theory and Ethics of the Economic Order*, ed. Peter Koslowski (Berlin, 1998), 73–95.

Manow, Philip, 'Ordoliberalismus als ökonomische Ordnungstheologie', *Leviathan* 29 (2001): 179–98.

Müller-Armack, Alfred, *Wirtschaftsordnung und Wirtschaftspolitik: Studien und Konzepte zur Sozialen Marktwirtschaft und zur Europäischen Integration* (Freiburg, 1966), 19–170.

———, 'Das gesellschaftspolitische Leitbild der Sozialen Marktwirtschaft', *Wirtschaftspolitische Chronik* 3 (1962), reproduced in idem, *Wirtschaftsordnung und Wirtschaftspolitik: Studien und Konzepte zur Sozialen Marktwirtschaft und zur Europäischen Integration* (Freiburg, 1966), 293–315.

———, 'Stil und Ordnung der Sozialen Marktwirtschaft', in *Wirtschaftliche Entwicklung und soziale Ordnung*, ed. E. Lagler and J. Messner (Vienna, 1952), reproduced in Alfred Müller-Armack, *Wirtschaftsordnung und Wirtschaftspolitik: Studien und Konzepte zur Sozialen Marktwirtschaft und zur Europäischen Integration* (Freiburg, 1966), 231–42.

———, 'Soziale Irenik', *Weltwirtschaftliches Archiv* 64 (1950), reproduced in idem, *Religion und Wirtschaft: Geistesgeschichtliche Hintergründe unserer europäischen Lebensform*, 3rd edition (Bern, 1981), 559–78.

———, 'Wirtschaftslenkung und Marktwirtschaft' (Hamburg, 1946), reproduced in idem, *Wirtschaftsordnung und Wirtschaftspolitik: Studien und Konzepte zur Sozialen Marktwirtschaft und zur Europäischen Integration* (Freiburg 1966), 19–170.

Piore, Michael, and Charles Sabel, *The Second Industrial Divide: Possibilities for Prosperity* (New York, 1984).

Prasad, Monica, *The Politics of Free Markets: The Rise of Neoliberal Economic Policies in Britain, France, Germany, and the United States* (Chicago, 2006).

Ptak, Ralf, 'Neoliberalism in Germany: Revisiting the Ordoliberal Foundations of the Social Market Economy', in *The Road from Mont Pèlerin: The Making of the Neoliberal Thought Collective*, ed. Philip Mirowski and Dieter Plehwe (Chicago, 2009), 98–138.

Rehling, Andrea, 'Die konzertierte Aktion im Spannungsfeld der 1970er Jahre: Geburtsstunde des Modells Deutschland und Ende des modernen Korporatismus', in *'Nach dem Strukturbruch'? Kontinuität und Wandel von Arbeitsbeziehungen und Arbeitswelt(en) seit den 1970er Jahren*, ed. Knud Andresen, Ursula Bitzegeio and Jürgen Mittag (Bonn, 2011), 65–86.

Rieter, Heinz, and Mathias Schmolz, 'The Ideas of German Ordoliberalism 1938–45: Pointing the Way to a New Economic Order', *European Journal of the History of Economic Thought* 1(1) (1993): 87–114.

Schefold, Bertram, 'Theoretical Approaches to a Comparison of Economic Systems from a Historical Perspective', in *The Theory of Ethical Economy in the Historical School*, ed. Peter Koslowski (Heidelberg, 1995), 221–47.

———, 'Vom Interventionsstaat zur Sozialen Marktwirtschaft: Der Weg Alfred Müller-Armacks', in *Vademecum zu einem Klassiker der Ordnungspolitik*, ed. Bertram Schefold (Düsseldorf, 1999), 5–42.

Schmidt, Vivien A., 'Discursive Institutionalism: The Explanatory Power of Ideas and Discourse', *Annual Review of Political Science* 11(2) (2008): 303–26.

Siebert, Horst, *The German Economy: Beyond the Social Market* (Princeton, NJ, 2005).

Sorge, Arndt, and Wolfgang Streeck, 'Industrial Relations and Technical Change: The Case for an Extended Perspective', in *New Technology and Industrial Relations*, ed. Richard Hyman and Wolfgang Streeck (Oxford, 1988), 19–47.

Soskice, David, 'Systemische Reform: Der Fall Deutschland', in *Gibt es einen deutschen Kapitalismus? Tradition und globale Perspektiven der sozialen Marktwirtschaft*, ed. Volker Berghahn and Sigurd Vitols (Frankfurt am Main, 2006), 215–24.

Spiethoff, Arthur, 'Die Allgemeine Volkswirtschaftslehre als geschichtliche Theorie: Die Wirtschaftsstile', *Schmollers Jahrbuch für Gesetzgebung, Verwaltung und Volkswirtschaft im Deutschen Reich* 56(2) (1932): 51–84.

Streeck, Wolfgang, *Re-Forming Capitalism: Institutional Change in the German Political Economy* (Oxford, 2009).

Streeck, Wolfgang, and Kathleen Thelen, 'Institutional Change in Advanced Political Economies', in *Beyond Continuity: Institutional Change in Advanced Political Economies*, ed. Wolfgang Streeck and Kathleen Thelen (Oxford, 2005), 1–39.

Van Hook, James C., *Rebuilding Germany: The Creation of the Social Market Economy 1945–1957* (Cambridge, 2004).

Vitols, Sigurt, 'Das "deutsche Modell" in der politischen Ökonomie', in *Gibt es einen deutschen Kapitalismus? Tradition und globale Perspektiven der sozialen Marktwirtschaft*, ed. Volker Berghahn and Sigurd Vitols (Frankfurt am Main, 2006), 44–61.

Vitols, Sigurt, and Lutz Engelhardt, 'National Institutions and High Tech Industries: A Varieties of Capitalism Perspective on the Failure of Germany's "Neuer Markt"', WZB Discussion Paper SP II 2005-03 (Berlin, 2005).

Watrin, Christian, 'The Social Market Economy: The Main Ideas and their Influence on Economic Policy', in *The Social Market Economy: Theory and Ethics of the Economic Order*, ed. Peter Koslowski (Berlin, 1998), 13–28.

Wehler, Hans-Ulrich, *Deutsche Gesellschaftsgeschichte. Bd.5: Bundesrepublik und DDR 1949–1990* (Bonn, 2009).

CHAPTER 3

Pioneers of Capitalism

The Reshaping of the East German Planned Economy and the Managers of the Treuhandanstalt between State, Market and Society (1990–1994)

MARCUS BÖICK

Old Enemies are the Best

In summer 2011, at the peak of the financial crisis in Greece and the euro area, a nearly forgotten institution resurfaced among the wider European public. Jean-Claude Juncker, prime minister of Luxembourg and then chairman of the Euro Group of finance ministers, in an interview with the German news magazine *Der Spiegel*, proposed a privatization programme for the Greek economy that was supposed to fill the empty coffers in Athens with about 50 billion euros.[1] This process of denationalization concerned transport and energy companies, ports and hospitals, and was to be carried out by an independent agency, run by economic experts and managers in an 'entrepreneurial' style. Juncker and other European politicians had a specific role model in mind: the German *Treuhandanstalt*, which had overseen the rapid transformation of nearly twelve thousand East German companies, with four million employees, from a planned to a market economy after the fall of the Iron Curtain in the early 1990s.

Notes for this section begin on page 70.

The reaction of the German press was somewhat ambivalent: a *Treuhand*-style privatization to contain the looming crisis in the euro zone? One German commentator called the suggestion 'adventurous'.[2] In a public speech to journalists, Nobel laureate Günter Grass sharply denounced the *Treuhand* as a 'semi-criminal enterprise', a gang of dubious capitalist managers who intended to expropriate from eastern Germans their state-owned properties.[3] Grass was attacking a familiar enemy: as one of the most prominent contemporary critics, the author never missed a chance to label the *Treuhand* a 'neoliberal conspiracy', especially in his much-debated novels *Ein weites Feld* (1995) and *Mein Jahrhundert* (2001).

Juncker's 'best practice' suggestion and Grass's sharp response in summer 2011 marked the different political poles of remembering and interpreting the history of the *Treuhandanstalt*: while foreign politicians, analysts and economists have praised the rapid and straight post-socialist 'turnaround' management of the *Treuhand* and its experts,[4] especially in comparison with other 'cases' in Eastern Europe, the wider German public remains deeply divided to this day. On the one hand, conservative and liberal politicians and academic economists, as well as the community of former *Treuhand* managers, still defend the post-socialist privatization programme as an 'extraordinary effort' for 'freedom and wealth' without any 'historical example'.[5] The dramatic breakdown of many traditional East German firms and the mass dismissals managed by the *Treuhand* in the early 1990s are, on this view, tragic but inevitable legacies of forty years of communist mismanagement. On the other hand, left-wing and post-communist politicians, journalists and many personally affected East Germans, who had opted for a gradual, more cautious reconstruction of post-socialist economy with a strong state as patient property owner, share Grass's angry verdict. They still condemn the accelerated mass privatizations as a 'Great Expropriation' on behalf of West German enterprises that left millions of Easterners on the streets.[6] Economic depression, 'deindustrialization', mass unemployment, disaffection and dissatisfaction in East Germany are interpreted as a dramatic failure of the 'neoliberal' management of transformation in the mode of 'shock therapy'.[7]

To summarize, the much debated legacy of the *Treuhandanstalt* proves at least that old enemies are the best. Even twenty years after its dissolution, the institution's name is likely to inflame an audience of (older) eastern Germans, while most western Germans only grimly recall the thousands of billions of 'taxpayers' money' that has been constantly flowing eastwards since 1990. Juncker's call for a Greek *Treuhand* was supposedly meant to signal approval of German achievements after reunification in the heated debate over how to rescue the Greek state from bankruptcy and perhaps the whole euro area from collapse. However, the prime minister inadvertently touched a raw nerve; to many Germans, east and west, the *Treuhandanstalt* was not success story.

Exploring the Traces of Post-socialist Managers

Needless to say, this brief chapter will definitely not settle the long-lasting conflict between 'affirmative' and 'critical' perspectives on the work and results of the 'Treuhand model' as simply a failure or a success. In focusing on *Treuhand* experts and managers from both east and west working in this remarkable institution during the early 1990s, I will try to develop a genuinely historical perspective on the topic. Apart from polemic speculations about 'gangsters', 'con artists' and 'adventurers',[8] the personnel of transformation, its recruitment, social background, motivations and experiences remain mostly in the shadows of competed history. Who were they, and where did they come from? What expectations and motivations took them there? Finally, what experiences did they have?[9]

From a conceptual perspective, the *Treuhand* experts are interpreted as one specific group of actors performing within a wider 'arena of transition'. Located at a critical intersection between state, economy and society in transition, this institutional arrangement proved to be a contact zone for a vast variety of different players: federal or local politicians and public officers, western enterprise managers as potential investors, eastern company managers, union leaders and other representatives of the employees of *Treuhand*-owned companies, as well as investigative journalists, social scientists and economists – all interacted on this crowded 'stage'. Altogether, they made the post-socialist transformation in terms of everyday business, and did so case by case. They reshaped, arranged and negotiated the processes of economic reconstruction after the fall of the Berlin Wall, in a material, but also in an ideational sense. They not only made 'hard' decisions on the future of single companies and their employees; at the same time they evoked and constructed a society and economy under transformation, ascribing and filling post-socialist blank spaces with significance.[10]

Heading back from the heights of theory to the field of empirical research, some severe challenges must be faced in order to identify the traces of these managers of post-socialism. Due to an unfortunate and currently insuperable lack of official material,[11] this chapter relies on a special set of sources, besides other published materials and voluminous documentation,[12] namely one hundred or so contemporary expert interviews with *Treuhand* employees, collected by social scientists and ethnologists between 1991 and 1995. Adopting the methods of oral history, which at that time were much discussed in Germany, these studies were aimed to 'conserve' different 'subjective' voices from within the *Treuhand* against the background of loud and highly emotional public discussions.[13] Thus, the interviewers focused on experts positioned in the middle ranks of the organizational hierarchy, just beneath the executive board, such as operational directors and department managers.[14]

To begin our journey into the impervious '*Treuhand* jungle', which will lead us to its exotic 'inhabitants', we will first sketch the conceptual debates of early 1990 and the emergence of the 'Treuhand model'. The following two sections will focus on the reorganization and practices of mass privatization, as well as the recruitment strategies of the *Treuhandanstalt* from late summer 1990. Finally, we shall pay attention to characteristic narratives concerning the personal motivations and socio-demographic backgrounds of the *Treuhand* staff.

Conceptual Debates: In the Spirit of Ludwig Erhard

Many *Treuhand* managers lamented the fact that there were whole libraries full of books that describe the revolutionary transition from a capitalist market economy to a socialist planned economy, but none that investigate the opposite.[15] Indeed, the Federal Republic of Germany and its government had made no specific preparations for reunification at the end of the 1980s. In the mid-1970s, with détente at its peak, nearly all official institutions and advisory councils that were supposed to deliver action plans and strategies were dissolved by the social-liberal government: the German Democratic Republic (GDR) was finally accepted as a stable and permanent German state. Significantly, the conservative Kohl government also did nothing to foster administrative preparations for an increasingly unlikely scenario, at least in the near future, of reunification. In contemporary perceptions, the abrupt breakdown of the East German regime in autumn 1989 came like a bolt out of the blue.[16]

Thus, 1990 was an eventful year of debated concepts under rapidly changing circumstances. Different groups, such as Eastern communists, dissidents and company managers, as well as Western politicians, economists, consultants and trade union officials competed with each other as they brought their different politico-economic concepts and ideas into the political arena. But in a time of revolution many pressing questions had to be answered, and economic reconstruction was *not* at the centre of public debate; with few exceptions – such as the heated public controversy about the conversion rate of the GDR's currency into deutschmarks that drove the East German population back out onto the streets – for most of 1990, complicated economic questions remained within the shadows of high politics.[17]

Ironically, the *Treuhandanstalt* was initially merely a by-product of these heated debates and negotiations.[18] In early spring 1990, the personally renewed communist government under Hans Modrow and members of the opposition in the central 'Round Table' agreed to establish a new kind of organization in order to hold in trust the vast state-owned assets of the GDR. Both sides deeply mistrusted each other, but accepted the *Treuhand* as lowest common denominator: a temporary trustee institution to prevent Western capitalist companies from taking over state-owned properties in confusing times – or so they hoped. Communists and dissidents were still in desperate search of a 'third way' between capitalism and socialism, with gradual economic reforms to sustain an autonomous GDR; they demanded more time for further discussions. Both were overcome by the political impact of the advanced *Volkskammer* election in March 1990 and its landslide victory for the political right.

The new conservative-dominated GDR government, with Lothar de Maizière at its head, now quickly set a course for rapid reunification of both German states in the form of the accession of the GDR to the Federal Republic. The newly elected GDR officials started negotiations with the liberal-conservative federal government under Helmut Kohl, who surprisingly had already, in February 1990, suggested an abrupt economic merger in order to support the conservative party group during the election campaign. Immediately beforehand, in January 1990, liberal and conservative politicians, as well as high-ranking government officials in Bonn, had found their own emblematic 'role model' for economic transformation: the currency reform of 1948. In an essay of 1953, Ludwig Erhard, the popular first federal minister of economic affairs, later glorified as the 'father' of the *Wirtschaftswunder*, reflected on the 'Economic Problems of Reunification'.[19] Given the confusing situation at the beginning of 1990, in the eyes of politicians and officials in Bonn this essay served as a strategic blueprint for post-socialist transformation. Erhard suggested a quick and radical merger of economies and currencies according to the regulatory principles of a 'social market economy' without any further state planning or transition periods; it was not the state and its officials, but private actors on free markets who should organize the economic venture from socialism to capitalism. A central planned economy, Erhard argued, could not be overcome by planners via planning – in his view, the political foxes should no longer keep the geese of the economy. 'In political, economic and human respects', he concluded, 'the Reunification of Germany will free resources, whose strengths and powers the erudition of planned economists could never dream of'.[20] Thus, Erhard's suggestions from 1953 played a crucial role in the prehistory of (economic) reunification.

Western opposition parties, Social Democrats and the Green Party criticized the envisioned path of rapid reunification, in dark remembrance of the annexation of Austria by Nazi Germany in 1938 as an overwhelming '*Anschluss*' (union or annexation). The political left demanded a gradual, long-lasting reform approach, with an independent and equal German state.[21] But while the left-wing opposition protested, the two conservative German governments created a fait accompli. A keystone of this 'fast track' to national reunification, they believed, was an irrevocable economic merger between East and West Germany. It was to communicate a strong message on both domestic and foreign policy: while the international negotiations between the Allied powers and the two German governments were still up in the air, this radical step would make a complete rollback quite complicated. Furthermore, a rapid merger would pose a definite answer to a more and more pressing domestic issue that bothered German politicians considerably in both East and West: the massive and continuing migration of disillusioned easterners to West Germany after the opening of the German borders. After hasty negotiations lasting a mere two months, the Treaty on Monetary, Economic and Social Union was signed in May 1990. On 1 July, the whole national economy of the GDR became part of the Western economic sphere, literally overnight and without any further precautions: a special German form of 'shock therapy' in the spirit of Ludwig Erhard.[22]

In the meantime, the newly founded *Treuhandanstalt* in East Berlin with its nearly one hundred staff members – all hastily recruited from the dissolving authorities of the central planned economy – desperately tried to transform over eight thousand East German enterprises, organized as 'nationally owned companies' (VEB), into adequate legal forms, such as limited liability companies (GmbH) or stock corporations (AG). Originally founded in March 1990 to conserve state-owned property, in late spring 1990 the *Treuhand* was given a completely different role during the negotiations in preparation for the economic merger. The organization was to be transformed into a central agency of privatization and liquidation of the companies in its trust. It was in May and June 1990 that the specific German 'Treuhand model' of economic transformation came to life during intergovernmental negotiations.

A cornerstone was the *Treuhand Gesetz* (Trustee Act), which passed the Volkskammer after heated and emotional debates on 17 June 1990, the highly symbolic 36th anniversary of the uprising in the GDR of 1953.[23] In its preamble, the bill declared as its main objectives the denationalization of the economy 'as far and as fast as possible', the restructuring of East German industry in order to regain its competitiveness, and the preservation of as many jobs as possible. The expected revenues were to be used for reconstructing defaulted companies, as well as to compensate for public expenditure on reunification. The bill prepared the ground for a new model of privatization: an autonomously acting agency under the formal control of the prime minister (later the Federal Ministry of Finance) was to organize the economic transformation in terms of mass privatization in the mode of entrepreneurial crisis management. In this way, elected German governments would only define abstract politico-economic objectives and then delegate practical implementation to non-elected economic experts. From a liberal-conservative perspective, free markets were to reorganize the East German economy according to their own rules and with their own personnel and instruments *without* 'dangerous' or 'distorting' public or political interference.

Thus far, the legislative and institutional framework of economic transformation in East Germany had been defined during the first half of 1990 – but how should the process go on? After the hasty rush to economic merger, with its dramatic consequences for ailing East German companies – such as exploding costs and boundless competition – some crucial questions remained to be answered. How should the institutional framework be implemented? And how should the abstract parameters laid down in the law be transformed into everyday practice?

Institution-Building under Pressure: Forming the 'Magic Square'

The two German governments, as well as many economists and managers from the West, quickly came to the conclusion that East German bureaucrats and company managers would be overwhelmed by this process because of their lack of managerial know-how and business expertise – a view confirmed by many East Germans working in the early *Treuhandanstalt*, such as a former high-ranking GDR economist, who in 1992 worked as a contributor: 'Everything was completely virgin soil to us', and all of them were forced into a 'very intensified learning process'.[24] Thus, the next step taken by the German governments was the appointment of a new top management. In July 1990, just a few days after the economic merger, two experienced West German industrial managers moved to East Berlin: Reiner Gohlke, former IBM manager and now chairman of the Bundesbahn, the state-owned rail company, replaced a panel of East German functionaries as president; and Detlev Rohwedder, former state secretary and popular CEO of crisis-ridden Westphalian steel company Hoesch, was appointed head of the newly formed board of directors of the *Treuhandanstalt*. Just four weeks later, an overburdened Gohlke surprisingly resigned. He had thrown himself head first into the chaotic business and vainly tried to transform the East German economy in a kind of 'one-man show', as a former assistant described it.[25]

Finally, Chancellor Helmut Kohl successfully urged Rohwedder to succeed the unfortunate first president. The new chief established a more managerial style of delegation. Instead of deciding individual cases on the spur of the moment in minute-cycles, like his predecessor had done, he concentrated on three main developments: first, the composition of an adequate strategic and conceptual framework for mass privatization; second, the reorganization of existing institutional structures to perform the new tasks; and third, the rapid recruitment of experienced West German managers and experts. Moreover, pressing emergency cases in the late summer of 1990 had to be handled as well. After 1 July, ten thousand East German firms now had to pay their employees and suppliers in Deutschmarks and were dearly in need of 'hard' liquidity without sufficient financial statements, and desperate company directors besieged the *Treuhand*. Simultaneously, more or less respectable Western investors literarily 'invaded' the scruffy and improvised offices at Alexanderplatz and demanded to buy companies, while the overstretched *Treuhand* staff sometimes hardly knew more than their names.[26]

Meanwhile, *Treuhand*'s hastily assembled new top managers were struggling to come to terms with the practice of mass privatization under the fairly unfavourable circumstances of post-socialism: the majority of East German industrial companies were suffering from massive overemployment, inefficient structures, outdated products and machinery, ecologically devastated facilities and collapsing key markets in the dissolving Comecon area – and all this in open market conditions that had been tending towards worldwide economic recession since 1991. Besides some attractive 'pearls' and specialized branches within the *Treuhand* portfolio, the arriving Western managers realized that the mass of industrial companies were risky cases with unforeseeable expenditure. The *Treuhand*'s standard procedures were formed in an interesting, two-sided process in early 1991: while the president and the executive board started to develop overall guidelines and rules of action to be implemented 'top–down', the operational departments functioned 'bottom-up'. Not long before his assassination, in a letter to the staff, the president coined the infamous phrase that 'privatization is the best form of reconstruction'.[27] Not surprisingly, especially at the dawn of the *Treuhandanstalt*, individual freedom of action without established rules or routines was preeminent: 'The freedom of action we have here', an operational director concluded, 'and the accompanying accountability are incomparable with anything you will find in normal businesses'.[28]

The practical core of the German 'Treuhand model' of mass privatization was shaped by the Western managing board and the new operational directors during the late autumn of 1990. It consisted of confidential and discrete bargains with one or more interested parties (mainly Western companies), negotiated by the staff of the operational departments. Employee representatives, company managers, and local politicians, as well as consultants and investment bankers, were also involved in these often long and changeful negotiations that took place under the gaze of the media. A so-called 'magic square', derived from the *Treuhand Gesetz*, made up the goal of the *Treuhand* negotiators; as Birgit Breuel, Rohwedder's successor, wrote: '[R]evenues, job tenures, investment consent and corporate concepts formed the corners of the square'.[29] But in practice, the particular course of these often long and intense negotiations was quite unforeseeable: mass privatization was a complex and hard-fought process with its own rules, routines and veto-players; it had developed its own 'psychology of negotiations', as one young manager put it.[30] Thus, it was quite difficult to explain its complicated outcomes to a more and more dissatisfied, even wrathful, public, unsettled by seemingly never-ending mass dismissals.

In short, the tasks to be implemented in eastern Germany were inscrutable, complex and risky. How could qualified managers and experts accustomed to the routines and customs of western economies be found for this challenge?

Recruitment and Reorganization: 'Chieftains' in Search of 'Tribesmen'

From the outset, Rohwedder gave recruitment top priority: strategies or concept papers, Rohwedder believed, are without value if the developed ideas are not transferred into action by convinced and experienced economic experts. Thus the president quickly launched a multilevel campaign to lure western managers eastwards: besides eye-catching advertisements in national and international newspapers, one showing a stunned Erich Honecker on a floral sofa,[31] the president also used his private networks within the highly cross-linked 'Deutschland AG', consisting of West German industry and finance. Later on, *Treuhand* managers reported sudden phone calls on Sunday evenings and conspiratorial meetings in airport lounges, in which they were asked to come to Berlin in a hit-and-run style.[32] Additionally, prominent headhunters and consultants were engaged to make systematic recommendations.

Nevertheless, the first results were fairly meagre. By German Unification Day on 3 October 1990, in addition to nearly 350 eastern German functionaries, barely a dozen westerners had come to East Berlin. Now Rohwedder pressed the federal government for official support, finally with success: in a 'national plea', Helmut Kohl called on the heads of German industry and finance to send able managers and experts eastwards in order to accelerate the reconstruction of East German industry. The chancellor's call did not go unheeded. Over the next few weeks, several hundred Western managers were delegated as 'one-dollar men' to support the *Treuhand*, most of them for only a few weeks or months. Additionally, miscellaneous ministries and administrations on the federal or *Länder* levels delegated public officers to support the task.

In December 1990, Rohwedder and his executive board completed the reorganization of the *Treuhandanstalt*, moving from a functional to a divisional structure. Instead of tracking cross-sectional tasks, such as finance, staff or privatization for the whole *Treuhand*, experienced operational directors were to be responsible for supervising and transforming particular industrial sectors. It was this special group of experts that accelerated the explosive growth of the *Treuhand* in personnel and structures from January 1991 onwards. These elderly managers, who had previously worked within the managements of large-scale enterprises, such as Siemens, Bayer and Krupp, or as chief executive officers in medium-sized companies, shaped their divisions and teams according to their own ideas, beliefs and experiences. They particularly pushed forward the recruitment of staff from East and West, using their own networks and tested strategies. One operational director described this impromptu process of ad hoc recruitment and reorganization in an interview, using a symptomatic frontier motif: 'The chieftains were here first, and then they began the search for their tribesmen on different levels'.[33]

As a result, the *Treuhand* experienced massive personnel growth during the following weeks and months. By the end of December 1990, there already were over a thousand staff members serving in the *Treuhand*, including about a hundred Westerners; a few days before Rohwedder's assassination on 1 April 1991, more than two thousand had already gathered at headquarters and in fifteen local offices, 360 of them from the West. The new president, Birgit Breuel, a distinguished 'neoliberal' politician and former minister of finance in Lower Saxony, continued the expansion. By the end of 1991, about 3,500 men and women had joined, nearly a third of them Westerners. The peak was reached in mid-1992, when 4,000 permanent employees were engaged with mass privatization. However, even this massive growth in personnel numbers was not enough to meet the tasks at hand. One could have doubled the number of permanent staff with thousands of external consultants and advisers who filled the personnel gaps at high cost.[34] Until the end, the *Treuhand* had severe problems in recruiting qualified experts. Also the systematic and symbolic reduction of staff beginning as early as 1992 was not an easy task: important employees, mainly well-networked Westerners, quit ahead of time; appropriate replacements limited to just one or two years' employment were hard to find. Other colleagues, especially the mass of East Germans, became more and more anxious at the

prospect of losing their jobs. 'To make ourselves superfluous as fast as possible' was a corporate motto of the *Treuhand*.[35] However, this proved to be
cataclysmic for the inner life of the institution and its members after 1993,
when the end was in sight.

Motivations and Social Background: Patriotism, Career, Security and Adventure

In these difficult conditions, a crucial question accompanied the
Treuhandanstalt right from the beginning: why should qualified managers
interrupt or give up their promising careers and move to the 'foul-smelling
cities' beyond the Elbe, as one Western manager put it?[36] Working in
Eastern Germany during the early 1990s proved to be an imposition on
Western managers, according to their accustomed standards of working
and living. Inhospitable grey housing complexes, broken streets, heavy air
pollution and poor leisure facilities dominated. But what brought them
eastwards anyway? In contemporary interviews, the *Treuhand* staff allowed
detailed insights into their motivations. The subjective incentives can be
closely connected to three distinct socio-demographic groups: older managers from the West, young West German graduates and East German
employees.[37]

For older managers over fifty years of age, the *Treuhand* offered a
late opportunity. Often stressing more or less close biographical links to
Germany's eastern regions, these men interpreted their engagement as a
mixture of practical patriotism and professional challenge: 'Maybe for the
first time in German history, merchants are in charge, not soldiers, officers
or bureaucrats', a top manager explained with the evident pride of a trades-
man.[38] Many of them described the widespread spirit of 'national break-up'
in early 1990: the chancellor's request indeed fell upon welcoming ears.[39]
Others stressed the notion of helping Easterners who had suffered for so
long. Approaching the end of their careers, many older managers acted on
long nascent fears of career deadlock in their former positions. These men
suddenly got an unexpected chance for professional reorientation, serving in
top positions in the *Treuhand*: a 'unique challenge' had arisen that demanded
all their experience and know-how, with work going on twelve, fourteen
or even sixteen hours a day.[40] Interestingly, the situation in East Germany
reminded many older managers of their own apprenticeships in post-war
Germany in the 1940s and 1950s. And indeed, within the group of older
Treuhand managers, diffuse hopes of a second '1948' seemed to be widespread, to some extent echoing the enthusiasm for Ludwig Erhard's suggestions within the conservative government. It was not without reason that

one business magazine portrayed the first Western managers moving east-wards as heroic '*Wirtschaftswunderdoktoren*'.[41]

This special mixture of patriotism, supportiveness and sense of a chal-lenge was not to be found among their younger associates. These men and women, most of them business economists or lawyers below thirty years of age, often entered the *Treuhand* directly after they had finished their last exams at university. Expressing no kind of patriotism and thus indi-cating a significant gap between the generations, they clearly interpreted their engagement as a means of kick-starting their careers. Significantly, the *Treuhand* aggressively courted this group of young people with high wages and the prospect of professional approbation: working as consultants in the middle ranks of the organization, they often had responsibilities and freedom of action that no established Western company or management would offer them. 'Go East, young man!' one young lawyer enthusiastically told the interviewer when he was asked about his motivations.[42] Not surprisingly, a latent conflict of generations gleamed through many interviews, in which brisk 'yuppies' battled with cranky 'seniors', and vice versa.[43]

By contrast, the age cohorts between thirty and fifty were underrepre-sented within the staff coming from the West. Already in the middle of their careers, not many followed the call to East Berlin, unless on compassionate grounds. On the other hand, the majority of East German associates staff-ing the lower and middle ranks of the *Treuhand* were part of this group of 'middle-agers'. Having served within the structures of the central planned economy for years or even decades, these men and women applied for the jobs mainly to avoid looming unemployment. Of course, East German associ-ates often enjoyed the instructive cooperation with their Western colleagues and embraced the opportunity to support economic reconstruction, some of them even regarding their *Treuhand* activities as a sequel to the communist reform experiments of the late 1960s.[44] But existential fears of suspension, political suspicions regarding their socialist past, and the dire public image of the *Treuhand*, especially within East German society, weighed heavily on their shoulders. When the interviewer asked one economist in his mid-fifties about his future prospects, he explained wearily: 'It will be very difficult for me. What chance do I have?'[45] Finally, many of them carefully hinted at the 'inner conflicts' they had to contend with while 'liquidating' Socialism – a system they had lived in and tried to maintain for so many years.[46]

Overall, in describing the 'chaotic' and 'adventurous' atmosphere, the early *Treuhand* staff in particular later glorified the dawn of the organiza-tion as a 'golden era' of short cuts, unconventional improvisation, quick decisions and extensive individual freedom of action. They had a 'jester's license in a good sense', as one experienced energy manager from the Ruhr described it.[47] One chief of a regional *Treuhand* branch office even felt like an 'oriental potentate', presiding high-handedly over applicants and making 'more or less accidental decisions that had a grave impact'.[48] Altogether, the 'spark of adventure'[49] and the 'common break-up'[50] in rapidly changing times fascinated Easterners and Westerners alike: 'I had the feeling that I was writing history one more time', one older Western manager explained.[51] Consistently, the interviewed managers solemnly evoked the exceptional 'pioneer spirit' that swiftly incorporated the newly arriving staff members, coming from divergent biographical and professional backgrounds: East and West, industry managers and public officers, young and old, women and men.

Conclusion: By the Many Hands of 'Pioneers'

Due to limited space, I have only been able to shed a narrow spotlight on the staff of the *Treuhandanstalt* to supplement the traditional narratives, oscillating between the 'heroic' and the 'villainous'. While the ambivalent economic results of the *Treuhandanstalt* continue to be discussed on a macro-level, the picture changes significantly when fading to the subjective perspectives of acting contemporaries and their perceptions, reflections and narratives. The group of economic experts and managers, who consistently interpreted themselves as 'pioneers' of capitalism with rolled-up sleeves,[52] operated under immense pressure of time and action on a hazardous 'frontier', in the ambiguous circumstances of confusing post-socialism with its manifold conflicts and opaque disarray. In the specific context of contemporary interviews, they tried to reflect and explain their thoughts and actions: 'We never had the time to talk about our experiences thoroughly', a director concluded at the end of a long interview;[53] one of his colleagues had, in fact, started to write a diary, but quickly gave it up because he was mostly 'too tired' to write when he came home.[54]

In contrast to what common economic narratives – from a bird's eye view – suggest, there was not one 'invisible hand' that ordered the post-socialist economies 'from plan to market', but thousands of them, which this chapter has tried to make a bit more visible. Acting at a contested intersection between economy, politics and society, these men and women were part of an organization that represented the contemporary mistrust of politicians, mainly conservatives and liberals, regarding state regulation. It was not, in practice, a political 'Ministry for Reunification' or a state-owned holding company that shaped the massive reconstruction of East German firms, as the left-wing opposition vehemently suggested, but would-be 'apolitical' economic experts and managers who were supposed to launch market forces within the East German economy and its mostly tattered companies on their own authority: 'There is no one else in the whole of Germany', a self-confident Rohwedder told *Der Spiegel* in January 1991, who was 'qualified, professional and dedicated enough to manage the business-related restructuring of the former GDR economy. No ministry could accomplish this task'.[55] In practice, this politico–economic assumption of economic empowerment without political interference did not work out so easily, as the *Treuhand* managers poignantly experienced and reported. In the hour of its great 'triumph' over its socialist competitors, it was this heterogeneous 'vanguard' of economic experts and managers who conceptually, practically and mentally struggled to bring capitalism back, in the context of the rough post-socialist passage, not only in East Germany, but in the whole of post-socialist Eastern Europe during the early 1990s.[56]

Marcus Böick is research associate at the chair for contemporary history, Ruhr University, Bochum. He has published texts in the field of the history of economic and cultural transformation after 1990, including 'Vermarktlichung/Marketization', edited with Ralf Ahrens and Marcel vom Lehn, in the journal *Zeithistorische Forschungen/Studies in Contemporary History* 12(3) (2015).

Notes

1. Björn Finke, 'Eine Treuhand für Griechenland', *Süddeutsche Zeitung*, 23 May 2011, 17.

2. Cerstin Gammelin, 'In fremden Händen', *Süddeutsche Zeitung*, 6 June 2011, 4.

3. Günter Grass, 'Die Steine des Sisyphos', *Süddeutsche Zeitung*, 4 July 2011, 11.

4. See Phyllis Dininio, *The Political Economy of East German Privatization* (Westport, CT, 1999).

5. Birgit Breuel and Michael Burda (eds), *Ohne historisches Vorbild: Die Treuhandanstalt 1990 bis 1994. Eine kritische Würdigung* (Berlin, 2005); Otto Depenheuer and Karl-Heinz Paqué (eds), *Einheit – Eigentum – Effizienz: Bilanz der Treuhandanstalt* (Berlin, 2012).

6. Rüdiger Liedtke (ed.), *Die Treuhand und die zweite Enteignung der Ostdeutschen* (Munich, 1993).

7. Andreas Pickel and Helmut Wiesenthal, *The Grand Experiment: Debating Shock Therapy, Transition Theory, and the East German Experience* (Boulder, CO, 1997).

8. Michael Jürgs, *Die Treuhändler: Wie Helden und Halunken die DDR verkauften* (Munich, 1997); Dirk Laabs, *Der deutsche Goldrausch: Die wahre Geschichte der Treuhand* (Munich, 2012).

9. For further methodological considerations, see Norbert Frei and Dietmar Süß (eds), *Privatisierung: Idee und Praxis seit den 1970er Jahren* (Göttingen, 2012); Hartmut Berghoff and Jakob Vogel (eds), *Wirtschaftsgeschichte als Kulturgeschichte: Dimensionen eines Perspektivenwechsels* (Frankfurt am Main, 2004); Christoph Kleßmann, 'Deutschland einig Vaterland? Politische und gesellschaftliche Verwerfungen im Prozess der deutschen Einigung', *Zeithistorische Forschungen/Studies in Contemporary Studies*, Online-Ausgabe 6(1) (2009).

10. Christopher Hann (ed.), *Postsozialismus: Transformationsprozesse in Europa und Asien aus ethnologischer Perspektive* (Frankfurt, 2002); Stephan Weingarz, *Laboratorium Deutschland?*

Der ostdeutsche Transformationsprozeß als Herausforderung für die deutschen Sozialwissenschaften (Münster, 2003).

11. Katrin Verch, 'Sicherung, Bewertung und Übernahme des Schriftgutes der Volkseigenen Betriebe der DDR ab 1990', *Archiv und Wirtschaft* 44 (2011), 177–86.

12. Treuhandanstalt, *Dokumentation 1990–1994* (Berlin, 1995); Birgit Breuel (ed.), *Treuhand intern: Tagebuch* (Berlin, 1993).

13. Dietmar Rost, *Innenansichten der Treuhandanstalt: Ergebnisse einer qualitativen Befragung von Führungskräften* (Berlin, 1994). The interviews quoted below were conducted by ethnologist Dietmar Rost between June 1992 and May 1993, and have been translated for this chapter.

14. In our context, we should understand and interpret them as scientifically produced individual self-representations and reflections, arranged and communicated in specific narratives. See Rüdiger Graf and Kim Christian Priemel, 'Zeitgeschichte in der Welt der Sozialwissenschaften: Legitimität und Originalität einer Disziplin', *Vierteljahrshefte für Zeitgeschichte* 59 (2011), 479–508.

15. Interview 43, 29 January 1993.

16. Dirk van Laak, 'Der Tag X: Vorbereitungen für die deutsche Wiedervereinigung vor 1989', in *Der Tag X in der Geschichte. Erwartungen und Enttäuschungen seit tausend Jahren*, ed. Enno Bünz, Rainer Gries and Frank Möller (Stuttgart, 1997), 256–86; Markus Gloe, *Planung für die deutsche Einheit: Der Forschungsbeirat für Fragen der Wiedervereinigung Deutschlands, 1952–1975* (Wiesbaden, 2005).

17. See Manfred Görtemaker, *Die Berliner Republik: Wiedervereinigung und Neuorientierung* (Berlin, 2009); Andreas Rödder, *Deutschland einig Vaterland: Die Geschichte der Wiedervereinigung* (Munich, 2009).

18. See Marc Kemmler, *Die Entstehung der Treuhandanstalt: Von der Wahrung zur Privatisierung des DDR-Volkseigentums* (Frankfurt am Main, 1994); Wolfgang Seibel, *Verwaltete Illusionen: Die Privatisierung der DDR-Wirtschaft durch die Treuhandanstalt und ihre Nachfolger 1990–2000* (Frankfurt am Main, 2005); Roland Czada, 'Vom Plan zum Markt: Die radikale Massenprivatisierung der DDR-Wirtschaft durch die Treuhandanstalt', *Jahrbuch für europäische Verwaltungsgeschichte* 7 (1995), 307–23.

19. Ludwig Erhard, 'Wirtschaftliche Probleme der Wiedervereinigung', in *Ludwig Erhard: Gedanken aus fünf Jahrzehnten. Schriften und Reden*, ed. Karl Hohmann (Düsseldorf, 1988), 381–86.

20. Erhard, *Wiedervereinigung*, 386.

21. Rudolf Hickel and Jan Priewe, *Nach dem Fehlstart: Ökonomische Perspektiven der deutschen Einigung* (Frankfurt am Main, 1994).

22. Wolfgang Seibel, 'Wenn ein Staat zusammenbricht: Über die Frühgeschichte und Funktion der Treuhandanstalt', in *Privatisierung: Idee und Praxis seit den 1970er Jahren*, ed. Norbert Frei und Dietmar Süß (Göttingen, 2012), 184–207.

23. 'Gesetz zur Privatisierung und Reorganisation des volkseigenen Vermögens (Treuhandgesetz)', *Gesetzesblatt der Deutschen Demokratischen Republik*, 22 June 1990.

24. Interview 17, 8 September 1992.

25. Interview 32, 22 December 1992.

26. Interview 22, 1 October 1992.

27. Detlef Rohwedder, 'Letter to the Staff', 27 March 1991, in *Treuhand intern*, Breuel, 224–26.

28. Interview 23, 1 October 1992.

29. Birgit Breuel, 'Die Treuhandanstalt – Zielvorgaben, Rahmenbedingungen und Ergebnisse', in *Ohne historisches Vorbild: Die Treuhandanstalt 1990 bis 1994. Eine kritische Würdigung*, ed. Birgit Breuel and Michael Burda (Berlin, 2005), 13–30.

30. Interview 22, 1 October 1992.

31. See *Handelsblatt*, 27 April 1991.

32. Interview 46, 10 February 1992.

33. Interview 49, 16 April 1993.

34. Seibel, *Verwaltete Illusionen*, 172–85.

35. Breuel, *Treuhand intern*, 273.

36. Interview 22, 1 October 1992.

37. Seibel, *Verwaltete Illusionen*, 172–85; Kemmler, *Die Entstehung*, 187–217.

38. Interview 46, 10 February 1992.

39. Interview 15, 1 September 1992.

40. Interview 13, 5 August 1992.

41. *Capital* 11 (1990), 11.

42. Interview 36, 11 January 1993.

43. Interview 15, 1 September 1992.

44. Interview 1, 10 July 1992; Interview 17, 8 September 1992.

45. Interview 28, 17 December 1992.

46. Interview 31, 21 December 1992.

47. Interview 15, 1 September 1992.

48. Interview 35, 7 January 1993.

49. Interview 18, 10 September 1992.

50. Interview 17, 8 September 1992.

51. Interview 15, 1 September 1992.

52. This theme appears in more than a dozen of the interviews conducted by Dietmar Rost: see, for example, Interview 2, 22 June 1992; Interview 9, 30 June 1992; Interview 20, 18 September 1992; Interview 21, 18 September 1992; and Interview 25, 13 October 1992.

53. Interview 43, 29 January 1993.

54. Interview 11, 31 July 1992.

55. *Der Spiegel* 5 (1991), 28 January 1991.

56. Anselm Doering-Manteuffel and Lutz Raphael, *Nach dem Boom: Perspektiven auf die Zeitgeschichte seit 1970* (Göttingen, 2008).

Bibliography

Berghoff, Hartmut, and Jakob Vogl (eds), *Wirtschaftsgeschichte als Kulturgeschichte: Dimensionen eines Perspektivenwechsels* (Frankfurt am Main, 2004).

Breuel, Birgit (ed.), *Treuhand intern: Tagebuch* (Berlin, 1993)

Breuel, Birgit, 'Die Treuhandanstalt – Zielvorgaben, Rahmenbedingungen und Ergebnisse', in *Ohne historisches Vorbild: Die Treuhandanstalt 1990 bis 1994. Eine kritische Würdigung*, ed. Birgit Breuel and Michael Burda (Berlin, 2005), 13–30.

Breuel, Birgit, and Michael Burda (eds), *Ohne historisches Vorbild: Die Treuhandanstalt 1990 bis 1994. Eine kritische Würdigung* (Berlin, 2005).

Czada, Roland, 'Vom Plan zum Markt: Die radikale Massenprivatisierung der DDR-Wirtschaft durch die Treuhandanstalt', *Jahrbuch für europäische Verwaltungsgeschichte* 7 (1995): 307–23.

Depenheuer, Otto, and Karl-Heinz Paqué (eds), *Einheit – Eigentum – Effizienz: Bilanz der Treuhandanstalt* (Berlin, 2012).

Dininio, Phyllis, *The Political Economy of East German Privatization* (Westport, CT, 1999).

Doering-Manteuffel, Anselm, and Lutz Raphael, *Nach dem Boom: Perspektiven auf die Zeitgeschichte seit 1970* (Göttingen, 2008).

Erhard, Ludwig, 'Wirtschaftliche Probleme der Wiedervereinigung', in *Ludwig Erhard: Gedanken aus fünf Jahrzehnten. Schriften und Reden*, ed. Karl Hohmann (Düsseldorf, 1988), 381–86.

Frei, Norbert, and Dietmar Süß (eds), *Privatisierung: Idee und Praxis seit den 1970er Jahren* (Göttingen, 2012).

Gloe, Markus, *Planung für die deutsche Einheit: Der Forschungsbeirat für Fragen der Wiedervereinigung Deutschlands, 1952–1975* (Wiesbaden, 2005).

Görtemaker, Manfred, *Die Berliner Republik: Wiedervereinigung und Neuorientierung* (Berlin, 2009).

Graf, Rüdiger, and Kim Christian Priemel, 'Zeitgeschichte in der Welt der Sozialwissenschaften: Legitimität und Originalität einer Disziplin', *Vierteljahrshefte für Zeitgeschichte* 59 (2011), 479–508.

Hann, Christopher (ed.), *Postsozialismus: Transformationsprozesse in Europa und Asien aus ethnologischer Perspektive* (Frankfurt, 2002).

Hickel, Rudolf, and Jan Priewe, *Nach dem Fehlstart: Ökonomische Perspektiven der deutschen Einigung* (Frankfurt am Main, 1994).

Jürgs, Michael, *Die Treuhändler: Wie Helden und Halunken die DDR verkauften* (Munich, 1997).

Kemmler, Marc, *Die Entstehung der Treuhandanstalt: Von der Wahrung zur Privatisierung des DDR-Volkseigentums* (Frankfurt am Main, 1994).

Kleßmann, Christoph, 'Deutschland einig Vaterland? Politische und gesellschaftliche Verwerfungen im Prozess der deutschen Einigung', *Zeithistorische Forschungen / Studies in Contemporary Studies*, Online-Ausgabe 6(1) (2009).

Laabs, Dirk, *Der deutsche Goldrausch: Die wahre Geschichte der Treuhand* (Munich, 2012).

Laak, Dirk van, 'Der Tag X: Vorbereitungen für die deutsche Wiedervereinigung vor 1989', in *Der Tag X in der Geschichte: Erwartungen und Enttäuschungen seit tausend Jahren*, ed. Enno Bünz, Rainer Gries and Frank Möller (Stuttgart, 1997), 256–86.

Liedtke, Rüdiger (ed.), *Die Treuhand und die zweite Enteignung der Ostdeutschen* (Munich, 1993).

Pickel, Andreas, and Helmut Wiesenthal, *The Grand Experiment: Debating Shock Therapy, Transition Theory, and the East German Experience* (Boulder, CO, 1997).

Rödder, Andreas, *Deutschland einig Vaterland: Die Geschichte der Wiedervereinigung* (Munich, 2009).

Rost, Dietmar, *Innenansichten der Treuhandanstalt: Ergebnisse einer qualitativen Befragung von Führungskräften* (Berlin, 1994).

Seibel, Wolfgang, *Verwaltete Illusionen: Die Privatisierung der DDR-Wirtschaft durch die Treuhandanstalt und ihre Nachfolger 1990–2000* (Frankfurt am Main, 2005).

———, 'Wenn ein Staat zusammenbricht: Über die Frühgeschichte und Funktion der Treuhandanstalt', in *Privatisierung: Idee und Praxis seit den 1970er Jahren*, ed. Norbert Frei and Dietmar Süß (Göttingen, 2012), 184–207.

Treuhandanstalt, *Dokumentation 1990–1994* (Berlin, 1995).

Verch, Katrin, 'Sicherung, Bewertung und Übernahme des Schriftgutes der Volkseigenen Betriebe der DDR ab 1990', *Archiv und Wirtschaft* 44 (2011), 177–86.

Weingarz, Stephan, *Laboratorium Deutschland? Der ostdeutsche Transformationsprozeß als Herausforderung für die deutschen Sozialwissenschaften* (Münster, 2003).

CHAPTER 4

Against the Deregulatory Tide

Privacy Protection Legislation in the Federal Republic of Germany in the 1970s and 1980s

Larry Frohman

In most scholarly writing, the concepts of deregulation and privatization are employed to theorize the limitations of nationally organized Keynesian welfare states and to capture the policy implications of neoliberalism, which sought to reassert the primacy of the market, rather than the state, as the organizing principle of society, the macroeconomy and individual subjectivity.[1] However, not only are these concepts sorely in need of historicization;[2] they are also particularly ill suited for capturing the main trends in the area of privacy protection legislation during these years. The most recent edition of one of the standard commentaries on German Federal Privacy Protection Law (*Bundesdatenschutzgesetz*, BDSG) is over 600 pages long.[3] However, even this pales in comparison to the thick volume edited by Spiros Simitis, the long-time Hessian privacy commissioner, which comes in at 1,886 pages.[4]

The 1970s and 1980s saw not the deregulation of the new information technologies that were coming into widespread use during these years, but rather the rapid formation of a new body of law governing the way that these technologies could be used in both the public and private sectors to collect, process and disseminate personal information. The big bang in European privacy legislation dates from the beginning of the 1970s.[5] West Germany was a pioneer both in the use of new information and communication technologies for population surveillance and in computer privacy laws to regulate the automated processing of personal information. What do these

Notes for this section begin on page 83.

precocious developments tell us about the political and regulatory culture of West Germany and the Western industrialized nations more generally?

In the following pages, I would like to make three arguments about the relationship between privacy protection legislation and the broader deregulation movement. First, although the debate on the usefulness of deregulation as a category of historical analysis has taken place primarily on the terrain of political economy, the development of privacy protection legislation was driven not by economic forces, but rather by a bundle of technological, administrative and political factors, which all followed a logic and temporality quite different from those of the economic sphere.

This is not to say, however, that privacy protection legislation was completely disconnected from economic developments, and my second argument is that the privacy movement theorized the externalities that had heretofore remained invisible to the economic and administrative systems. But while privacy legislation may in some ways have blocked or limited the use of new information technologies, by codifying the community's understanding of the conditions under which they could be deployed and the uses to which they could be put, privacy *regulation* – as much as, if not more than, *deregulation* – facilitated the introduction and spread of these technologies.

Thirdly, much of the scholarly literature has focused on explaining why the deregulatory dog did not bark – that is, why dogmatic neoliberalism never had such a pronounced effect on public policy in West Germany as it did in Britain and the United States. I will argue that the Federal Republic opted for comprehensive state regulation rather than a market model because the country's political culture and constitutional tradition led privacy advocates there to theorize both the privacy problem and available remedies in ways that were quite different from those that dominated American thinking on the question.

Although the larger state bureaucracies in West Germany had been experimenting with the use of computers since the 1950s, the situation changed dramatically at the turn of the 1970s with the introduction of third generation computers, which employed integrated circuits and randomly accessible memory, and with advances in communications technology, which permitted the networking of computer databases and decentralized, real-time access through the use of cathode ray terminals. In the 1980s, the Ministry for Post and Telecommunications under the Christian Democrat Christian Schwarz-Schilling pushed aggressively for the creation of a nation-wide cable network and the partial privatization of telecommunications services.[6] After the United States and Japan, Germany was the world's third largest producer of information technology products,[7] and it was also one of the most advanced countries in the deployment of these technologies to automate both production and public administration, though as yet there has been no systematic study of the computerization of the Federal Republic.[8]

But what brought about the burst of privacy legislation at the beginning of the 1970s was not the use of these new technologies for accounting, payroll and inventory purposes, but rather public concern about the expansion and intensification of population surveillance. This was driven by a number of different factors. First, the deepening of the welfare state, the growing interest in social planning, and the informationalization of capitalism all gave rise to an unquenchable thirst for personal information. The most important state initiative in the informational domain was the plan to automate the local population registries and then link them together to create a national population information and identification system, which would, it was hoped, provide the raw data needed for expanded social planning. Second, in response to the emergence of domestic terrorism, the governing Social Democratic–Liberal coalition announced an ambitious programme to expand and modernize the police, and in the autumn of 1972 the Federal Criminal Police (*Bundeskriminalamt*) rolled out its new computer system INPOL, which linked the information held by the individual state police forces to form a national police information system.[9] Third, in early 1972 the West German government committed itself to halting the long march of the New Left through the country's decision-making institutions by mandating the investigation of the political loyalties of all applicants for public employment; as a result, between 1972 and 1975 the domestic intelligence agency screened the personal and political activities of 430,000 people.[10] Fourth, there were also conflicts over the collection of personal information by the private sector, especially in the consumer credit reporting field.[11] These concerns about state surveillance were driven to new heights by the September 1977 kidnapping of, and the subsequent nationwide search for, the industrialist Hanns Martin Schleyer, and all of these accumulated tensions were then unleashed – to the great surprise of all – by the 1983 census.

None of these factors is related in any direct manner to a desire to either reassert the primacy of the market over the welfare state or create a more entrepreneurial subject, and they reflect a general concern, which was shared by all of the major political parties, about the impact of the new information and communication technologies on individual privacy, the concentration of power in the hands of the executive, and the subordination of individual liberties to administrative efficiency. The real line of political conflict in this area ran between the free-market wings of both the liberal Free Democrats (FDP) and the conservative Christian Democratic Union (CDU) and what might be termed the civil liberties wings of both parties. However, although the FDP remained committed in principle to the limitation of state surveillance, by the early 1980s the CDU's growing concern with law and order had led it to vigorously oppose the further extension of privacy protection legislation. Neoliberal ideas played at best a subordinate role in these developments.

Although the factors outlined above may explain why West Germans felt that it was important to regulate the use of information technologies for the collection of personal information, they do not explain why German regulations took the form that they did, and we can perhaps learn more about the German path by looking first at contemporary debates on computer privacy on the other side of the Atlantic. In the United States, the debate on privacy was driven by a number of issues, including intrusive credit reporting practices and the proposal to create a national data centre that would collect individual microdata for use in social scientific and policy research. Concerns about government surveillance then rose to an entirely new level in the wake of the Watergate scandal.[12] After the 1970 Fair Credit Reporting Act, the first major attempt to regulate the new information technologies came in 1973, when a government committee proposed that federal agencies be required to adhere to a code of fair information practices. These practices, which were codified in the 1974 Privacy Act,[13] represented the minimum consensus on privacy on both sides of the Atlantic.

While the leading Congressional proponents of privacy protection legislation called for the creation of an independent oversight agency to monitor the collection and use of personal information by federal agencies, the administration maintained that this was not necessary, and, after he succeeded Richard Nixon as President, Gerald Ford threatened to veto any

Table 4.1 Code of Fair Information Practices

There must be no personal data record-keeping systems whose very existence is secret.
There must be a way for individuals to find out what information about them is in a record and how it is used.
There must be a way for individuals to prevent information about them that was obtained for one purpose from being used or made available for other purposes without their consent.
There must be a way for individuals to correct or amend a record of identifiable information about them.
Any organization creating, maintaining, using or disseminating records of identifiable personal data must ensure the reliability of the data for their intended use and must take precautions to prevent misuse of the data.

Source: US Department of Health, Education & Welfare, Records, Computers, and the Rights of Citizens. Report of the Secretary's Advisory Committee on Automated Personal Data Systems (1973), xx–xxi.

privacy bill calling for the creation of such an agency. As Ford explained, he preferred to rely on the adversarial mechanism of the courts, rather than regulation and supervision by the state:

> I do not favour establishing separate Commission or Board bureaucracy empowered to define privacy in its own terms and to second guess citizens and agencies. I vastly prefer an approach which makes Federal agencies fully and publicly accountable for legally mandated privacy protections and which gives the individual adequate legal remedies to enforce what he deems to be his own privacy interests.[14]

The Privacy Act, which was approved during the final weeks of the legislative session, was a hastily adopted compromise solution that did a poor job of reconciling the versions of the law passed by the House and Senate. The law placed responsibility for enforcing the Privacy Act in the hands of the Office of Management and Budget (OMB), but sidestepped more controversial measures by creating a politically ineffectual Privacy Policy Study Commission to make recommendations regarding the many privacy-related issues that were not satisfactorily addressed by the law itself.[15] However, the primary responsibility of the OMB, which was part of the executive branch, was to promote the efficiency of government operations; making such an agency responsible for enforcing privacy law was tantamount to leaving the fox to guard the informational hen house.

This eschewal of a state role in protecting and promoting individual rights can be characterized as a classic liberal approach. However, the Privacy Act was primarily a data protection law, which sought to assuage public concerns by regulating the use of the new information and communication technologies rather than by imposing systematic limits upon the collection of personal information by the state, and it did not specify precisely what kinds of information could be collected, how this information could be used or under what circumstances. Consequently, with the exception of the recognition of the constitutional rights to privacy and self-determination in the domains of reproduction and sexuality, which were codified by the Supreme Court beginning with Roe v. Wade (1973), the absence of a constitutional foundation has led to the steady erosion of privacy rights in the United States in the areas of media and information technology.

Although the West Germans approached the privacy problem from a very different direction, they were not intrinsically predisposed to a regulatory approach to such matters, and in other areas they adopted a more market-oriented approach. For example, in the domain of consumer protection West Germany opted for what Gunnar Trumbull has called an information model, which was based on the assumption that consumer citizens would make wise decisions concerning quality, safety and price if they were given adequate information on the products they were considering for purchase.[16]

In contrast, in the field of privacy protection, the West German legislature argued that the state had a positive obligation to protect citizens from novel, complex technologies whose workings the public could not be expected to understand because this was necessary to ensure the constitutional right to the development of the personality. This reliance on expert knowledge and the adoption of a preventive approach were two things that privacy legislation had in common with other bodies of law intended to govern the externalities of the industrial economy, especially environmental law.

The German Privacy Protection Law, which was adopted at the turn of 1976/77 and which went into force at the beginning of 1978, was based on a blanket prohibition (§3) of the storage and processing of personal information, except where specifically permitted by law or where the individual had given informed consent. The law was from the very beginning conceived as applying equally to the public and the private sectors. It covered all information organized as addressable, sortable files containing formalized data; this included all electronic databases and some manual record-keeping systems. And the final version of the law provided for the creation of a federal privacy commissioner (*Datenschutzbeauftragter*), an innovation that was borrowed from the 1970 Hessian state privacy law. The commissioner, who was to be nominated by the administration and confirmed by the Bundestag, had the authority to audit compliance with the law and make recommendations to the executive and the legislature regarding privacy policy. However, the commissioner could not compel federal agencies to adopt his recommendations and interpretations of the law. He could only influence policy through his annual reports to the legislature. Table 4.2 compares some of the essential features of the American and West German privacy laws.

In her 1995 *Legislating Privacy*, Priscilla Regan argued that in the United States the conception of privacy as a subjective right or interest provided only a weak foundation for privacy protection legislation because it set the rights of the individual against other collective interests, such as security, the right to information, and the efficient functioning of public administration and private enterprise all of which were frequently found to be more compelling. However, she also suggested that a firmer foundation for such legislation could be established by focusing instead on the social value of privacy – that is, on the role played by personal privacy in the realization of collective values and ends.[17] I would like to suggest that the diverse arguments regarding the anti-social implications of privacy rights largely missed the mark because the most sophisticated West German arguments advanced on behalf of the right to informational self-determination regarded privacy rights as the condition for the meaningful participation of the individual in society, rather than as a means of escaping from it.[18]

Table 4.2 Key Features of United States and West German Privacy Law

	United States Privacy Act of 1974	**West Germany Federal Privacy Protection Act**
Type of protection	Self-regulation by government agencies on the basis of fair information practices. Individuals may then have recourse to the courts if they feel that their rights have been violated.	Categorical prohibition on the processing of personal information except: – when specifically permitted by law – with informed consent of the individual
Scope of protection	Limited to federal agencies	BDSG applied directly to federal agencies and to the private sector. The states (*Länder*) were to pass laws to apply the principles of BDSG to their own administrative activities.
Enforcement mechanism	Office of Management and Budget to issue regulations to guide agency self-regulation.	Federal and state privacy commissioners with consultative and audit authority. Recommendations could only be translated into policy via annual reports to the legislature and the public.

Note: Office of Management and Budget, 'Privacy Act Implementation: Guidelines and Responsibilities', *Federal Register* 40:132 (9 July 1975), 28948–78. Available online at http:// www.whitehouse.gov/sites/default/files/omb/assets/omb/inforeg/implementation_guidelines.pdf (accessed 22 December 2012).

Since the early 1970s, German privacy protection legislation had been stranded in a conceptual no man's land between the limited protection of personal information against unauthorized use and disclosure and the assertion of a stronger constitutional right to privacy. The issue was brought to a head by the legal challenges to the 1983 census. In this case, the complainants, academic privacy advocates and the boycotters all argued that new information technologies were generating new kinds of disciplinary, normalizing power that were incompatible with the country's constitutional commitment to human dignity and the development of the individual personality.[19]

In its final decision on the matter, the country's Constitutional Court adopted this line of reasoning and overturned the census law in the name of a new constitutional right to privacy, or what it called the right to 'informational self-determination' (*informationelle Selbstbestimmung*), which the court defined as 'the principle that the individual himself has the authority to determine what personal information to reveal and how it can be used'.[20]

Such a right might appear to be close to the subjectively individualist conception of privacy criticized by Regan, and, in the immediate aftermath of the decision, many critics argued that a strong reading of this right would paralyse the state and bring an end to statistical civilization as they knew it. However, as the court itself made clear, its ruling did not imply that the individual enjoyed unlimited, sovereign control or ownership over personal information. Rather, the court regarded the individual as 'a personality, which develops within a social community and which, therefore, depends on communication. Information – even that which can be attributed to a specific individual – constitutes a representation of social reality, a representation that cannot be ascribed exclusively to the individual concerned'.[21] The court also went on to argue that, to the extent that the new information technologies were diminishing the political capacity of the individual, the right to informational self-determination was essential both to the dignity and self-realization of the individual and to the broader social or collective interest in the proper functioning of a democratic society.[22]

So, what does this all mean for understanding the question of deregulation in the Federal Republic? In the declaration of principles and intentions for the new administration, which he delivered in May 1983, the new chancellor, Helmut Kohl, proclaimed that the goal of his administration was 'to reduce the scope of state activity to its essential functions'.[23] This statement has been understood as an endorsement of the neoliberal economic ideas and policies that were the basis of the CDU–FDP coalition. The problem is that no systematic reorientation of economic policy followed in the wake of this declaration. This was the case, I argue, because the governing coalition was subject to the same fiscal constraints and global economic pressures as its predecessor and because the understanding of the essential functions of the state that Kohl had in mind was quite different from both the American liberal tradition and the neoliberalism espoused by Ronald Reagan and Margaret Thatcher. The Christian Democrats would never have agreed with Thatcher's polemical claim that there is 'no such thing as society',[24] and in many of its broader policy initiatives the Kohl administration struggled to strike a satisfactory balance between the promotion of market incentives and its deep-seated belief in the role of the state in regulating social and economic life.

Moreover, even before the census decision, the Federal Privacy Protection Law had been a broad statement of principles that had virtually demanded supplementary, domain-specific legislation. However, the census decision set in motion an entirely new regulatory dynamic. As Hans Peter Bull, the first federal privacy commissioner and later interior minister of Schleswig-Holstein, has recently explained, ever since the Constitutional Court ruled that, in the absence of explicit legislative authorization, the collection and processing of personal information constituted an infringement of the rights of the individual,

> legislators have been unceasingly occupied with regulating processes that had previously been regarded as legally permissible. The legislative machine has been running at high speed because we now have higher expectations for the exhaustive legal codification (*Durchnormierung*) of all spheres of social life – and because sufficient authorization is indispensable for countless state activities, especially for the security agencies.[25]

As a result, the 1980s was anything but a decade of deregulation, at least in the domain of privacy protection law.

Lastly, it is important to enquire into the significance of this legislation. Like its predecessor, the Kohl administration was committed to the modernization and rationalization of the civil administration and the security agencies. The new information technologies played a central role in these plans. However, the census decision meant that every major initiative in these areas would have to be accompanied by flanking legislation spelling out the conditions under which personal information could be collected, used and exchanged and that a number of existing laws would have to be revised in order to bring them into compliance with the principles laid out by the court. These included the packet of security laws that was the top domestic priority of the Kohl administration, the country's statistical, census and archive laws, and the laws regulating the country's population information and identification system (the national population registry law, the ID card law, the passport law), as well as police laws and the code of criminal procedure. Not only did this lead to the proliferation of privacy legislation. Concerns about terrorism and the prevailing balance of parliamentary power insured that, rather than narrowing the scope of state surveillance, this legislation instead provided legal authorization for the novel surveillance practices that had been developed by the police and the intelligence agencies since the 1970s. Although privacy appeared to recede as a political issue after the 1987 census boycott,[26] since 2001 the issue has returned with a vengeance. Over the past decade the Constitutional Court has extended the original right to informational self-determination to include the confidentiality and integrity of information technology systems and placed limits on the bulk collection of telephony metadata (*Vorratsdatenspeicherung*). In addition, recent revelations concerning the scope of American surveillance of the digital domain and the infiltration and co-optation of encryption technologies by the National Security Agency are again making surveillance and privacy into important political issues, although the implication of the German intelligence agencies in the scandal, and a sense of resignation regarding the possibility of actually holding the American government accountable for its actions, have so far limited the extent to which public outrage has been translated into political action.

Larry Frohman is associate professor of History at the State University of New York at Stony Brook. His research interests include Modern Europe (especially Germany and France), welfare and social policy, intellectual history, and historiography. He is currently working on a study of surveillance, privacy and the politics of personal information in the Federal Republic. His first book was *Poor Relief and Welfare in Germany from the Reformation to World War I* (Cambridge University Press, 2008).

Notes

All translations from German are by the author.

1. For a recent account of neoliberal theory and policy, see Daniel Stedman Jones, *Masters of the Universe: Hayek, Friedman, and the Birth of Neoliberal Politics* (Princeton, NJ, 2012). Thomas Biebricher, *Neoliberalismus* (Hamburg, 2012), and Wendy Brown, *Undoing the Demos: Neoliberalism's Stealth Revolution* (New York, 2015). See also Norbert Frei and Dietmar Süß (eds), *Privatisierung: Idee und Praxis seit den 1970er Jahren* (Göttingen, 2012) and, on the forging of the neoliberal subject, Ulrich Bröckling, *Das unternehmerische Selbst: Soziologie einer Subjektivierungsform* (Frankfurt, 2007) and Donncha Marron, *Consumer Credit in the United States: A Sociological Perspective from the 19th Century to the Present* (New York, 2009).

2. For the recent debate over the usefulness of such social scientific concepts for the writing of contemporary history, see Bernhard Dietz and Christopher Neumaier, 'Vom Nutzen der Sozialwissenschaften für die Zeitgeschichte: Werte und Wertewandel als Gegenstand historischer Forschung', *Vierteljahrshefte für Zeitgeschichte* 60(2) (2012), 293–304; and Rüdiger Graf and Kim Christian Priemel, 'Zeitgeschichte in der Welt der Sozialwissenschaften: Legitimität und Originalität einer Disziplin', *Vierteljahrshefte für Zeitgeschichte* 59(4) (2011), 479–508. On the development of the West German economy in the 1970s and 1980s, see Anselm Doering-Manteuffel and Lutz Raphael, *Nach dem Boom: Perspektiven auf die Zeitgeschichte*, 3rd enlarged edn (Göttingen, 2012), and Andreas Wirsching, *Abschied vom Provisorium: Geschichte der Bundesrepublik Deutschland 1982–1990* (Munich, 2006).

3. Peter Gola and Rudolf Schomerus, *BDSG – Bundesdatenschutzgesetz: Kommentar*, 10th edn (Munich, 2010).

4. Spiros Simitis (ed.), *Bundesdatenschutzgesetz*, 7th edn (Baden-Baden, 2011).

5. 'Gesetz zum Schutz vor Mißbrauch personenbezogener Daten bei der Datenverarbeitung/Bundesdatenschutzgesetz' (*Bundesgesetzblatt* I, 1977, No. 7, 201). An English translation is available in Ulrich Dammann et al. (eds), *Data Protection Legislation: An International Documentation* (Frankfurt: Metzner, 1977), and an English version of the law as revised in 1990 and 1994 is available online at http://www.iuscomp.org/gla/statutes/BDSG.htm. The German word '*Datenschutz*' is variously translated as 'privacy protection' or 'data protection', depending on whether one wishes to emphasize the goal of the law (protection of the private sphere or the legitimate privacy interests of the individual) or the role of the law in ensuring the accuracy, completeness and confidentiality of the personal data being processed.

6. Gabriele Metzler, 'Ein deutscher Weg: Die Liberalisierung der Telekommunikation in der Bundesrepublik und die Grenzen politischer Reformen in den 1980er Jahren', *Archiv für Sozialgeschichte* 52 (2012), 163–90; and Frank Bösch, 'Politische Macht und gesellschaftliche

Gestaltung: Wege zur Einführung des privaten Rundfunks in den 1970/80er Jahren', *Archiv für Sozialgeschichte* 52 (2012), 191–210.

7. Bundestag Drucksache 10/1281 (11 April 1984).

8. This promises to change substantially in the next few years, when the dissertations and other monographs completed at the Potsdam Center for Contemporary History under the auspices of its project on Journeys into the Digital Society begin to appear in print.

9. On the discourse and policy of domestic security in the 1970s, see Karrin Hanshew, *Terror and Democracy in West Germany* (Cambridge, 2012), and Stephan Scheiper, *Innere Sicherheit: Politische Anti-Terror-Konzepte in der Bundesrepublik Deutschland während der 1970er Jahre* (Paderborn, 2010).

10. 'Bericht über das Ergebnis der Umfrage zur Praxis der Überprüfung der Gewähr der Verfassungstreue bei Einstellungsbewerbern (fall 1975)', Bundesarchiv Koblenz B106, Nr. 95951. Derogatory information was reported in 5,678 cases, and 235 applicants were denied positions based on doubts about their political loyalty. Gerard Braunthal, in *Political Loyalty and Public Service in West Germany: The 1972 Decree against Radicals and Its Consequences* (Amherst, 1990), p. 93, claims that somewhere between 2 and 2.4 million people were reviewed 1972–79, and that by 1985 the total had reached 3.5 million. See also Dominik Rigoll, *Staatsschutz in Westdeutschland: Von der Entnazifizierung zur Extremistenabwehr* (Göttingen, 2013).

11. Larry Frohman, 'Virtually Creditworthy: Privacy, the Right to Information, and Consumer Credit in West Germany, 1950–1985', in *The Development of Consumer Credit in Global Perspective: Business, Regulation, and Culture*, ed. Jan Logemann (New York, 2012), 129–54.

12. On American privacy policy, see Priscilla Regan, *Legislating Privacy: Technology, Social Values, and Public Policy* (Chapel Hill, NC, 1995), and Colin Bennett, *Regulating Privacy: Data Protection and Public Policy in Europe and the United States* (Ithaca, 1992), 68f. Between 1965 and 1974 there were forty-seven separate sets of Congressional hearings and reports on a variety of privacy-related issues.

13. See http://www.justice.gov/opcl/privstat.htm (accessed 22 December 2012).

14. Cited in Bennett, *Regulating Privacy*, 198.

15. For the legislative history of the Privacy Act, see US Congress. Senate. Committee on Government Operations, *Legislative History of the Privacy Act of 1974 S. 3418. Source Book on Privacy* (Washington: USGPO, 1976), available online at http://www.loc.gov/rr/frd/Military_Law/pdf/LH_privacy_act-1974.pdf (accessed 22 December 2012).

16. Gunnar Trumbull, *Consumer Capitalism: Politics, Product Markets, and Firm Strategy in France and Germany* (Ithaca, NY, 2006), 15–17, 170–71.

17. Regan, *Legislating Privacy*, 22–23, 212ff.

18. Larry Frohman, 'Rethinking Privacy in the Age of the Mainframe: Integrated Information Systems, the Changing Logic of Privacy, and the Problem of Democratic Politics in Surveillance Societies', in *Im Sog des Internets: Privatheit und Öffentlichkeit im digitalen Wandel*, ed. Ulrike Ackermann (Frankfurt, 2013), 71–92.

19. Larry Frohman, '"Only Sheep Let Themselves Be Counted": Privacy, Political Culture, and the 1983/87 West German Census Boycotts', *Archiv für Sozialgeschichte* 52 (2012): 335–78.

20. Entscheidungen des Bundesverfassungsgerichts (BVerfGE) 65, 43.

21. BVerfGE 65, 1, 44.

22. BVerfGE 65, 1, 42–43.

23. '...den Staat auf den Kern seiner Aufgaben zurück[zu]führen', Bundestag Sten. Ber. 10. Wahlperiode, 4. Sitzung (4 May 1983), 56.

24. In her September 1987 interview with Woman's Own (http://www.margaretthatcher.org/document/106689).

25. Hans Peter Bull, 'Konkreter Realismus statt abstrakter Polemik: Ist Datenschutz ein Grundrecht?', Neue Gesellschaft/Frankfurter Hefte 12 (2009): 35.
26. Wirsching, Abschied vom Provisorium, 434–44, provides a good account of this shift.

Bibliography

Biebricher, Thomas, *Neoliberalismus* (Hamburg, 2012).

Bösch, Frank, 'Politische Macht und gesellschaftliche Gestaltung: Wege zur Einführung des privaten Rundfunks in den 1970/80er Jahren', *Archiv für Sozialgeschichte* 52 (2012), 191–210.

Bennett, Colin, *Regulating Privacy: Data Protection and Public Policy in Europe and the United States* (Ithaca, 1992).

Braunthal, Gerard, *Political Loyalty and Public Service in West Germany: The 1972 Decree against Radicals and Its Consequences* (Amherst, MA, 1990).

Bröckling, Ulrich, *Das unternehmerische Selbst: Soziologie einer Subjektivierungsform* (Frankfurt, 2007).

Brown, Wendy, *Undoing the Demos: Neoliberalism's Stealth Revolution* (New York, 2015).

Bull, Hans Peter, 'Konkreter Realismus statt abstrakter Polemik: Ist Datenschutz ein Grundrecht?', *Neue Gesellschaft/Frankfurter Hefte* 12 (2009), 34–37.

Dammann, Ulrich, et al. (eds), *Data Protection Legislation: An International Documentation* (Frankfurt, 1977).

Dietz, Bernhard, and Christopher Neumaier, 'Vom Nutzen der Sozialwissenschaften für die Zeitgeschichte: Werte und Wertewandel als Gegenstand historischer Forschung', *Vierteljahrshefte für Zeitgeschichte* 60(2) (2012): 293–304.

Doering-Manteuffel, Anselm, and Lutz Raphael, *Nach dem Boom: Perspektiven auf die Zeitgeschichte*, 3rd enlarged edn (Göttingen, 2012).

Frei, Norbert, and Dietmar Süß (eds), *Privatisierung: Idee und Praxis seit den 1970er Jahren* (Göttingen, 2012).

Frohman, Larry, '"Only Sheep Let Themselves Be Counted": Privacy, Political Culture, and the 1983/87 West German Census Boycotts', *Archiv für Sozialgeschichte* 52 (2012): 335–78.

——, 'Virtually Creditworthy: Privacy, the Right to Information, and Consumer Credit in West Germany, 1950–1985', in *The Development of Consumer Credit in Global Perspective: Business, Regulation, and Culture*, ed. Jan Logemann (New York, 2012), 129–54.

——, 'Rethinking Privacy in the Age of the Mainframe: Integrated Information Systems, the Changing Logic of Privacy, and the Problem of Democratic Politics in Surveillance Societies', in *Im Sog des Internets: Privatheit und Öffentlichkeit im digitalen Wandel*, ed. Ulrike Ackermann (Frankfurt, 2013), 71–92.

Gola, Peter and Rudolf Schomerus, *BDSG – Bundesdatenschutzgesetz: Kommentar*, 10th edn (Munich, 2010).

Graf, Rüdiger, and Kim Christian Priemel, 'Zeitgeschichte in der Welt der Sozialwissenschaften: Legitimität und Originalität einer Disziplin', *Vierteljahrshefte für Zeitgeschichte* 59(4) (2011): 479–508.

Hanshew, Karrin, *Terror and Democracy in West Germany* (Cambridge, 2012).

Jones, Daniel Stedman, *Masters of the Universe: Hayek, Friedman, and the Birth of Neoliberal Politics* (Princeton, NJ, 2012).

Marron, Donncha, *Consumer Credit in the United States: A Sociological Perspective from the 19th Century to the Present* (New York, 2009).

Metzler, Gabriele, 'Ein deutscher Weg: Die Liberalisierung der Telekommunikation in der Bundesrepublik und die Grenzen politischer Reformen in den 1980er Jahren', *Archiv für Sozialgeschichte* 52 (2012): 163–90.

Regan, Priscilla, *Legislating Privacy: Technology, Social Values, and Public Policy* (Chapel Hill, NC, 1995).

Rigoll, Dominik, *Staatsschutz in Westdeutschland: Von der Entnazifizierung zur Extremistenabwehr* (Göttingen, 2013).

Scheiper, Stephan, *Innere Sicherheit: Politische Anti-Terror-Konzepte in der Bundesrepublik Deutschland während der 1970er Jahre* (Paderborn, 2010).

Simitis, Spiros (ed.), *Bundesdatenschutzgesetz*, 7th edn (Baden-Baden, 2011).

Trumbull, Gunnar, *Consumer Capitalism: Politics, Product Markets, and Firm Strategy in France and Germany* (Ithaca, NY, 2006), 15–17, 170–71.

Wirsching, Andreas, *Abschied vom Provisorium: Geschichte der Bundesrepublik Deutschland 1982– 1990* (Munich, 2006).

CHAPTER 5

Changes in Business Organization

Integration in the American Workplace in the Early 1970s

ENRICO BELTRAMINI

Introduction

On 18 February 2009, in his first major speech since being confirmed as the United States' first black attorney general, Eric Holder took the opportunity when celebrating Black History Month to define American people as 'essentially a nation of cowards' on matters of race.[1]

Probably in order to balance the highly controversial – for some, even incendiary – nature of his powerful opening statement, Holder immediately limited the extension of the issue. He stated that:

> As a nation we have done a pretty good job in melding the races in the workplace. We work with one another, lunch together and, when the event is at the workplace during work hours or shortly thereafter, we socialize with one another fairly well, irrespective of race. ... Outside the workplace the situation is [however] bleak in that there is almost no significant interaction between us.

What is significant in this statement is the choice of the workplace as a fine example of racial integration. According to Holder, work is an island of racial decency and mutual understanding in an ocean of social shaming and public embarrassment. Remarkably, fifty years ago the situation was quite different. African Americans were not only severely unemployed, but when employed it was rarely in secure, remunerative jobs.

Notes for this section begin on page 103.

First, this chapter sustains the view that, despite the immense job opportunities provided by the furious economic growth of the post-war economy, the American workplace was still segregated in the early 1960s. Second, it recognizes that the relationship between federal government and business institutions in terms of job desegregation changed suddenly in the 1960s, beginning with the establishment of the new Committee on Equal Employment Opportunity in 1961 and the subsequent civil rights legislation, making 'equal employment opportunity' a convincing goal. Third, beyond the dominant narrative that economic parity in the workplace is the result of the important colour-blind civil rights legislation of the 1960s, this chapter points out that it was a colour-conscious item of legislation in terms of 'preferential employment treatment' that ultimately opened up access to jobs for African Americans, ultimately allowing the nation's first black attorney general under the nation's first president to identify himself as black, to exemplify 'melding the races in the workplace'.

A Segregated Workplace

Probably nothing symbolized the promise and optimism of post-war America more than employment. This was a time of low unemployment, increasing consumerism and a positive attitude about the future. It was a time of great expectations, faith in progress and the American Dream. It was also a time of grace: Americans had triumphed over the Great Depression and then Fascism and Nazism; they had won the war against Japan; and they believed they had become the healthiest, wealthiest and happiest nation in the world, which was inevitably destined to win the Cold War. Fundamental changes were at work in the very fabric of American society, and the economy was booming. The spectacular economic growth was opening up more and better-paid jobs to black people and increasing their social status and self-confidence. In the aftermath of the Second World War, there was a general confidence that black people could benefit from society's dramatic increase in affluence that had resulted from the strength of the national economy. Yet, the workplace in the United States was still predominantly segregated in the early 1960s.

A long period of consistent economic growth in American capitalism began at the end of the Second World War and ended in the early 1970s (although there are some debates on dating).[2] The nation's gross national product (GNP) rose from about $200,000 million in 1940 to $300,000 million in 1950 and to more than $500,000 million in 1960. At one point, in the late 1940s, American capitalism accounted for 57 per cent of the world's steel, 62 per cent of its oil and 80 per cent of its cars. The United States had three-quarters of the planet's gold reserves. GNP grew in the 1940s

– especially in the first half of the decade – and by 1950 it had increased by 56.3 per cent for the 1940s as a whole.[3] The 1950s was 'an age of astonishing material affluence'.[4] The Eisenhower administration carefully monitored inflation through fiscal restraints, while technological advancements maintained unemployment at a very low level, between 4.1 and 4.4 per cent between 1955 and 1957 (in the recession year of 1958, however, unemployment suddenly rose to 6.8 per cent). This prosperity accelerated even more rapidly in the 'golden age' of the 1960s, when per capita income increased by 41 per cent. Prices remained stable until the late 1960s and unemployment stayed quite low, falling to 3.5 per cent in 1969. Poverty, as measured by the government, declined from 22 per cent of the population in 1960 to 12 per cent in 1969.[5] Fundamental in the 'golden age' to sustaining and securing economic growth was the tax cut proposed by John Kennedy in 1963 and passed early the following year. It was designed to stimulate production, not consumption, as happened in the 1980s. It was supposed to increase GNP, the number of jobs, personal and family disposable income, and corporate profits – and it worked. GNP increased by more than 10 per cent in 1965 and disposable personal income by 12 per cent in the year following. By December 1965, the unemployment rate was 4.1 per cent, although a month later it fell to 3.9 per cent.[6]

The black job landscape was affected by these gigantic shifts. In 1939, 42.5 per cent of African Americans were still employed in agriculture, forestry and fisheries. Twenty years later, it was only 12.5 per cent. In the meanwhile, blacks lost interest in agricultural opportunities for employment and placed all their hope on industrial work. In the 1940s and early 1950s, they left the South and migrated north to find industrial work in the supposedly booming manufacturing sector. As a result, by 1970, only 53 per cent of black people lived in the South compared to 77 per cent in 1940.[7] This massive migration did not necessarily convey employment opportunities to all. While the black population increased – in 1950, African Americans numbered 15.8 million, and 19 million a decade later – unemployment remained a curse: in 1960, unemployment was twice as high for blacks as for whites, and poverty afflicted 50 per cent or more of blacks. The problem was that the US economy was already involved in another major change, deindustrialization, with subsequent modification of job patterns. At the very moment that blacks were repositioning themselves as a potential labour force for the industrial complex, the whole country was moving away from industrialization.

In the 1950s, automation was already the single most influential factor in the deindustrialization of the American economy. Automation increased output and reduced labour costs – ultimately the number of workers. A closer investigation of the period following the Second World War reveals that manufacturing employment reached its peak in the early 1950s, only to drop rapidly from that point on, falling back to pre-war levels by the end of the next decade. Accordingly, the American workforce changed significantly. During the 1950s, the number of workers providing services grew until it equalled and then surpassed the number who produced goods. It became fashionable to propose the advent of some sort of post-industrial society, in which corporations depended less on manual labour and more on services and office-based workers. By 1956, a majority of US workers held white-collar rather than blue-collar jobs. However, while 'white-collar' clearly referred to people who perform professional, managerial or administrative work, the designation was fairly vague: almost 50 per cent of the total of 27.2 million workers in 1960 (14.4 million) were considered 'white-collar' workers, including clerical and sales workers. At the same time, blue-collar workers remained central to the economy of the 1950s, and only in the 1960s did the shift become evident. In fact, although the percentage of people defined by occupation as 'manual' workers declined over time, the absolute number continued to increase, from 23.7 million in 1950 to 25.6 million in 1960 and 29.1 million in 1970.[8] Nevertheless, the transition from a manufacturing-based economy to a service-based economy was gigantic in size and extensive in terms of effect. The industrial boom of the early twentieth century and the promise of well-paying jobs for unskilled labourers had boosted the urban population and the interest of the North's labour-hungry industries in unskilled workers. For decades, millions of immigrants from Europe had benefited from the opportunity of unskilled, heavy-lifting jobs in the booming industries of steel, railroads and mining. In the 1950s, however, American jobs initiate a slow and inexorable migration from the urban manufacturing centres, while the early impact of automation (or cybernation) caused the decline of manufacturing employment and created a new job crisis for those workers without advanced education or vocational training. The decline of manufacturing employment by the late 1950s and early 1960s had created a sense of desperation in urban black communities and pressure for some sort of relief. Blacks had moved into the city centres at the very moment when whites were moving out to the suburbs. 'There is an irony in this for the Negro', noted a Chicago Urban League forum years later: 'He may be winning the right to get a job just at the time when the job itself is disappearing'.[9] Of course, here 'job' should be understood as 'manufacturing job'.

The exclusion of black workers from employment was matched only by their exclusion from employment in *good* jobs. When African Americans were employed, it was rarely in secure, remunerative jobs. Black workers tended to be taken on in unskilled industrial and service activities, while white employers maintained the monopoly of white employees in sales, management and professional jobs. In the 1950s, it was rare to see black professionals, black white-collar workers or even skilled black blue-collar workers. In 1950, only 2.2 per cent of black men and 5.7 per cent of black women worked as professionals, nearly all of them in black-owned businesses.[10] African Americans were assigned to less desirable job categories, such as maid, cook and porter. Managers refused to hire blacks for sales and clerical jobs because they would often involve contact with – and an inevitable reaction from – white clientele and white co-workers. For African Americans, it was a humiliating experience, as well as a practical barrier to better jobs. Herbert Hill, the labour director of the *National Association for the Advancement of Colored People* (NAACP), a civil rights organization, envisioned 'a permanent black underclass', a group in 'permanent unemployment' or underemployed, *a segment of American society that would be at risk of failing to participate fully in the economic prosperity of the country*. To avoid that risk, black activists elaborated two different options: they demanded fair hiring and promotion policies; and they asked for jobs specifically for blacks. The latter ultimately succeeded.[11]

The Option of Fair Employment Opportunity Policy

In the 1950s, labour and civil rights leaders were already sharing the idea of fair employment practices legislation – a set of laws prohibiting racial discrimination and promoting equal opportunity in the workplace. Not only that, they also articulated the idea of agencies responsible for enforcing those laws that would move a step further the fundamental assumptions and the underlying philosophy of the two original pieces of federal action to promote equal opportunity and prohibit employment discrimination, especially in the national defence industry: the Executive Order No. 8802 and the Fair Employment Practices Commission (FEPC) signed by Franklin D. Roosevelt on 25 June 1941.[12] Labour and civil rights leaders envisioned a federal legislation that might establish and enforce non-discriminatory hiring and promotion practices in the workplace, with equal treatment and fair employment in both the public and private sectors. The major obstacle was the existing low degree of democratization in the job market. Black workers, especially but not exclusively in the South, felt trapped by a federal government that was too timid in enforcing economic rights, while aggressively defending white privileges in the economy. Determined to protect the South's racial hierarchy and low-wage regional economy in an age of economic growth and technological innovation, southern Democrats in Congress had joined with conservative Republicans to stress the traditions of economic liberty, small government and privileged access to better employment and high-wage jobs. Numan Bartley writes aptly: 'In 1940 the raison d'être of Southern state governments was the protection of white supremacy and social stability; thirty years later their central purpose was the promotion of business and industrial development'.[13] Bartley maintains that the South was trying to modernize economically while retaining 'white supremacy and social stability'. However, when the forces of boosterism collided with the emerging civil rights movement in the 1950s and 1960s, as Elizabeth Jacoway acknowledges, 'white businessmen across the South found themselves pushed – by the federal government and civil rights forces as well as by their own economic interests (and values) – into becoming reluctant advocates of a new departure in southern race relations'.[14] In other words, when it became clear that economic development coincided with racial justice, the wall of segregation crumbled.

It was only with the election of President John F. Kennedy that a revival of public affairs over corporate authority finally put an end to the federal government's passivity. With renewed government-backed equal job rights, momentum for business hegemony suddenly dissolved. For the first time since the Labor–Management Relations Act (also, the Taft–Hartley Act of 1947), friends of business did not dominate government in Washington. In March 1961, President Kennedy issued Executive Order No. 10925 to create a Presidential Committee on Equal Employment Opportunity (CEEO). Kennedy's order was based on precedents that included President Roosevelt's Fair Employment Practices Commission in 1941 and President Eisenhower's Committee on Government Employment Policy in 1953, chaired by Vice President Nixon. Consequently, Vice President Johnson was designated to chair the newly established committee.

In the absence of enforcing legislation, workplace desegregation was left to social forces rather than to the CEEO. In Birmingham, Alabama, protest actions began in 1962, when students from local colleges arranged for a year of staggered boycotts. They caused downtown business to decline by as much as 40 per cent, which attracted attention from Chamber of Commerce president Sidney Smyer, who commented that the 'racial incidents have given us a black eye that we'll be a long time trying to forget'.[15] The Southern Christian Leadership Conference (SCLC), the civil rights organization in which Martin Luther King, Jr., played a key role, was established in 1957 to coordinate the action of local protest groups throughout the South. They decided that economic pressure on Birmingham businesses would be more effective than pressure on politicians.[16] In May 1963, in the aftermath of the campaign for the desegregation of Birmingham's downtown merchants, one of the most influential campaigns in the history of the civil rights movement, the Kennedy administration proclaimed itself to be eager to engage more deeply in civil rights issues.[17] The attorney general, Robert Kennedy, sent

Burke Marshall, his assistant attorney general for civil rights, to Birmingham to survey the situation. Marshall complained that he did not find any black employees in the federal offices in the city. On 29 May 1963, at the CEEO meeting, Robert Kennedy acknowledged that only fifteen out of two thousand federal employees in Birmingham were black – which was just 1 per cent in a city that was 37 per cent black. On the same occasion, the attorney general confronted Johnson, the CEEO chairman, and mentioned, among the other statistics, that NASA had only two people working on equal employment, with $3.5 billion in contracts. Short of results, the CEEO was on the verge of becoming quite an embarrassment for the Administration; on the advice of his brother, President Kennedy decided to expand the CEEO's jurisdiction and include not only government contracts but also highway and other programmes which were entitled to receive even a portion of federal funds.[18] Then, President Kennedy called the Civil Rights Bill a priority. 'We face a moral crisis', he told the nation on 11 June 1963; 'It is time to act in Congress'.[19] But his bill did not comprise a number of provisions deemed essential by civil rights leaders, including ending discrimination in private employment or granting the Justice Department power to initiate desegregation or job discrimination lawsuits, or an FEPC provision.[20] In the aftermath of the string of protests that in the summer of 1963 caused thousands of protesters to join months-long campaigns to provide jobs to blacks, organizations not involved in the Birmingham events, such as the NAACP and the Congress on Racial Equality (CORE), began demanding 'full and non-discriminatory employment' and the 'vital right to earn money'.[21]

The national business press took note. *Fortune* magazine predicted that 'the problem of race relations may become a major – at times *the* major – preoccupation of top management for a number of years to come'. *Business Week* pointed out that businesspeople might recognize the increasing pressure on individuals and organizations for more and better jobs for blacks. This campaign 'is comparable to the American worker's drive to unionize at the turn of the century'.[22] Many businesses decided that temperance and accommodation would have been a better option than disorder and turbulence. Business leaders tried to convince local governments to negotiate their differences with civil rights leaders peacefully.

While the attempts to prevent boycotts and avoid retaliation by black customers were a major cause of the conciliatory efforts of small, local, white-owned businesses, in the same period American corporations played a complex role in promoting or resisting the opening of the American workplace to racial minorities. On the one hand, there was a genuine interest in racial integration among executives and businesspeople in the corporate world. As pressure from civil rights organizations and federal government increased in the late 1950s and early 1960s, executives at the largest corporations began integrating their organizations. They were responding to the pressure of civil rights activists, and to the incoming legislation of the federal government and the enforcing actions of its agencies, but they were also moved 'by the desire to be well regarded' and by a moral obligation to do the right thing.[23] According to Jennifer Delton, corporations were in many regards at the forefront of racial integration, together with civil rights activists, federal government and labour unions, despite having been portrayed as impediments to it. On the other hand, fair employment was pursued as a pre-emptive strategy. In other words, executives were claiming alignment with the philosophy of racial integration in the workplace, while pursuing fair employment free from the constraints of government coercion, and thus ultimately maintaining control of their organizations. This is an important point, because most scholarship addresses the political and cultural white defence of segregation, not the protection of economic power inside the enterprise.[24] Enemies of fair employment practices and pro-business con-servatives did not oppose the civil rights movement to defend segregation. The sovereignty of the corporate executives in the workplace, and ultimately the principles of the free market and the independence of the enterprise from the influence of federal government were at stake.[25] Businesspeople argued that government legislation was an intolerable intrusion into the traditional prerogatives of management over hiring, promoting and firing, as well as a direct attack on the authority of corporate executives. They claimed it was a violation of one of the most protected values of American capitalism, the notion of merit and business as a meritocracy.[26] According to this notion, the workplace has always been colour-blind. People succeed or fail, move up or out, are promoted or fired, according to the principles of scientific manage-ment – a rational technique for efficiency.

The labour scholar, David Roediger, who researches the relationship between labour management and the formation of racial identities in the United States, holds the opposite view. Despite the claims of merit as an indisputable value, the history of management in the United States has been an uninterrupted attempt to control the workers. Managers explicitly ranked racial groups, both in terms of which type of labour they were best suited for, and in terms of their relative value compared to others. White executives relied on such alleged racial knowledge to manage workers, and believed that the 'lesser races' could only benefit from their tutelage. These views were woven into managerial strategies that promoted white supremacy, not only ideologically but also in the everyday practical processes used in many work-places. Even in factories governed by 'scientific management', the impulse to play the races against each other, and to slot workers into jobs categorized by race, were powerful management tools used to enforce discipline, keep wages low, keep workers in dangerous jobs, and undermine working-class solidarity.[27] The myth of merit at work has never had any substantial foundation; it simply serves to allow executives and businesspeople to maintain control of the workplace.

It is important to realize that important social and economic forces were at work in that period, and institutions and organizations were 'fighting the good fight' on both sides, to increase or reduce the influence of the federal government in the workplace. On one side are the efforts of the federal government and its allies to establish hiring and promotion practices that do not depend on the corporation's internal rules, but are set by law. On the other side, there were the business-friendly conservatives and corporate executives opposing this trend and fighting to retain control of the workplace. While claiming to protect merit as the basic principle of American enterprise, and in pursuit of efficiency, corporate executives explicitly ranked racial groups by profiling workers, deciding who was best suited to each job. The executives ultimately merged managerial strategies and white supremacy for the sake of controlling the workplace.

Putting it into context, the 1960s was a decade not only of dominant liberal consensus, but of resurgent business-friendly conservatism. Well before phrases such as 'free market economy' and 'free enterprise' entered popular parlance, hundreds of legislators, businesspeople and executives made it a common cause to promote an economic system that provided individuals with the opportunity to make their own economic decisions free of government constraints, for the sake of private profit. A resurgent Republican Party and the business community fought to block or reverse expansion of the New Deal and to re-establish managerial autonomy and corporate political hegemony in the workplace. The primary belief of the pro-business conservative movement was that the market, not the government, was the centre of gravity of American capitalism.

Assassinated in Dallas, Kennedy did not live to see his civil rights legislation approved. The Civil Rights Act (technically, the Mansfield–Dicksen–Humphrey–Kuchel amendment), approved in 1964 under the Johnson administration, stated in Title VII the principle of equality of opportunity in employment, and made it clear that employers were not obliged to redress racial imbalances caused by past discriminatory practices. The general counsel of the CORE, Carl Rachlin, explained that in Title VII 'preferential treatment to right past wrong is not required'.[28] Title VII also created the Equal Employment Opportunity Commission (EEOC) to process and respond to charges of employment discrimination. During the Senate debate, Republican Senator Everett Dirksen endorsed the creation of an EEOC in order to limit the action of the Justice Department, and made sure that the federal government was called in only if local agencies proved themselves unable to handle job discrimination complaints. Congress also stripped out of this section authority for the EEOC to file suit in its own right (a power gained in 1972) and issue 'cease and desist' orders, and forced individuals to go to court to defend their rights in instances where discriminatory behaviour persisted.[29] Basically, as Herbert Hill argued, 'Title VII is not self-enforcing'.[30] However, Title VII provided the right to sue for unfair treatment. In 1965, in order to replace the CEEO – the commission created by executive order under President Kennedy and chaired by then Vice President Johnson – President Johnson signed Executive Order 11246 transferring responsibility for monitoring and regulating non-discrimination for business contractors and sub-contractors dealing with the federal government to the Secretary of Labor, who established the Office of Federal Contract Compliance (OFCC).[31]

After the passage of the Civil Rights Act and the creation of the EEOC and OFCC, an epic shift occurred, as they helped to recognize racial inequality in the workplace and provided mechanisms for correcting it. In fact, Title VII had awarded blacks and other minorities the right to sue for fair job employment, while EEOC and OFCC had encouraged workers to apply for jobs and supported them in case of resistance. Lawsuits became a concrete threat for corporate executives, together with acts of protest such as nationwide boycotts of downtown stores by black consumers until they hired black cashiers and workers. However, despite the historic importance and practical results achieved by Title VII (and EEOC and OFCC) to provide black workers with a better chance of obtaining a job, Title VII was rapidly succeeded by affirmative action – another policy promoted by the federal government.

The Option of Preferential Treatment and Affirmative Action

Although the project of federal fair employment practices legislation remained the main goal of liberal politicians and the federal government, civil rights and union leaders, preferential treatment and affirmative action slowly established themselves as a valid alternative option. When Vice President Johnson was designated to chair the newly established CEEO, he privately advised Kennedy that the Eisenhower administration's non-discrimination clause for governmental contractors should 'be revised to impose not merely the negative obligation of avoiding discrimination but the affirmative duty to employ applicants'.[32] Thus the term 'affirmative action' entered the lexicon of public policy in the early 1960s. In fact, it was adopted for the very first time by Hobart Taylor, Jr., a young black lawyer from Houston, on a draft of the Executive Order written for Lyndon Johnson in 1961. However, under the language of the Executive Order No. 10925, the term affirmative action, allied as it appeared to be to phrases such as 'positive effort' and 'affirmative program', did not mean compensatory actions or special group treatment. It meant only positive action against race discrimination.[33]

The idea to guarantee jobs specifically for blacks was conceived at the time of the Great Depression and was pursued as federal government policy and through civil rights activism. In the first case, racial quotas were implemented by the federal government in the 1930s, as both the Tennessee Valley Authority and the Public Works Administration practised a quota system that reserved jobs for blacks.[34] In the second case, black activists aimed to convince employers to reserve jobs for blacks through boycotts, protests, and acts of civil disobedience. The 'Don't Buy Where You Can't Work' movement, which was successfully organized in Chicago in 1929, established the right to work on blacks' status as consumers. The movement became a major form of black activism in cities across the country, and achieved important results in Philadelphia, Atlanta and New York. At times the adoption of an intimidating approach – that is, demanding that white store owners hire blacks in proportion to the black population in the area, or in proportion to their consumer power (patronage) – was offered as an alternative to retaliatory boycotts.

Racial quotas resurged as an option in coincidence of the economic growth and the rising expectations of economic justice in the late 1950s and 1960s. *New York Herald Tribune* columnist Walter Lippmann described, in a nutshell, his understanding of post-scarcity economics in regards to the 1960s: 'A generation ago it would have been taken for granted that a war on poverty meant taxing money away from the haves and turning it over to the have nots ... But in this generation a revolutionary idea has taken hold. The size of the pie can be increased by intention'.[35]

While Lippmann was not speaking about jobs and employment specifically, in his article he clearly defined the fundamental assumption that lies behind the economic sustainability and _political_ legitimacy of racial quotas: for the very first time in the history of the country, the possibility of expanding job opportunities for African Americans could happen with no consequences for white workers. The equation appeared to have validity due to the previous quarter-century of extraordinary economic growth. Ultimately, the purpose of this economic growth was a society that was capable of providing access to employment for all Americans. The post-war economy was booming, and full employment seemed at hand without the threat of a racial conflict.

As a practical solution to job discrimination, civil rights leaders such as A. Philip Randolph and Martin Luther King, Jr., pointed out that fair employment opportunity was not enough, and they lobbied for preferential treatment. They both recommended that President Johnson 'make work available for those in the ghetto' and 'provide a job for every person who needs work' – that is, also for black workers.[36] They envisioned a reformed and expanded role for government that would lead to some kind of restructuring of American society – in the words of King, 'a restructuring of the architecture of American society' – in order to provide a higher level of economic justice.[37] Already in 1963, King had elaborated the proposal that some sort of special treatment or 'affirmative action' might be implemented to promote workplace integration. In his book *Why We Can't Wait*, King pointed out:

> The nation must not only radically readjust its attitude toward [African Americans] in the compelling present, but must incorporate in its planning some compensatory consideration for the handicaps [that African Americans have] inherited from the past. It is impossible to create a formula for the future [that] does not take into account that our society has done something special against [African Americans] for hundreds of years. How then can [African Americans] be absorbed into the mainstream of American life if we do not do something special for [them] now, in order to balance the equation and equip [them] to compete on a just and equal basis? Whenever this issue of compensatory or preferential treatment for [African Americans] is raised, some of our friends recoil in horror. [African Americans] should be granted equality, they agree; but [they] should ask nothing more. On the surface, this appears reasonable, but it is not realistic. For it is obvious that if a [person] entered at the starting line in a race three hundred years after another [person], the [former] would have to perform some impossible feat in order to catch up with his fellow runner.[38]

Liberals such as President Johnson seemed to agree with King and the other civil rights leaders that some sort of special treatment was necessary to heal the scars of racial discrimination in the workplace. In his Commencement Address at Howard University on 4 June 1965, Johnson explained:

> You do not wipe away the scars of centuries by saying: 'Now you are free to go where you want, and do as you desire, and choose the leaders as you please'. You do not take a person who, for years, has been hobbled by chains and liberate him, bring him to the startling line of the race and then say, 'You are free to compete with all the others', and still justly believe that you have been completely fair. Thus it is not enough just to open the gates of opportunity. All our citizens must have the ability to walk through those gates.

However, President Johnson did not mean 'preferential treatment', but rather 'compensatory treatment'. Here is the source of disagreement between King and Johnson. For the latter, the role of the government was compensatory, in line with the liberal tradition that goes back to Roosevelt. Since the Great Depression, the federal government had been actively involved in handling the economy, during the New Deal through a regulated form of capitalism, and then – inspired by economist John Maynard Keynes – through managerial government. With regard to this approach, Alan Brinkley has noted:

> In its pursuit of full employment, the government would not seek to regulate corporate institutions so much as it would try to influence the business cycle. It would not try to redistribute economic power and limit inequality so much as it would create a compensatory welfare system (what later generations would call a 'safety net') for those whom capitalism had failed. It would not reshape capitalist institutions. It would reshape the economic and social environment in which those institutions worked.[39]

Then Brinkley explains how the federal government moved carefully from a regulatory strategy to compensatory policy. Accordingly, Johnson never really agreed with civil rights leaders such as King that American society needed radical change, that capitalism was unable to deliver economic justice, and that the problems of poverty and minority unemployment might be solved – in King's words – with 'public service employment for those less able to compete in the labour market', and income guarantees for those unable to 'participate in the job economy'.[40] In contrast, he strongly believed that capitalism was fundamentally sound and only in need of specific reforms and adjustments in order to provide opportunity for everyone. According to scholar James T. Patterson, '[t]he essence of Great Society liberalism was that government had the tools and the resources to help people help themselves. It sought to advance equality of opportunity, not to establish greater equality of social condition'.[41]

The system was in place to provide equality of opportunity, and therefore the right to work was meant to be the right to have the same opportunity as anyone else to be hired, promoted and obtain a better salary; the system was not in place to provide equality of outcome.

King, Randolph and other civil rights and labour union leaders, including Bayard Rustin, argued instead in favour of 'special and preferential treatment, in the form of preparation in training and education to enable it [Negro labour] effectively to move forward'.[42] The point resonated also with the New York Commission on Human Rights, who mention the option of 'preferential treatment' of 'qualified' blacks 'for a limited period'. In the form articulated by unions and civil rights organizations, the concept of affirmative action came to designate effective affirmative action employment policies, and found its way in the media and political landscape. An editor of *Fortune* magazine, Charles E. Silberman, was already, in 1963, considering 'it inevitable ... that Negro organizations would use their power to increase job opportunities for Negroes. Indeed, Negroes are not content with equal opportunity anymore; they are demanding preference, or 'positive discrimination' in their favour'.[43] He was right. The statement that detailed the compromise that ended the protest in Birmingham ('The Birmingham Truce

Agreement', 10 May 1963) explicitly mentioned an ongoing 'program of upgrading Negro employment', which was supposed to mean awarding a set number of jobs to eligible black applicants.[44]

While the history of the slow and imperfect reception of Title VII in labour management remains a testament to the strength and stubbornness of corporate executives in defending their prerogatives, the rise of racial quotas, or affirmative action, in the workplace is a remarkable case of unintended consequences. Initiated by Johnson as a compensatory policy and strongly supported by King as a preferential treatment, affirmative action was soon abandoned by Johnson because it clearly violated the 1964 Civil Rights Act.[45] Without the support of the Johnson administration, the efforts of the labour unions and civil rights organizations to promote racial quotas and end the monopoly of whites on managerial roles was a final, epic challenge to employers' authority, and their power to hire and promote according to internal, corporate criteria. Not surprisingly, American executives' efforts to limit unions ran second only to their dislike of anti-discrimination legislation.

The whole context changed with Richard Nixon, a Republican with a more liberal record on civil rights and black support than Adlai Stevenson or John Kennedy in the 1950s. His administration began surfing the waves of partisan realignment, and liberal-conservative lines simply became unsustainable. According to David Chappell, 'Nixon's political masterstroke was affirmative action'.[46] As president, Nixon endorsed affirmative action for several reasons. Philosophically, the president sought to replace the melting pot concept, and re-establish 'distinct ethnic and racial cultures', and he 'played down the importance of integration'.[47] He also pursued a sort of championing affirmative action to the liberal coalition of pro-government liberals, labour unions, and the civil rights movement. Nixon used affirmative action as a political tool to promote minority employment and ignite a white backlash. Historian Katznelson adds that during the Nixon administration, action against 'specific, intentional acts of discrimination was supplanted by policies that gave advantages, even actual points, to membership in a specific racial group. Compensatory policies were adopted where black individuals could be chosen even if white applicants had more appropriate qualifications judged by customary measures'.[48]

The Nixon administration also enforced the Philadelphia Plan, first drafted by the Department of Labor in 1967, which required that minority workers in the construction trade be hired in proportion to their percentage in the local labour force.[49] The goals were modest: the percentage of minority employees on Philadelphia Plan projects was to rise from 1.6 to 4 per cent (minimum) to 9 per cent (maximum) in 1970, and from 19 per cent (minimum) to 26 per cent (maximum) by the end of 1973. All were to be hired to fill new vacancies; no white workers were to be displaced.

An increasing percentage of whites started to believe that affirmative action meant quotas, and quotas exceeded equal opportunity, while its practical result translated into little progress for black workers. Not surprisingly, the white backlash against government bureaucracies, civil rights and race relations skyrocketed. Construction unions and contractors joined forces to oppose what they called 'reverse discrimination'. Appealing to whites who were uneasy about competition in the workplace, the Philadelphia Plan ignited racial tensions and further racial backlash, the ultimate goal of the Nixon administration.

With the conservative coalition inside and outside Congress opposing and weakening fair employment legislation, and Americans becoming increasingly less sympathetic to the 'rights narrative' after passage of the Voting Rights Act on 6 August 1965 and the riot that broke out in Watts only five days later, a broader consensus coalesced on preferential treatment and racial quotas. While the Nixon administration adopted affirmative action in order to generate the split between labour unions and civil rights leaders, and within the Democratic coalition, organized business embraced it as a less threatening option than a potential form of enforced fair employment legislation.[50] Accordingly, the 1970s were marked by increasing adoption of affirmative action. In *Griggs* v. *Duke Power Company* in 1971, for example, the Supreme Court found that the Civil Rights Act of 1964 applied not only to intentional acts of job discrimination but also to recruitment procedures. The decision marked an important constitutional turning point because it shifted the burden of proof from individuals to employers.[51] In *Bakke* v. *University of California – Davies* in 1978, the Supreme Court articulated a new justification for preferential programmes and affirmative action; as Justice Harry Blackmun pointed out: 'In order to treat some persons equally, we must treat them differently'.[52]

In the 1970s, the United States became a more racially inclusive and less egalitarian society.[53] While it is difficult to quantify the importance of affirmative action for black employment, it is also difficult to underestimate it.[54] Despite the three recessions between 1970 and 1980, the number of employed blacks increased by 1.3 million (17 per cent). The largest employment gains for blacks occurred in white-collar occupations, where their advancement was proportionately greater than among whites. The number of black men in professional positions grew at a slightly faster pace than that of white males during the decade. Relative to their white counterparts, black women strengthened their foothold as professional workers. Jobs for managers and administrators also increased during the decade, and black men and women shared more than proportionately in the gains. Employment in clerical occupations rose rapidly between 1972 and 1980. Among women, the increase was proportionately much greater for blacks than for whites.

Black men also increased their participation in this field, while white men experienced a decline. There was a similar occurrence in sales, where both black men and women increased their representation, while white participation declined.[55] As stated by Diane Nilsen Westcott:

> Clearly, the movement out of the lower paying non-farm-labor, service, and farm jobs and into mid- and upper-level jobs in the white-collar occupations and craft trades was sustained during the 1970s, although the changes were not as dramatic as those [that had] occurred in the previous decade. ... [W]hile blacks moved into higher skilled (and more highly paying) occupations in greater numbers, [they] correspondingly diminished their proportions in the less desirable job groups.[56]

Conclusion

The reform of the job market and the regulation of the discrimination practices in the workplace were supposed to be the intended result of equality of opportunity policies sponsored by a broad alliance of federal government, labour unions and the civil rights movement. It happened, instead, to be a result of the unpredictable convergence of a conservative business-friendly coalition around legislation proposed by liberals and issued by the Johnson administration in the 1960s — specifically, affirmative action. The Nixon administration adopted affirmative action as a political tool to split the alliance between civil rights leaders and labour unions, already in decline and in transition from a strictly liberal orthodoxy, and establish a two-party political dynamic, thereby rendering them toothless.

Declining liberalism was unable to challenge the growing appeal of a rising business-friendly conservatism to the economic soul of America, and the struggle between fair employment and preferential treatment as the most effective strategy to deliver more and better jobs to black workers ended with the success of the latter. Surprisingly, despite the classical, colour-blind narrative empathetically embraced by the civil rights movement, and especially by Martin Luther King, it was in effect a colour-conscious strategy that ultimately succeeded, both on the legislative floor and in the boardroom.

Enrico Beltramini is lecturer at the Department of Philosophy and Religious Studies of Notre Dame de Namur University in Belmont, California. He has published essays on the history of economic civil rights in the United States, including financial, housing and employment: 'Consumer Credit as a Civil Right in America – 1968–1976', in Thomas Luckett, Chia Yin Hsu and Erika Vause (eds), *The Cultural History of Money and Credit: A Global Perspective*, Lanham, MD: Lexington Books, 2015; and 'Operation

Breadbasket in Chicago: Between Civil Rights and Black Capitalism', in Michael Ezra (ed.), *The Economic Civil Rights Movement*, London and New York: Routledge, 2013.

Notes

1. The whole statement says: 'Though this nation has proudly thought of itself as an ethnic melting pot, in things racial we have always been and continue to be, in too many ways, essentially a nation of cowards'. Attorney General Eric Holder at the Department of Justice African American History Month Program. Remarks as prepared for delivery. US Department of Justice.

2. The traditional narrative is that America enjoyed constant growth from 1945 to 1972. In reality, based on the definition of recession as 'a significant decline in economic activity spread across the economy, lasting more than a few months, normally visible in real gross domestic product (GDP), real income, employment, industrial production, and wholesale–retail sales', as proposed by the National Bureau of Economic Research, then in fact America suffered recessions in 1945, 1949, 1953, 1958, 1960–61 and 1969–70.

3. The source of most statistics is: *Statistical History of the United States, from Colonial Times to Present* (New York: Bureau of the Census, 1976). Also: James T. Patterson, *Grand Expectations: The United States, 1945–1974* (New York, 1996), 1 and 312.

4. David Halberstam, *The Fifties* (New York, 1993), jacket.

5. Patterson, *Grand Expectations*, 316 and 451.

6. John A. Andrew, *Lyndon Johnson and the Great Society* (Chicago, 1998), 14–15.

7. Patterson, *Grand Expectations*, 380–81. Between 1910 and 1920, the first migration brought more than half a million blacks northward, and in the 1920s another three-quarters of a million followed. Harvard Sitkoff, *The Struggle for Black Equality, 1954–1992* (New York, 1995), 9. For an overview of the workforce composition in the United States since the 1945, see Michael French, *US Economic History since 1945* (Manchester and New York, 1997), 81–108.

8. Patterson, *Grand Expectations*, 323.

9. The National Urban League, formerly known as the National League on Urban Conditions among Negroes, is a non-partisan civil rights organization that advocates on behalf of African Americans against racial discrimination in the United States. It is the oldest and largest community-based organization of its kind in the nation. As for 'he may be …', see: Nancy MacLean, *Freedom Is Not Enough: The Opening of the American Work Place* (New York, 2006), 56–57. At the close of the 1950s, whites already outnumbered blacks in the suburbs by a ratio of more than 35 to 1. Sitkoff, *Struggle for Black Equality*, 13. On the same topic, see William J. Wilson, *When Work Disappears: The World of the New Urban Poor* (New York, 1996).

10. MacLean, *Freedom Is Not Enough*, 19.

11. Herbert Hill, 'Race, Ethnicity and Organized Labor: The Opposition to Affirmative Action', *New Politics* (Winter 1987), 33 (blaming racial practices of organized labour for 'permanent conditions of poverty and social disorganization' in the black community).

12. Executive Order 8802 was the first federal action, though not a law, to promote equal opportunity and prohibit employment discrimination in the United States. The order also established the Fair Employment Practices Commission (FEPC) to investigate incidents of discrimination.

13. Numan Bartley, 'In Search of the New South: Southern Politics after Reconstruction', in *The Promise of American History: Progress and Prospects*, ed. Stanley I. Kutler and Stanley Nider Katz (Baltimore, MD, 1982), 150–63.

14. Elizabeth Jacoway and David R. Colburn (eds), *Southern Businessmen and Desegregation* (Baton Rouge, LA, 1982), 1. On the same topic: Gavin Wright, 'The Economics of the Civil Rights Revolution', in *Toward the Meeting of the Waters: Currents in the Civil Rights Movement of South Carolina during the Twentieth Century*, ed. Winfred B. Moore and Orville Vernon Burton (Columbia, SC, 2008), 267–89. On the economic transformation of the South, see for example: Philip Scranton, *The Second Wave: Southern Industrialization from the 1940s to the 1970s* (Athens, GA, 2001); James C. Cobb, *The Selling of the South: The Southern Crusade for Industrial Development, 1936–1980* (Baton Rouge, LA, 1982); Bruce J. Schulman, *From Cotton Belt to Sunbelt: Federal Policy, Economic Development, and the Transformation of the South, 1938–1980* (New York, 1991); Mary E. Frederickson, *Looking South: Race, Gender, and the Transformation of Labor from Reconstruction to Globalization* (Gainesville, FL, 2011); Donald Holley, *The Second Great Emancipation: The Mechanical Cotton Picker, Black Migration, and How They Shaped the Modern South* (Fayetteville, AR, 2000).

15. Adam Fairclough, *To Redeem the Soul of America: The Southern Christian Leadership Conference and Martin Luther King, Jr.* (Athens, GA, 1987), 113.

16. In spring 1963, before Easter, the Birmingham boycott intensified during the second-busiest shopping season of the year. Pastors urged their congregations to avoid shopping in Birmingham stores in the downtown district. For six weeks supporters of the boycott patrolled the downtown area to make sure blacks were not patronizing stores that promoted or tolerated segregation. If black shoppers were found in these stores, organizers confronted them and shamed them into participating in the boycott. Reverend Fred Shuttlesworth, the legendary native pastor of Birmingham, recalled a woman whose $15 hat was destroyed by boycott enforcers. Campaign participant Joe Dickson recalled, 'We had to go under strict surveillance. We had to tell people, say look: if you go downtown and buy something, you're going to have to answer to us'. After several business owners in Birmingham had taken down 'white only' and 'colored only' signs, Commissioner of Public Safety, Eugene 'Bull' Connor, told the others that if they did not obey the segregation ordinances they would lose their business licenses. Source: Fairclough, *To Redeem the Soul of America*, 113.

17. The Birmingham Campaign was a series of lunch counter sit-ins, marches on City Hall and boycotts of downtown merchants, coordinated by Martin Luther King's SCLC, to protest segregation laws in the city. It was met with violent attacks on black men, women and children alike, using high-pressure fire hoses and police dogs, and producing some of the most iconic and troubling images of the civil rights movement. President John F. Kennedy would later say, 'The events in Birmingham ... have so increased the cries for equality that no city or state or legislative body can prudently choose to ignore them'. It is considered one of the major turning points in the civil rights movement, and led to the Civil Rights Act of 1964.

18. Robert Dallek, *Flawed Giant: Lyndon Johnson and His Times, 1961–1973* (New York, 1998), 35–36.

19. MacLean, *Freedom Is Not Enough*, 65.

20. As for FEPC, see note 12.

21. For NAACP, 'full and nondiscriminatory employment', see Jack Greenberg, 'An NAACP Lawyer Answers Some Questions', *New York Times Magazine*, 18 August 1963, 85; For CORE's leader James Farmer, 'vital right to earn money', see Timothy J. Minchin, *The Color of Work: The Struggle for Civil Rights in the Southern Paper Industry, 1945–1980* (Chapel Hill, NC, 2001), 11.

22. Charles E. Silberman, 'The Businessman and the Negro', *Fortune* (September 1963), 3 and 4; 'The Negro Drive for Jobs', *Business Week* (17 August 1963), 52.

23. Jennifer Delton, *Racial Integration in Corporate America, 1940–1990* (New York, 2009), 163. Professor Delton is part of a new wave of economic historians, such as Frank Dobbin, Anthony Chen and Lauren Edelman, who have recently reframed our understanding of the history of corporate workplace integration.

24. Among the recent literature on the defence of segregation, see Kevin Michael Kruse, *White Flight: Atlanta and the Making of Modern Conservatism* (Princeton, NJ, 2005); Joseph Crespino, *In Search of Another Country: Mississippi and the Conservative Counterrevolution* (Princeton, NJ, 2007); George Lewis, *Massive Resistance: The White Response to the Civil Rights Movement* (London, 2006); Jason Sokol, *There Goes My Everything: White Southerners in the Age of Civil Rights, 1945–1975* (New York, 2006); Clive Webb, *Massive Resistance: Southern Opposition to the Second Reconstruction* (New York, 2005).

25. On the rising business and free market friendly movement, see Angus Burgin, *The Great Persuasion: Reinventing Free Markets since the Depression* (Cambridge, MA, 2012); David Harvey, *A Brief History of Neoliberalism* (Oxford, 2005); Robert Leeson, *The Eclipse of Keynesianism: The Political Economy of the Chicago Counter-Revolution* (Basingstoke, 2000); idem, *The Anti-Keynesian Tradition* (Basingstoke, 2008); Mark Skousen, *Vienna & Chicago, Friends or Foes?: A Tale of Two Schools of Free-Market Economics* (Washington, DC, 2005); Kim Phillips-Fein, *Invisible Hands: The Making of the Conservative Movement from the New Deal to Reagan* (New York, 2009).

26. For literature focused on resistance to desegregation, see note 14.

27. David R. Roediger and Elizabeth D. Esch, *The Production of Difference: Race and the Management of Labor in U.S. History* (New York, 2012).

28. Ira Katznelson, *When Affirmative Action Was White: An Untold History of Racial Inequality in Twentieth-Century America* (New York, 2005), 216, note 3.

29. Andrew, *Lyndon Johnson*, 26 and 29–30.

30. Herbert Hill to branch presidents, 27 July 1965, box A180, group 3, NAACP.

31. The Office of Federal Contract Compliance and the Equal Employment Opportunity Commission were the two arms of the federal government that had authority over matters of employment discrimination. As part of the United States Department of Labor, the OFCC was created to handle the responsibilities of making sure employers were complying with the laws covering non-discrimination in their operations as they were conducting business with the federal government. On the other hand, the EEOC was an independent agency under the federal government that made sure non-discrimination was practised and enforced in the workplace for all independent businesses and employers that were not contracted with the federal government. Subsequent legislation expanded the role of the OFCC and EEOC.

32. Johnson to the president, 14 February 1961, VPP/CRF, Box 8, LBJ Library, cited in Hugh David Graham, *The Civil Rights Era: Origins and Development of National Policy, 1960–1972* (New York, 1990), 39.

33. Katznelson, *When Affirmative Action Was White*, 144 and 216, note 2.

34. Delton, *Racial Integration*, 23.

35. Walter Lippmann, 'Today and Tomorrow', *New York Herald Tribune*, 17 March 1964.

36. MacLean, *Freedom Is Not Enough*, 105–106.

37. The whole quote is: 'It was easier to integrate public facilities, it was easier to gain the right to vote, because it didn't cost the nation anything, and the fact is that we are dealing with issues now that will call for something of a restructuring of the architecture of American society. It is going to cost the nation something'. Martin Luther King, Hearings before the Subcommittee on Executive Reorganization of the Committee on Government Operations, United States Senate, Eighty-Ninth Congress, Second Session, 15 December 1966, Part 14. Washington, DC: United States Government Printing Office, 1967, 2967–82.

38. Martin Luther King, Jr. *Why We Can't Wait* (New York, 1963), 38. Chappell makes the important point that the later affirmative action, as well as the constitutional justification, the coalition of beneficiaries and the cultural appeal of affirmative action are radically different from the affirmative action that King supported. Source: David L. Chappell, 'Waking from the Dream', presented at the Historical Society Annual Meeting, 5–8 June 2008, Baltimore, MD.

39. Alan Brinkley, *The End of Reform: New Deal Liberalism in Recession and War* (New York, 1995), 7.

40. Martin Luther King, Jr. 'Statement on resolutions passed at annual Southern Christian Leadership Conference Board meeting', 14 April 1966, Miami (3 pp. Martin Luther King Center: Box 118. 660414-001). Also, Thomas F. Jackson, *From Civil Rights to Human Rights: Martin Luther King, Jr., and the Struggle for Economic Justice* (Philadelphia, PA, 2007), 270. The differences between King and Johnson in terms of economic policy are important. As for Johnson, see, for example, James E. Anderson and Jared Hazleton, *Managing Macroeconomic Policy: The Johnson Presidency* (Austin, TX, 1986).

41. Patterson, *Grand Expectations*, 590.

42. Quote from A. Philip Randolph, *The Civil Right Revolution and Poverty*, 8, 13 June 1964, box 3, Haughton Papers. A. Philip Randolph is a towering figure in the civil rights and African American history. He organized and led the first predominantly black labour union and was instrumental in the two 'Marches on Washington', which convinced President Roosevelt to issue Executive Order 8802 in 1941, and led Reverend King to deliver his 'I Have A Dream' speech, in 1963. Randolph inspired the Freedom Budget, sometimes called the 'Randolph Freedom Budget', which aimed to deal with the economic problems facing the black community, particularly workers and the unemployed. There is an increasing literature on Asa Philip Randolph. See, for example, Kenneth A. Kovach, 'Manager, Political Activist, Labor Leader, Statesman: All in One Lifetime', *Journal of Management History* 2(4) (1996): 48–58. Sarah A. Wright, *Philip Randolph: Integration in the Workplace* (Englewood, NJ, 1990).

43. City Commission on Human Rights of New York, Policy Statement on the State of the Negro Today, 23 October 1963, box 4, Haughton Papers; Charles E. Silberman, *Crisis in Black and White* (New York, 1964), 237 and 241.

44. The Birmingham Truce Agreement states: '1. Within 3 days after close of demonstrations, fitting rooms will be desegregated. 2. Within 30 days after the city government is established by court order, signs on wash rooms, rest rooms and drinking fountains will be removed. 3. Within 60 days after the city government is established by court order, a program of lunchroom counter desegregation will be commenced. 4. When the city government is established by court order, a program of upgrading Negro employment will be continued and there will be meetings with responsible local leadership to consider further steps', in Carson Clayborne, *The Eyes on the Prize – Civil Rights Reader: Documents, Speeches, and Firsthand Accounts from the Black Freedom Struggle, 1954–1990* (New York, 1991). MacLean, *Freedom Is Not Enough*, 71.

45. Chappell, 'Waking from the Dream'. See note 38.

46. Ibid.

47. Dean Kotlowski, 'Black Power – Nixon Style: The Nixon Administration and Minority Business Enterprise', *The Business History Review* 72(3) (1998), 411.

48. Katznelson, *When Affirmative Action Was White*, 146.

49. Ibid., 146–47.

50. MacLean, *Freedom Is Not Enough*, 95 and 101. Historian Chen maintains that the emergence of the affirmative action had more to do with the conservative coalition than the civil rights organizations. See Anthony S. Chen, *The Fifth Freedom: Jobs, Politics and Civil Rights in the United States, 1941–1972* (Princeton, NJ, 2009).

51. Katznelson, *When Affirmative Action Was White*, 147–48.

52. Quoted in Thomas Borstelmann, *The 1970s: A New Global History from Civil Rights to Economic Inequality* (Princeton, NJ, 2012), 315.

53. This is the main thesis of Borstelmann, ibid.

54. For cases of affirmative action in the corporate world, see Delton, *Racial Integration*, Part II: Color-Conscious Ascendancy, 1961–1990.

55. Source of data and comments: Diane Nilsen Westcott, 'Blacks in the 1970s: Did They Scale the Job Ladder?', *Monthly Labor Review* 105(6) (1982): 29–30.

56. Ibid., 30.

Bibliography

Anderson, James E., and Jared Hazleton, *Managing Macroeconomic Policy: The Johnson Presidency* (Austin, TX, 1986).

Andrew, John A., *Lyndon Johnson and the Great Society* (Chicago, 1998).

Bartley, Numan, 'In Search of the New South: Southern Politics after Reconstruction', in *The Promise of American History: Progress and Prospects*, ed. Stanley I. Kutler and Stanley Nider Katz (Baltimore, MD, 1982), 150–63.

Borstelmann, Thomas, *The 1970s: A New Global History from Civil Rights to Economic Inequality* (Princeton, NJ, 2012).

Brinkley, Alan, *The End of Reform: New Deal Liberalism in Recession and War* (New York, 1995).

Burgin, Angus, *The Great Persuasion: Reinventing Free Markets since the Depression* (Cambridge, MA, 2012).

Chen, Anthony S., *The Fifth Freedom: Jobs, Politics and Civil Rights in the United States, 1941–1972* (Princeton, NJ, 2009).

Clayborne, Carson, *The Eyes on the Prize – Civil Rights Reader: Documents, Speeches, and Firsthand Accounts from the Black Freedom Struggle, 1954–1990* (New York, 1991).

Cobb, James C., *The Selling of the South: The Southern Crusade for Industrial Development, 1936–1980* (Baton Rouge, LA, 1982).

Crespino, Joseph, *In Search of Another Country: Mississippi and the Conservative Counterrevolution* (Princeton, NJ, 2007).

Dallek, Robert, *Flawed Giant: Lyndon Johnson and His Times, 1961–1973* (New York, 1998).

Delton, Jennifer, *Racial Integration in Corporate America, 1940–1990* (New York, 2009).

Fairclough, Adam, *To Redeem the Soul of America: The Southern Christian Leadership Conference and Martin Luther King, Jr.* (Athens, GA, 1987).

Frederickson, Mary E., *Looking South: Race, Gender, and the Transformation of Labor from Reconstruction to Globalization* (Gainesville, FL, 2011).

French, Michael, *US Economic History since 1945* (Manchester and New York, 1997).

Graham, Hugh David, *The Civil Rights Era: Origins and Development of National Policy, 1960–1972* (New York, 1990).

Halberstam, David, *The Fifties* (New York, 1993).

Harvey, David, *A Brief History of Neoliberalism* (Oxford, 2005).

Hill, Herbert, 'Race, Ethnicity and Organized Labor: The Opposition to Affirmative Action', *New Politics* (Winter 1987): 31–82.

Holley, Donald, *The Second Great Emancipation: The Mechanical Cotton Picker, Black Migration, and How They Shaped the Modern South* (Fayetteville, AR, 2000).

Jackson, Thomas F., *From Civil Rights to Human Rights: Martin Luther King, Jr., and the Struggle for Economic Justice* (Philadelphia, PA, 2007).

Jacoway, Elizabeth, and David R. Colburn (eds), *Southern Businessmen and Desegregation* (Baton Rouge, LA, 1982).

Katznelson, Ira, *When Affirmative Action Was White: An Untold History of Racial Inequality in Twentieth-Century America* (New York, 2005).

Martin Luther King, Jr. *Why We Can't Wait* (New York, 1963).

Kotlowski, Dean, 'Black Power – Nixon Style: The Nixon Administration and Minority Business Enterprise', *The Business History Review* 72(3) (1998): 409–45.

Kovach, Kenneth A., 'Manager, Political Activist, Labor Leader, Statesman: All in One Lifetime', *Journal of Management History* 2(4) (1996): 48–58.

Kruse, Kevin Michael, *White Flight: Atlanta and the Making of Modern Conservatism* (Princeton, NJ, 2005).

Leeson, Robert, *The Eclipse of Keynesianism: The Political Economy of the Chicago Counter-Revolution* (Basingstoke, 2000).

———, *The Anti-Keynesian Tradition* (Basingstoke, 2008).

Lewis, George, *Massive Resistance: The White Response to the Civil Rights Movement* (London, 2006).

MacLean, Nancy, *Freedom Is Not Enough: The Opening of the American Work Place* (New York, 2006).

Minchin, Timothy J., *The Color of Work: The Struggle for Civil Rights in the Southern Paper Industry, 1945–1980* (Chapel Hill, NC, 2001).

Patterson, James T., *Grand Expectations: The United States, 1945–1974* (New York, 1996).

Phillips-Fein, Kim, *Invisible Hands: The Making of the Conservative Movement from the New Deal to Reagan* (New York, 2009).

Roediger, David R., and Elizabeth D. Esch, *The Production of Difference: Race and the Management of Labor in U.S. History* (New York, 2012).

Schulman, Bruce J., *From Cotton Belt to Sunbelt: Federal Policy, Economic Development, and the Transformation of the South, 1938–1980* (New York, 1991).

Scranton, Philip, *The Second Wave: Southern Industrialization from the 1940s to the 1970s* (Athens, GA, 2001).

Silberman, Charles E., *Crisis in Black and White* (New York, 1964).

Sitkoff, Harvard, *The Struggle for Black Equality, 1954–1992* (New York, 1995).

Skousen, Mark, *Vienna & Chicago, Friends or Foes?: A Tale of Two Schools of Free-Market Economics* (Washington, DC, 2005).

Sokol, Jason, *There Goes My Everything: White Southerners in the Age of Civil Rights, 1945–1975* (New York, 2006).

Webb, Clive, *Massive Resistance: Southern Opposition to the Second Reconstruction* (New York, 2005).

Westcott, Diane Nilsen, 'Blacks in the 1970s: Did They Scale the Job Ladder?', *Monthly Labor Review* 105(6) (1982): 29–38.

Wilson, William J., *When Work Disappears: The World of the New Urban Poor* (New York, 1996).

Wright, Gavin, 'The Economics of the Civil Rights Revolution', in *Toward the Meeting of the Waters: Currents in the Civil Rights Movement of South Carolina during the Twentieth Century*, ed. Winfred B. Moore and Orville Vernon Burton (Columbia, SC, 2008), 267–89.

Wright, Sarah A., *Philip Randolph: Integration in the Workplace* (Englewood, NJ, 1990).

Part II

CONCEPTUAL TRANSITION IN (STATE) REGULATION FROM THE 1970S TO THE 1980S

CHAPTER 6

Helmut Schmidt, the 'Renewal' of European Social Democracy, and the Roots of Neoliberal Globalization

GIOVANNI BERNARDINI

> The Free World has been lucky to enjoy the benefit of your leadership and advice during the recent times of economic recession. I can assure you that I am storing away all the economic experience that I have been absorbing from you. Who knows, it might be useful some day.
>
> —Henri Kissinger to Helmut Schmidt[1]

Between Crisis and Revolution

A large part of Western historiography portrays the 1970s as the decade when 'thirty glorious years' of unprecedented economic growth came to an end. The ensuing crisis did not bring capitalism to an end, as some had forecast at that time; instead, a series of unpredictable events and deliberate acts brought about the decline of *one* historically determined form, later called 'embedded liberalism', which was characterized by a shared urge for incresed control of market mechanisms by the state.[2] After the Second World War, illustrious intellectuals such as John M. Keynes came up with this solution in order to consolidate the capitalist economy and to avoid the disruptive effects of its cyclical crises. As a result, Western economies witnessed a rapid recovery characterized by the constant introduction of new investments and technologies, substantial full employment, and a dramatic rise in productivity that ensured profits grew at a faster pace than wages. A democratically elected political power was charged to manage the excesses by investing in a welfare state, and granting social rights on a universal base. In short, sustained economic growth and the solidity of democratic institutions guaranteed each other.

During the 1970s, the simultaneous manifestation of recessionary tendencies, falling investment and productivity, as well as widespread inflation, challenged the Fordist–Keynesian paradigm. It became apparent that the system was facing a whole new situation, without the theoretical tools to find a solution. However, if one looks at the new course of the international economy from the 1980s onwards, the world economic crisis assumes the character of a typical process of 'creative destruction'. The 1980s were the years of the 'great leap backward' to laissez-faire and to the *credo* of the hidden hand of the market as the sole solution for the problems of economic redistribution. Interventions by governments and international institutions were deemed responsible for inefficiency, whereas only the free flow of goods and capital could provide an efficient allocation of resources.[3] This was not a novelty of the 1970s: economists such as Friedrich von Hayek had been supportive of such approaches since the foundation of the post-war system.[4] However, the relative success of 'embedded capitalism' had pushed the radical liberal approach into the background of history for a quarter of a century. By contrast, after the crisis of the 1970s it was adopted progressively by the government of the United States and the other most influential economies around the world, with different degrees and timing, and then spread quickly through free adoption or imposition by international institutions.

Was the neoliberal approach the only viable one for coping with the crisis? The Reagan administration and Margaret Thatcher's cabinet were skilful in introducing public opinion to the acronym 'TINA' (There Is No Alternative). Nevertheless, the 1970s witnessed a bourgeoning of claims of a New International Economic Order (NIEO) in order to promote a more equitable wealth distribution, fairer conditions for international trade and new democratic rules for international economic institutions.[5] The sharp and largely unforeseen rise in oil and raw material prices partially reflected the increased awareness of some countries that they had contributed to boosting the development of the West with cheap energy sources, without adequate compensation for the development of their national economy.[6] Thus, the eventual victory of neoliberalism did not come about as a result of competitors, but by its deliberate adoption in the most important countries of the industrialized world, and by the reorganization of a social block keen to obtain a bigger profit margin compared to the one allowed by 'embedded capitalism'.[7] According to an authoritative analysis by Michael Cox, during the 1970s '[t]he bourgeoisie overall abandoned Fordist industrial strategies designed to incorporate workers by guaranteeing full employment and welfare, and adopted fiscally tight policies whose purpose was to impose political and economic discipline'.[8]

German Social Democracy and the Crisis

The third quarter of the twentieth century also witnessed the progressive ideological and political identification of social democracy with the 'embedded capitalism' model. Social democracy faced post-war reconstruction with a strong commitment to maintain its profile distinct from both liberalism and Soviet communism, and to 'shift from the phase of propaganda to the phase of achievement' of socialism linked with democratic freedoms. Even if a large number of social democratic parties did not gain control of their national governments until the 1960s, a large part of the original 'short-term' programme of the Second International became reality after the Second World War in a great part of Western Europe: universal suffrage, eight-hour working days and free participation in political life were granted by law, as well as the regulation of the labour market.[9] However, these advancements were not the products of social democracy alone. As an example, full employment during the 1950s and 1960s could not be credited to one political family alone, although its 'inclusive nature' (women, less qualified and non-unionized workers) was something towards which social democracy strove. Besides, concerning the limits of the welfare state, Andrew Glyn says that 'the Left has traditionally argued for much more than a minimal safety net for those incapable of looking after themselves and, by extension, for redistribution to offset the disadvantages of those who, even with equal opportunity, suffer from a weak position in the market'.[10]

Even conservative parties were keen to reach compromise solutions in order to avoid fuelling social conflict: as an example, in 1951 the moderate parliamentary majority in West Germany approved a law for the joint supervision of companies between employers and employees – so-called *Mitbestimmung* – after a huge trade union mobilization.[11] However, the crisis of the 1970s was bound to jeopardize the post-war consensus: while the confrontation between conservatives and social democrats had been centred on the redistribution of surplus over the previous thirty years, the 1970s saw a more radical conflict concerning the reorganization of capitalist relations and a revision of the balance between the state and the market.[12]

What role did social democratic parties play during the crisis? Looking at later periods when they were in government simultaneously in the most important West European countries (for example, during the late 1990s), it becomes apparent how they had absorbed some of the precepts of the neoliberal 'counterrevolution' because very modest shifts in economic policy could be noted in comparison with their political opponent. Although a complete overview of this subject goes beyond the scope of this chapter, archival sources allow the examination of the conduct of the major social democratic party in Europe, the Sozialdemokratische Partei Deutschlands (SPD), which ruled the Federal Republic of Germany uninterruptedly before and during the 1970s economic crisis.

The first systematic attempt to cope with the new economic challenges was the '*Orientierungsrahmen 85*' (Orientation Framework 85), a report adopted by the SPD national congress in 1975 and described by Willy Brandt as 'a middle way between everyday politics and a fundamental programme'. Although the document would eventually exert influence over other European socialist parties, it fell short in both of Brandt's categories: it could not be compared with the Bad Godesberg resolutions of 1959, because it lacked elaboration of the basic concepts of 'democratic socialism' and 'reformist party'; furthermore, it was limited to the reaffirmation of the fundamental values of freedom, equality and solidarity, which could no longer give the party a distinctive personality. Nor did the document represent a guide for everyday politics, because it ignored the symptoms of the failure of traditional Keynesian recipes. Consequently the 'Orientation Framework' proved outdated at the very time of its publication.[13] For all these reasons, it was strongly criticized by Chancellor Helmut Schmidt, the main representative of the SPD's moderate wing. Although not the only expert on international economics in the German Social Democratic leadership at that time, Schmidt's prestige in this field increased dramatically both at home and abroad from 1972, when he was appointed minister of finance. After that and until his designation as chancellor in 1974, Schmidt played an important role in international accommodation to the demise of the Bretton Wood system, and developed strong personal contacts with his American, French and British colleagues in the so-called 'Library Group', which paved the way for the establishment of the G5 (later G7) group.[14]

Subsequently, Schmidt established himself successfully as a pragmatic leader interested in 'working further on the German model' and thus not prone to substantial experiments with progressive socio-economic reforms. During a conversation with other SPD leaders, the chancellor heavily criticized 'Orientation Framework 85' as it failed to face the completely new nature of the economic crisis; according to Schmidt, the crisis demanded the abandonment of Keynesian policies on work and wages, a strong reduction in the role of the state in the economy, and a commitment to freeing up the flow of goods and capital.[15] On the international level, it was not long before the chancellor proved himself to be the most reliable partner of Gerald Ford's administration; both bilaterally and multilaterally, Schmidt played his part in directing the capitalist economy towards greater laissez-faire, which had little in common with previous definitions of social democracy.[16]

In fact, the vagueness of 'Orientation Framework 85' on economic matters left considerable room for manoeuvre. Furthermore, Schmidt gained great prestige on the economy within his party because of his experience as finance minister during the second Brandt government; the relative speed with which West Germany seemed to overcome the early 1970s 'economic storm' – compared with the hard times of most European partners – paved the way for his personal management of the international economy.[17] Schmidt was genuinely concerned that the economic crisis of the West could slip into 'the greatest depression since 1932', as he confessed to President Ford.[18] The experience of the Weimar Republic proved how economic hardships could eventually lead to serious social and political disorder. Thus all governments had to desist from implementing 'the methods of recent years for a situation that none of us have lived through', explicitly referring to the coexistence of recession, low employment rates and high inflation. If Keynes' methods worked in the 1930s, they did not seem to work in the 1970s, and there was 'no new Keynes'. Therefore the first task was to bring the whole West back to unity in order to face the new menaces to its welfare. Hence, the chancellor took advantage of his speech at the North Atlantic Council in May 1975 to state that the Atlantic Alliance was not likely to confront geopolitical threats, 'but rather the state of the world economy on which the prosperity of all of us depends. … The present-day situation of the world economy is unforeseen by any economic textbook, be it printed at the Sorbonne or at Harvard'.[19] As a starting point, Western governments had to adopt two measures in order to overcome the serious problems that were endangering the economy: concerted planning of future intervention on an international scale, and stricter control of the management of national economies.[20]

The Unity of the West and the Birth of the G7

Schmidt conceived the economic crisis as a political rather than a technical matter, which only the major Western authorities could confront and overcome. In this situation, however, from 1974 he seems to have favoured a restrictive and elitist response: the chancellor was keen to exclude the involvement of minor partners in Europe and Less Developed Countries (LDC) from the international programme that would rewrite the rules of the international economy.[21] Although the idea of a summit of the Western world's five (later seven) most industrialized countries came from the

French government in 1975, the German government offered its immediate support. Furthermore, Schmidt seemed willing to confine the solution of the economic problems to a 'circle' in which social democratic partners were a minority; due to the seriousness of the British economic situation, the Labour government was not in a position to make a stand against the US Republican administration, the moderate French president Giscard D'Estaing, the Japanese liberal government or the precarious Italian 'centre-left' coalition.

During the first G6 meeting in Rambouillet, as well as during other international conferences, Schmidt urged that coping with inflation should be the top priority in order to overcome the crisis. In historical perspective, the chancellor blamed the US authorities for permitting inflation to spread globally as a result of their uncontrolled military expenditure. Thus, the subsequent crisis of the system of fixed exchange rates among currencies was 'inevitable'.[22] Such an explanation hardly corresponded to reality, because it overlooked the United States' responsibility for the eventual demise of the system.[23] On the contrary, the end of fixed exchange rates was provoked intentionally by the Nixon administration's initiative to suspend indefinitely the conversion of the US dollar into gold in order to solve US balance of payments problems. This unilateral decision restated Washington's position of unimpaired primacy in the international system: without the cornerstone on which the post-war monetary architecture had been built, its end came as a consequence, as well as the ultimate transition to flexible exchange rates.[24] The Federal Republic of Germany refrained from criticizing the US decision for its own convenience, as it was protected from the relative strength of its national currency. However, ideology was also a component of Schmidt's indulgent analysis, since he had professed to be 'a staunch supporter' of flexible changes.[25] The German constitutional system assigns to the government the task of determining the value of the Deutsche Mark, while the independent authority of the Bundesbank is charged with assuring its stability.[26] After 1971 it became clear that the government had abandoned its prerogative, while the constant apprehension over inflation (a feature of German authorities since the crises of 1923 and 1932) allowed the Bundesbank to increase its strict control over the monetary liquidity. Schmidt pointed at the German solution as an example for other countries as well as for the international system: exchange rates should not be fixed by governments, but by the free market and by the evaluations of investors.[27] Countries capable of 'putting their houses in order' would attract international investment: its increased mobility through the removal of all obstacles was affirmed as a goal of the Rambouillet meeting.[28] Thus, governments had to renounce their prerogatives in the monetary field and to commit its management to 'technical' authorities, such as the central banks. Following this line, an essential tool of political control over the economy traditionally claimed by social democrats was progressively abandoned with the consent of the German Social Democratic chancellor.

Concerning the granting of credits to countries in particularly dramatic circumstances, such as Italy and the United Kingdom during the 1970s, Schmidt did not disregard the utility and even the necessity of strong intervention by international authorities. The chancellor favoured the assignment of this role to the International Monetary Fund (IMF), a decision debated at the second G7 summit held in Puerto Rico in 1976.[29] Although the Federal Republic had granted credit on a bilateral basis in the past, Schmidt believed that his country was not willing to become the only 'global creditor': nevertheless, the problem was not German unwillingness to contribute, but the necessity that credit concessions come with the commitment of the recipient countries to pursue anti-inflationary policies and introduce austerity measures. Only the IMF would have had the necessary authority to impose such measures and, after the summit held in Puerto Rico, the institution began to elaborate coherent rules that the Italian government had to follow in order to obtain the loan it had asked for.[30] The 1976 IMF loan to Italy was conditional on the acceptance of the first prototype 'structural adjustment plan', worked out by the IMF and strongly sponsored by the German government. It was aimed not only at providing liquidity to a country experiencing payment difficulties under the guarantee of restitution, but also at changing by external constraints some features of the country's domestic economy: the wage indexation system through which salaries kept up with inflation, the opening of the financial and trade markets, and the privatization of parts of the public sector.[31] The chancellor, in full agreement with the main supporters of the 'neoliberal revolution' in the US Treasury Department, appreciated this formula and promoted a further limitation of national government sovereignty over management of the economy.[32]

Furthermore, Schmidt approved the application of the same scheme to Third World countries asking for international help in order to boost their development: their 'education towards the market and its rules' had to be undertaken by the industrialized countries and the IMF. During a meeting with Willy Brandt – former chancellor, and recently appointed leader of the Independent Commission on International Development Issues – Schmidt expressed his scepticism of every design for a 'New International Economic Order' that did not contemplate a precautionary adhesion on the part of the 'less developed countries' (LDC) to the principles of a free market economy, as well as to their opening up to the flow of international private capital.[33] LDCs were called on to acknowledge that only 'IMF experts' could underline the distortions in every country's economic management, therefore 'recommending' – if not imposing – the correct remedies. Once accepted, the IMF measures would contribute to the creation of an ideal 'climate' capable of bringing to the country the private capital, thereby avoiding the need for new credit in the future. Schmidt's hostility to the demands of the LDCs and the petroleum producers gathered in the Organization of the Petroleum Exporting Countries (OPEC), responsible for the 1973 oil shock, was evident. Unlike other social democratic leaders, such as Brandt, the chancellor was distrustful of the ideological character of the 'Group of 77' LDC itself and of its aim of improving economic self-determination: it was basically an 'unholy alliance' that the West had to break, separating the OPEC members from the LDCs, who could not rely on considerable amounts of raw materials.[34] The latter could obtain the support of the West for development on condition that they abided by the IMF's recommendations and renounced the self-determination of their economies, indiscriminately opening up to private capital. A serious collective dialogue with OPEC was postponed indefinitely until the day industrialized Western countries recovered their cohesion and made clear to the world that a new petroleum crisis would first of all affect the people responsible for it.[35]

The Future of Social Democracy

The understanding of how traditional measures were ineffective in coping with the crisis, and the elaboration of new solutions, were not exclusive prerogatives of the German chancellor; because the Keynesian economic policy of public intervention aimed at 'stimulating aggregate demand' did not seem suitable anymore, several European social democratic parties and movements envisioned a more forceful public intervention over the supply side.[36] From selective nationalization to the introduction of workers' control over ownership, from the containment of international corporations to compulsory planning agreements between state and private actors, during the 1970s the European social democratic and labour family explored new solutions to regain regular economic growth and full employment, while trying to increase the democratization of the economy. The programme of the 'Union of the Left' in France and the Alternative Economic Strategy in Britain were only the most authoritative examples.[37]

The German response was the international promotion of the methods established in the country by the Christian Democratic governments, such as the aforementioned *Mitbestimmung*. Schmidt himself publicly and privately praised the German trade unions' responsible conduct in accepting a wage moderation that had saved the country from inflation, and he urged both the other social democratic governments and the European trade unions to follow this path.[38] Thus, regardless of other peculiarities of the German experience of *Mitbestimmung*, the chancellor proved its staunch supporter against more radical projects because it promoted a self-limitation of wage claims and limited workforce participation in the management of companies. If, on one hand, the positive results of the German economy were evident, on the other that model could hardly be applied elsewhere because of the distinctive features of the Federal Republic labour market: during the recessionary phase examined here, the high employment rate was somehow 'disguised' by the dismissal of half a million foreign workers employed in industry who did not feature in the official statistics.[39]

However, such considerations did not prevent Schmidt from promoting wage moderation and workforce discipline as means for achieving the ideal 'climate' for attracting the private investment fundamental for a concrete recovery without state intervention.[40] As has been suggested, the economic policy action inspired by neoliberal doctrines focused on the creation of 'corporate welfare' to replace 'people welfare'. The state was consistently advised to progressively withdraw from productive activities, in which only the free market could guarantee an optimal allocation of resources. Within this context, Schmidt also exhorted governments and trade unions to realize how unattractive some advanced Western industrial sectors had become for international investment: the decision to keep them in artificial 'hothouses' in order to avoid dismissals only prolonged the inevitable agony, imposing further burdens on the state. The 'selfishness of the few' – in other words, the workers involved – had to be put after the general need to create 'coherent and consistent development plans' whose profits for investors were the only economic judgement. The crisis had above all to push social democrats towards a greater 'economic sense' to replace their 'economic rhetoric'. The prize for such a new orientation was supposed to be a return to economic growth capable of solving the unemployment problem.[41] However, a substantial difference can be noted in the language adopted by Schmidt, depending on his interlocutors: while 'the return to full employment' remained the main theme in his speeches to a Social Democratic audience, this was replaced by a more modest 'recuperation of employment' in his contributions at G7 summits.[42] A further step towards the abandonment of this social democracy cornerstone was taken in Schmidt's conversations with his closest economic collaborators; there they explicitly wondered whether the moment had come for Western governments to abandon the aim of full employment in order to accept that in the very near future 'production [would be assigned] to a reduced workforce'.[43]

During the 'Conference of Social Democratic Parties and European Trade Unions' held in Oslo in 1977, the chancellor blamed the crisis on the cultural backwardness of those Social Democratic governments that did not manage to 'tell the truth': the benefits obtained during the 'Thirty

Glorious [Years]' were probably a one–off, something that the other leaders of the left had to confess to their electors. Schmidt exhorted them to accept a deliberate and peaceful reduction of the privileges obtained during those years, in order to secure the return to an economic growth guaranteed by a system in which public control would be reduced dramatically.[44] By choosing a 'supply-side oriented' intervention, Schmidt had opted for a line that not only resulted in something completely different from the options suggested by many social democratic currents, but also inevitably verged on neoliberal solutions. This was enough to provoke the reaction of traditional social democratic leaders, such as the Austrian chancellor, Bruno Kreisky, who pointed out how the inflation problem, ascribed by Schmidt to the social democratic management of economic policy, had, on the contrary, a clear origin in the decline of the dollar and of the American economy in general; besides, many countries ruled by social democratic governments were overcoming the crisis better than those with moderate leaderships. On the one hand, Kreisky believed that the increasing pace and extent of global speculation – which endangered the economic recovery – and the 'waste of workforce' were the first by-products of the new laissez-faire. On the other hand, he blamed the German chancellor for staunchly supporting this new approach, instead of dedicating himself to working out new solutions in the direction of a genuinely Social Democratic economic policy.[45] More generally, the presence of Helmut Schmidt at international socialist meetings during the second half of the 1970s was rewarded with accusations of promoting 'uncritical capitalism', even from those parties (such as the Danish and Dutch) that the SPD strove to involve in a northern, moderate socialist block against the more extreme tendencies in the south.

By contrast, Schmidt considered such resistance responsible for hindering acceptance of the new rules necessary for economic recovery: the responsibility for such a legacy was attributed to that generation of social democrats (from whom clearly Schmidt excluded himself) that had studied economics in the period when Keynes and Roosevelt's New Deal enjoyed cultural hegemony, as well as National Socialist welfare. This led to obligatory economic development characterized by inflationary public financing and increasing state intervention in economic management.[46] Such a parallel between traditional social democratic and fascist economic cultures was traditionally dear to the main supporters of a return to the most extreme forms of liberalism.[47] However, Schmidt was still confident in social democracy, which he saw as already supplied with 'honest intellectuals' among the new generations. The latter were already learning the lessons of the recent past and were ready to implement everywhere the new rules that the governments of the most industrialized countries were already writing.[48]

Conclusions

Federal Chancellor Helmut Schmidt was one of the political characters who cooperated during the 1970s to overcome both the economic crisis and the model of 'embedded capitalism' that had been predominant in Western Europe during the third quarter of the twentieth century. Far from being a passive recipient of solutions from outside, Schmidt leveraged Germany's economic and political power to introduce a more laissez-faire-oriented economic approach on a global scale. Although Schmidt's record on internal economic policy was more nuanced, the rhetoric he displayed in international fora merged into a shifting political discourse that was bound to become mainstream during the late 1970s, and especially during the following decade. The success of this new 'economic revolution' was fostered by the adoption of principled positions by some of the most powerful and influential characters and institutions of international politics, such as Helmut Schmidt and the G7 summits.

As a leading figure of European social democracy, the chancellor urged the continental political movement in the same direction, in order to benefit from a cultural renewal that was needed to cope with new and unprecedented challenges. At a moment when 'old measures' did not seem to work anymore, Schmidt believed that only the unity of the most industrialized countries of the West, irrespective of their political differences, would be able to steer such a global transition; this policy would have basically led to an improvement of economic conditions in the LDCs, provided that they preventively renovated their economies in accordance with the new doctrine. In the West, although the golden days of the post-war era were gone forever, the retrenchment of the state and the moderation of working-class demands would have led to an increase in private investment and, ultimately, to the revival of stable economic development, as well as the return to acceptable levels of employment and welfare. Thus, moving away consistently from the traditional precepts and the goals of social democracy, Schmidt's approach ended up promoting a sort of new 'bipartisan consensus', although this time in terms of the reborn neoliberal doctrine.

Giovanni Bernardini is researcher at the Italian–German Historical Institute – FBK in Trento, Italy. He has published extensively on West German foreign policy, transatlantic relations during the Cold War, European social democracy after the Second World War, and the history of the South Tyrol question in international perspective. His most recent publication is 'Principled Pragmatism: The Eastern Committee of German Economy and West German–Chinese relations during the early Cold War, 1949–1958', in *Modern Asian Studies*, 1/2017.

Notes

1. Kissinger to Schmidt, 14 January 1977, Helmut Schmidt Archiv-Bundeskanzler (HSA-BK), Box 6388, Archiv der sozialen Demokratie, Bonn (AdsD).

2. John Gerard Ruggie, 'International Regimes, Transactions, and Change: Embedded Liberalism in the Postwar Economic Order', *International Organization* 36(2) (1982): 386.

3. Andrew Glyn, *Capitalism Unleashed: Finance, Globalization, and Welfare* (Oxford, 2006).

4. Serge Halimi, *Le grand bond en arrière: Comment l'ordre libéral s'est imposé au monde* (Paris, 2004).

5. The proposal of a New International Economic Order (NIEO) was advanced officially at the United Nations Assembly by Third World countries in 1974. Its main demands included 'the creation of a World commodity system to bolster the prices of LDC exports and the establishment of a "special fund" to support the incomes of the poorest countries'. Whether interpreted as an outright repudiation of liberalism, or as a reformist project aimed at improving the Third World's prospects within the status quo, the NIEO was a constant intellectual and political challenge to the liberal international economy throughout the 1970s. Daniel Sargent, 'The Cold War and the International Political Economy in the 1970s', *Cold War History* 2(13) (2013): 393–425.

6. Giuliano Garavini, 'The Colonies Strike Back: The Impact of the Third World on Western Europe 1968–1975', *Contemporary European History* 3(16) (2007): 299–319.

7. David Harvey, *A Brief History of Neoliberalism* (Oxford, 2005), 62.

8. Michael Cox, 'Interregnum, Prediction, Decline and the Lessons of History – Reflections on the 1970s'. Paper presented at the conference Re-Thinking the 1970s: Origins of a New Cycle of US Hegemony or Beginning of American Decline?, Bologna, 28 March 2004.

9. Donald Sassoon, *One Hundred Years of Socialism: The West European Left in the Twentieth Century* (London, 1996), 133–34.

10. Andrew Glyn, 'Aspirations, Constraints, and Outcomes', in *Social Democracy in Neoliberal Times: The Left and Economic Policy since 1980*, ed. A. Glyn (Oxford, 2001), 1–20.

11. Enzo Collotti, 'Il mito della società omogenea', in *La Germania socialdemocratica: SPD, società e Stato*, ed. E. Collotti and L. Castelli (Bari, 1982), 9–28.

12. Sassoon, *One Hundred Years*, 514.

13. See Heinrich Potthoff and Susanne Miller, *The Social Democratic Party of Germany, 1848–2005* (Bonn, 2006), 229ff.

14. Harold James, *International Monetary Cooperation since Bretton Woods* (Oxford, 1990), 266.

15. An illuminating example of Schmidt's economic ideas for the future of social-liberal governments is the so-called 'Marbella Paper', a programme for the following years written by the chancellor. See Helmut Schmidt, 'Erwägungen für 1977', 5 January 1977, HSA-BK, Box 9302, AdsD.

16. Duccio Basosi and Giovanni Bernardini, 'The Puerto Rico Summit of 1976 and the End of Eurocommunism', in *The Crisis of Détente in Europe: From Helsinki to Gorbachev, 1975–1985*, ed. Leopoldo Nuti (London, 2009), 256–67.

17. Sassoon, *One Hundred Years*, 590.

18. Memorandum of Conversation between Ford, Kissinger and Schmidt, 29 May 1975, National Security Assistant (NSA), Box 12, Gerald Ford Library (GFL).

19. Helmut Schmidt's speech at the North Atlantic Council, 30 May 1975, HSA-BK, Box 9302, AdsD.

20. 'Konferenz der Staats- und Regierungschefs aus sechs Industriestaaten auf Schloss Rambouillet', 16 November 1975, Document 348, Akten zur Auswärtigen Politik der Bundesrepublik Deutschland (AAPD), 1975.

21. 'Gespräch des Bundeskanzlers Schmidt mit Staatspräsident Giscard d'Estaing, Premierminister Wilson und Präsident Ford in Helsinki, 31 July 1975', AAPD, 1975.

22. Document 348, cit., AAPD, 1975.

23. For Bonn reactions to the 15 August 1971 Nixon decision, see William G. Gray, 'Floating the System: Germany, the United States, and the Breakdown of Bretton Woods, 1969–1973', *Diplomatic History* 31(2) (2007): 295–323.

24. Duccio Basosi, *Il governo del dollaro: Interdipendenza economica e potere statunitense negli anni di Richard Nixon* (Florence, 2007).

25. Memorandum of Conversation between President Ford and Chancellor Schmidt, 5 December 1974, NSA, Box 7, GFL.

26. Gray, 'Floating the System'. For an assessment of monetarist theories and practice, see Kevin Hickson, *The IMF Crisis of 1976 and British Politics* (London, 2005).

27. Robert Hormats, 'Notes on the Economic Summit. Second Session, Monetary Issues, 16 November 1975', secret/NODIS, attached to Hormats to Scowcroft, 'Copy of the Notes', 2 December 1975, Memcons, Rambouillet, Box 16, NSA, GFL.

28. Helmut Schmidt's speech at the North Atlantic Council, 30 May 1975.

29. For a memorandum of the official conversations in Puerto Rico, see 'Konferenz der Staats- und Regierungschefs aus sieben Industriestaaten in San Juan, 27/28 June 1976', Document 208, AAPD, 1976.

30. Memorandum of Conversation between Chancellor Schmidt and Prime Minister Andreotti of Italy, 18 January 1977, HSA, Box 7251, AdsD.

31. Margaret Garritsen De Vries, *The International Monetary Fund, 1972–1978* (Washington DC, 1985), 446.

32. 'The best institutional arrangement for producing conditional financing is the IMF. It … cloaks the conditionality in a multinational mantle that dilutes opposition within a borrowing country to conditions imposed by the US or other outsiders.' Undersecretary of the Treasury Yeo to Ford, 24 June 1976, Declassified Documents Reference System (DDRS).

33. Memorandum of Conversation between Schmidt and Brandt, 27 September 1979, HSA, Box 9417, AdsD.

34. 'Konferenz der Staats- und Regierungschefs aus sechs Industriestaaten auf Schloss Rambouillet, 16 November 1975', Document 349, AAPD, 1975.

35. David E. Spiro, *The Hidden Hand of American Hegemony* (Ithaca, NY, 1999).

36. Glyn, 'Aspirations, Constraints, and Outcomes', 5.

37. For a stimulating analysis of the Labour AES, see Hickson, *The IMF Crisis*, Chapter 7.

38. Speech of Chancellor Schmidt at the 'Conference of Social Democratic Parties and European Trade Unions' in Oslo, 1 April 1977, Parteivorstand (PV), Box 285, AdsD.

39. Sassoon, *One Hundred Years*, 602.

40. Helmut Schmidt's speech at the North Atlantic Council, 30 May 1975.

41. As Note 38 above.

42. Meeting between Kissinger and Schmidt, 21 May 1975, Digital National Security Archive (DNSA).

43. Talking point for Chancellor Schmidt in preparation for the Conference of the Socialist International in Copenhagen, 19 January 1976, FES, Box 6669, AdsD.

44. As Note 38 above.

45. Report on Oslo conference for Chancellor Schmidt, 2 April 1977, Nachlass Bruno Friedrich (NBF), Box 441, AdSD.

46. Schmidt, 'Erwägungen für 1977'.

47. See, for instance, the comparison with the totalitarian regimes of the Scandinavian social democratic governments expressed by the US Treasury Secretary, William Simon, in his autobiography. William E. Simon, *A Time for Truth* (New York, 1978).

48. Schmidt, 'Erwägungen für 1977'.

Bibliography

Basosi, Duccio, *Il governo del dollaro: Interdipendenza economica e potere statunitense negli anni di Richard Nixon* (Florence, 2007).

Basosi, Duccio, and Giovanni Bernardini, 'The Puerto Rico Summit of 1976 and the End of Eurocommunism', in *The Crisis of Détente in Europe: From Helsinki to Gorbachev, 1975–1985*, ed. Leopoldo Nuti (London, 2009), 256–67.

Collotti, Enzo, 'Il mito della società omogenea', in *La Germania socialdemocratica: SPD, società e Stato*, ed. E. Collotti and L. Castelli (Bari, 1982), 9–28.

Cox, Michael, 'Interregnum, Prediction, Decline and the Lessons of History – Reflections on the 1970s'. Paper presented at the conference Re-Thinking the 1970s: Origins of a New Cycle of US Hegemony or Beginning of American Decline?, Bologna, 28 March 2004.

Garavini, Giuliano, 'The Colonies Strike Back: The Impact of the Third World on Western Europe 1968–1975', *Contemporary European History* 3(16) (2007): 299–319.

Garritsen De Vries, Margaret, *The International Monetary Fund, 1972–1978* (Washington, DC, 1985).

Glyn, Andrew, 'Aspirations, Constraints, and Outcomes', in *Social Democracy in Neoliberal Times: The Left and Economic Policy since 1980*, ed. A. Glyn (Oxford, 2001), 1–20.

———, *Capitalism Unleashed: Finance, Globalization, and Welfare* (Oxford, 2006).

Gray, William G., 'Floating the System: Germany, the United States, and the Breakdown of Bretton Woods, 1969–1973', *Diplomatic History* 31(2) (2007): 295–323.

Halimi, Serge, *Le grand bond en arrière: Comment l'ordre libéral s'est imposé au monde* (Paris, 2004).

Harvey, David, *A Brief History of Neoliberalism* (Oxford, 2005).

Hickson, Kevin, *The IMF Crisis of 1976 and British Politics* (London, 2005).

James, Harold, *International Monetary Cooperation since Bretton Woods* (Oxford, 1990).

Potthoff, Heinrich, and Susanne Miller, *The Social Democratic Party of Germany, 1848–2005* (Bonn, 2006).

Ruggie, John Gerard, 'International Regimes, Transactions, and Change: Embedded Liberalism in the Postwar Economic Order', *International Organization* 36(2) (1982): 386.

Sargent, Daniel, 'The Cold War and the International Political Economy in the 1970s', *Cold War History* 2(13) (2013): 393–425.

Sassoon, Donald, *One Hundred Years of Socialism: The West European Left in the Twentieth Century* (London, 1996).

Simon, William E., *A Time for Truth* (New York, 1978).

Spiro, David E., *The Hidden Hand of American Hegemony* (Ithaca, NY, 1999).

CHAPTER 7

The Changing Corporate Tax Order of the European Community

HANNA LIERSE

The Changing Corporate Tax Order of the European Community since the 1970s

Taxes are an important economic tool of income redistribution and are thus at the heart of the democratic nation state. Although taxes are still mainly decided and enforced by nationally elected governments, the revenue extraction process has become subject to a number of new international forces since the 1970s. One of the main changes stems from European integration, which has altered the conditions under which the national tax state operates.[1] Although the European Union does not collect taxes, it has implemented a range of tax legislation to which the member states need to comply. For instance, EU law requires that the standard VAT rate must be at least 15 per cent and the reduced rate at least 5 per cent.

Besides European tax legislation, the creation of the common market and, above all, of capital liberalization, has brought about intensified tax competition among the member states. Financial-market liberalization has made it easier to move capital across borders within the European Union. At the same time, it has become more difficult to subject it to national tax regulation. By moving investments and capital to those jurisdictions in which the tax rate is lowest, it is possible to avoid high taxes, especially for mobile tax bases such as capital and other investments.[2] As a consequence, governments

Notes for this section begin on page 135.

may be inclined to lower taxes in the hope of exerting a positive impact on domestic growth, employment and revenue.

In fact, most member states have engaged in competitive rate cuts: Germany has cut its corporate tax rate from about 56 per cent to about 30 per cent, and the UK from about 53 to 24 per cent.[3] Even though a general downward trend can be observed in the EU, corporate tax rates vary, with Malta (35 per cent) and France (34.4 per cent) at the top, and Italy and Bulgaria (10 per cent) at the bottom.[4] Most European governments have lowered corporate tax rates considerably since the 1970s in order to remain competitive in global capital markets. Others, such as Luxembourg, can even be considered tax havens, offering very low or no taxes at all to international investors, who furthermore benefit from banking secrecy. Due to the country's economic and political stability, combined with attractive tax exemptions, Luxembourg has successfully lured internationally mobile capital from other countries with higher tax burdens. Hence, European integration has not only changed the national tax state due to the enforcement of supranational regulations, but it has also increased market pressures leading to increased tax competition.[5]

The ways in which the member states of the European Community have attempted to address problems associated with differences in corporate taxation have undergone a considerable ideational shift. In the 1970s, the Community attempted to harmonize corporate taxes among the member states in order to maintain high corporate tax rates and to achieve a more equal distribution of income. The reform was based on an interventionist perspective, according to which European tax harmonization was desirable. However, the reform was never passed, and in the 1990s a new approach to corporate taxation was put on the European agenda. The new reform no longer involved corporate tax harmonization, but on the contrary acknowledged the merits of tax competition. In other words, in the early years of integration, the heads of state and government aimed for a more interventionist and redistributive kind of European taxation. In light of high corporate tax rates among the members, this was a real alternative. However, the Commission did not capitalize on this window of opportunity, and in the 1990s a more market-liberal approach came to the fore.

It is the aim of this chapter to shed light on the evolution of the European tax order. What has been the driving force leading to a more market-liberal form of taxation? I argue that the new agenda is an expression of the dominance of market-liberal ideas among European elites, as well as of the European decision-making structure. To address the research questions, I analyse and compare tax policy ideas in the European Union between the 1970s and the 1990s. I explore the Commission's approach to corporate taxation, which is the main agenda-setter. However, because tax matters are subject to the unanimity rule in the European Council, I also analyse the views of the heads of government, as well as the attitudes of corporate actors in Germany and the United Kingdom. However, before evaluating why a market-liberal turn has taken place, it is crucial to compare the market-liberal tax approach with a more interventionist one. This is the focus of the next section.

Defining a Market-Liberal European Tax Agenda

Scholars distinguish between two main paradigms that have shaped tax policy-making since the post-war era: the progressive and the neutral approach.[6] Up until the 1980s the progressive approach was dominant, according to which redistribution and economic growth are compatible goals. This approach lays out mechanisms, mainly built-in stabilizers, through which progressive income taxes bring about economic prosperity. However, a more efficiency-oriented approach to taxation slowly came to the fore, which highlights how taxes affect peoples' decisions concerning work, saving and investing.

According to the efficiency school, taxes are still considered necessary to generate public revenue and to provide public goods; however, redistribution from high incomes is considered a hindrance to economic growth. The argument is that economic growth is welfare enhancing as such and thus distributional concerns should be secondary. Moreover, a trend towards shifting the tax burden onto consumption from direct taxes has occurred.[7] This shift is recommended by international organizations, such as the OECD, as indirect taxes, such as VAT, have a smaller negative effect on growth than direct taxes.[8] However, an increase in indirect taxes, particularly in VAT, has a more regressive effect on income distribution than raising taxes on high incomes. Compared to the progressive approach, the efficiency approach can be classified as being more market-liberal. It places less emphasis on the state's role in the economy and in redistribution between different incomes.

The set-up of the tax system is contested not only at the national but also at the European level. Due to increased capital liberalization in the European Union, the member states have investigated possibilities for European-wide corporate tax rules and standards. However, the extent to which they should commonly apply is hotly debated. While some hope that joint intervention can prevent a fiscal race to the bottom, others reject any kind of European cooperation as they believe that tax competition is beneficial, forcing governments to operate more efficiently. Moreover, many governments fear that tax harmonization would take away a substantial part of their sovereignty as it would constrain their ability to adjust taxes to national preferences.

Has a change towards a more market-liberal corporate tax regime occurred in the European Union? If yes, why has this change taken place? To understand the reasons for the current European set-up, we need to investigate the ideas and interests of the actors involved, as well as the rules underlying the decision-making process. In the community, tax matters are based on a formal, institutionalized procedure that requires unanimity among the Council members.[9] Although this can be a long and cumbersome process, the Commission has far-reaching possibilities to shape tax outcomes. It can decide how to word and frame a policy proposal, thus decisively determining the success or failure of an agreement in the Council.[10] In what follows, I discuss and compare the viewpoints on European corporate taxation of the Commission, the Council members and corporate actors in the 1970s and 1990s. The focus is on the United Kingdom and Germany: the former is typically very Euro-sceptical, but the latter more pro-European; they therefore often represent veto-players in the decision-making process.

European Corporate Taxation in the 1970s

Having defined an interventionist and a market-liberal approach to European corporate taxation, this section aims to evaluate aims and conflicts in the 1970s. To do so, I first evaluate the kind of tax approach that was proposed by the commission before analysing the viewpoints of national actors.

The Community's Tax Agenda

The 1975 Directive on the Harmonisation of Systems of Company Taxation was the commission's main reform proposal prior to 1990.[11] It was published in April 1975 and worked out under the Belgian Tax Commissioner, Henri Francois Simonet, who was a member of the Socialist Party and vice-president of the Ortoli Commission (1973–77), which dealt with the first enlargement of the Community, the oil crisis and the following economic downturn.

Table 7.1 summarizes the main ideas of the Commission's reform, and compares it to the reform ideas of the 1990s. The directive drew attention to the problems associated with existing tax differences of the European member states. They are not only considered a constraint on the free movement of capital, but the Commission is also concerned about the 'abnormal' movements of capital that occur when a company chooses a jurisdiction due to favourable tax conditions instead of other, more traditional investment motives. In other words, they are concerned about tax competition, although this term is not used by the Commission.

Consequently, the Community suggests harmonizing corporate taxes, which referred to the implementation of a common tax system and the approximation of the tax rates. To prevent different tax rates from influencing investment decisions,[12] the Commission suggested that the member states adopt a corporate tax rate not lower than 45 per cent and not higher than 55 per cent. Moreover, the directive suggests the adoption of a common imputation system instead of a classic system. Although the system considered to give rise to some technical problems, the benefits of partly relieving economic double taxation of dividends and encouraging distribution are seen to outweigh the classic system. By doing so, the Commission aimed to maintain high corporate tax rates and to align them with personal income tax, thus achieving a more equal distribution of income.[13]

In sum, the policy ideas of the 1975 directive have a fairly interventionist perspective, according to which tax harmonization is desirable at the European level. It involves the approximation of tax rates and the introduction of a common tax system. The delegation of tax sovereignty is not only justified with reasons related to tax competition but the reform is supposed to promote vertical and horizontal equity, redistribution and high corporate tax rates. The directive was the community's official agenda for fifteen years, when it was finally withdrawn without being acted upon.

Viewpoints of Political Leaders and Elites

In the early 1970s, the environment was generally favourable towards fiscal harmonization. The heads of state jointly agreed to initiate and promote the harmonization of fiscal policies, including corporate taxes, which was regarded as an integral part of European economic and monetary integration.[14] In Germany, a social–liberal coalition had been in power since 1969, first under Chancellor Willy Brandt (1969–74) and then under Helmut Schmidt (1974–82). Consequently, two Social Democrats shaped Germany's European policy in the 1970s, with an overall positive stance towards integration.[15] Brandt's European agenda was characterized by an emphasis on a common stabilization policy and on the establishment of monetary union. The first phase of EMU, in which fiscal and tax harmonization was to be achieved, was a crucial element of his agenda.

The British Conservative government under Edward Heath also supported the European plans to harmonize corporate taxes. In fact, it pro-actively sought an agreement with the French and the German governments, although it had not yet joined the community.[16] The positive stance of the Conservative leader was in line with Heath's general approach towards European integration. He strongly promoted Britain's membership, hoping to promote economic progress.[17] The Confederation of British Industry (CBI) also supported European integration, believing that tax harmonization would 'promote the free circulation of capital within the Community and help to eliminate distortions of competition'.[18] The support for tax harmonization by the conservatives and the business elite must be viewed in the historical context: the British corporate tax rate was then high, at 52 per cent. A European agreement would therefore, if anything, have put downward pressure on the tax rate. This was in their interest, hoping as they did that the modernization of the British economy and of companies would progress faster if they were exposed to European competition.

The pro-European stance of the British government ended in 1974 when Harold Wilson, of the Labour Party, took over.[19] In contrast to his Conservative predecessor, Wilson did not support European integration per se, being worried about negative effects on food prices, which were particularly low in the United Kingdom, and the freedom to engage in industrial policies. Also, the British Trades Union Congress (TUC) was sceptical about the European project, fearing that it would undermine British social policies.[20] At the same time, the German government was taken over by Schmidt, who had a more pragmatic approach towards integration than Brandt. In his first government declaration he announced that 'in a time of growing global problems, we need realism and sobriety, and should focus on the essentials of what is needed now and leave other things aside'.[21]

Although the 1975 directive was generally in line with the interests of the member states, the Commission was too slow in drafting the reform and missed a window of opportunity. By the time the Commission finally published the directive in 1975, conditions had changed. First, the political support for it had faded with Wilson in office. The social-democratic leader was a Euro-sceptic, fearing that European integration would undermine the high social and tax standards that characterized Britain at the time. Secondly, the 1973 oil crisis shifted priorities to other policy issues. With rising unemployment and inflation rates throughout Europe, the focus moved from plans to harmonize taxation to more urgent matters, such as restabilizing domestic economies.

In light of high corporate taxes in all European member states and a pro-integrationist stance on the part of the heads of state, European tax harmonization was a real alternative. Certainly, we can only speculate what would have happened if the external environment had been more favourable and the commission had taken a more proactive stance. However, it is certain that the community did once envisage a corporate tax order that was to maintain high rates and support income redistribution, and this received widespread support from the main decision-making actors.

European Corporate Taxation in the 1990s

After the withdrawal of the 1975 directive, the discussion on tax harmonization stalled, above all, due to the Parliament, which refused to issue an opinion on the proposed directive in the absence of specific proposals on tax base harmonization. During the 1980s the community focused on a number of other corporate-tax-related issues, such as the parent–subsidiary flows of dividends, fiscal treatment of cross-border mergers and acquisitions, and transfer pricing. However, as this chapter is interested mainly in the Community's discussion of tax competition versus harmonization, I will not elaborate on these reforms. In what follows I will show that, while the member states believed that tax harmonization would form a logical part of monetary and fiscal integration in the early years of integration, tax harmonization increasingly acquired negative connotations in the European Community, and a more market-liberal approach became dominant.

The New Approach to Community Taxation

In the early 1990s, the European Commission launched a new approach, entitled 'Towards Tax Coordination in the European Union: A Package to Tackle Harmful Tax Competition', which was approved by the council in 1997 (for an overview, see Table 7.1).[22] The commission saw the need to act due to the completion of the internal market but regarded the old approach as too centralized. The new approach would prioritize 'the coordination and approximation of policies rather than systematic use of harmonisation'.[23] In 1995, Mario Monti took over the Directorate of Taxation and published a draft proposal for a tax package, including a Code of Conduct for business taxation.[24]

The code highlights the need to reduce distortions in the single market, so that taxes do not influence economic decisions. Moreover, it draws attention to redistributive effects caused by tax competition, which may cause a shift of the tax burden towards less mobile taxes. Overall, the Commission took an ambiguous approach to tax competition, which 'is generally to be welcomed as a means of benefiting citizens and of imposing downward pressure on government spending'.[25] However, it was against unrestrained competition, as market integration 'without any accompanying tax coordination is putting increasing constraints on member states' freedom to choose the appropriate tax structure'.[26] The Commission thus introduced the concept of 'fair competition', which does not aim for tax harmonization among the member states but strives for the banning of unfair tax measures.[27]

The Code of Conduct is not legally binding. By introducing a nonbinding agreement, the Commission sought to persuade domestic veto-players, who feared the loss of tax sovereignty. In turn, it is based on a voluntary commitment by the member states to inform each other about existing and proposed tax measures, as well as an agreement to avoid harmful tax measures both by not introducing new ones and by eliminating any already existing within a determined period. However, the implementation of these principles is voluntary due to the non-binding nature of the code. It was hoped that, similar to best practice, the code would work on the basis of 'naming and shaming' without encountering too much resistance.

A comparison of the Commission's corporate tax agenda in the 1970s and in the 1990s indicates that an ideational shift occurred. The Community's goal changed from an interventionist to a more market-liberal solution. The 1975 reform based on the goals of tax harmonization and tax equity; in accordance with this, high corporate taxes and progressive income taxes contribute to stability and growth. In contrast, the Code of Conduct is based a non-binding agreement and an efficiency perspective, according to which tax competition and low corporate taxes are beneficial, with the idea that low corporate taxes attract businesses, stimulate investment and create growth. Although neither reform argues for the market or European intervention alone, their policy suggestions differ considerably. The first agenda assigns the EU a proactive role in the management of macroeconomic goals, while the latter argues for a minimization of joint intervention.

Viewpoints of Political Leaders and Elites in the 1990s

In 1997, when the Code of Conduct was published by the commission, the Labour Party had just won the national elections in the United Kingdom and Tony Blair became prime minister. Previously, the British government under Margaret Thatcher had liberalized the economy, reduced the corporate tax rate to 35 per cent and signed the Single European Act (1986). Similar to the Tories, Blair supported the creation of the single European market but opposed any further ceding of national sovereignty.[28] The Labour government stressed that it would not give up the veto in vital policy areas, such as taxation: 'As far as Britain is concerned, tax policy is made in Britain, not in Europe. It is by cutting taxes, not raising them, that is the way forward to create jobs'.[29] Also the CBI, which had welcomed the 1975 directive, was

Table 7.1 The Commission's Reform Ideas on European Business Taxation

	Overall Approach	Objective
1975 Directive	Progressivity	Tax harmonization and binding tax rate band
1997 Code of Conduct	Market-liberal	Non-binding rules to prevent *unfair* tax competition.

Source: Author's own work

now in favour of tax competition as a means 'to keep governments on the straight and narrow, charge lower taxes and consume less'.[30]

In Germany, various corporate tax reforms reduced the rate from 56 to 45 per cent throughout the early 1990s. However, relatively to the OECD average, Germany's corporate tax rate remained comparatively high until the late 1990s. The German government under Helmut Kohl (1982–98) believed that taxation should remain a national matter. However, they acknowledged that unfair tax dumping and tax havens constituted a problem that needed to be addressed by the EU.[31] Similarly, the new government under Gerhard Schröder (1998–2005) supported tax competition and low corporate tax rates.[32] Only a small minority – including the German and the European trade unions – pushed for tax harmonization with minimum standards to prevent tax dumping, and believed that 'one member state's tax cuts can indeed result in another's public service cuts'.[33] However, this was an isolated position in Europe, where the majority of political leaders and elites had become supportive of the effects of tax competition.

In sum, political and socio-economic leaders were less favourable towards European intervention and instead supported tax competition. This change was not limited to conservatives but also encompassed part of the left. Thus, there was widespread consensus, with the exception of the trade union movement, that tax decisions should be a national matter and that tax competition among EU members was beneficial.

The idea of 'unfair tax competition' introduced by the commission with the market-liberal Code of Conduct of 1997 was in line with the tax interests of economic and political leaders of the time. Tax competition is regarded as positive as such, and linked to efficiency, economic growth and employment. The commission built on the positive idea of tax competition and singled out only certain harmful tax measures. These were thought of as hidden state aid, distorting the efficient functioning of the single market. By making use of established rules linked to the common market, and by safe-guarding national tax sovereignty due to the non-binding nature of the code, the Commission achieved a consensus among supporters and opponents of tax competition.

Conclusion: The Ideational Shift and European Decision-Making

The Community's tax goals shifted from a more interventionist to a more market-liberal solution. The 1975 reform based on goals of tax harmonization and the introduction of minimum corporate tax standards. Moreover, the reform was built on ideals of uniformity, redistribution and high corporate taxes. In contrast, the Code of Conduct was based on a non-binding agreement and related to a neutrality perspective, according to which tax competition and low corporate taxes are beneficial. It is based on the idea that low taxes attract businesses, stimulate investment and create growth and jobs. The argument is that economic growth is welfare-enhancing in itself and thus concerns about the distribution of the economic pie are secondary. In sum, the Community's agenda clearly shifted from an interventionist tax approach in the 1970s to a more market-liberal one in the 1990s.

The analysis demonstrates that the Commission's reforms reflect an ideational shift among political and socio-economic leaders in the EU. While tax harmonization was regarded as appropriate by the Council members and by corporate actors in the 1970s, their support for joint standards in corporate taxation diminished over the years. In fact, the investigation shows that a drastic shift occurred as regards the benefits of tax harmonization, which in the early 1970s had been the main and pretty much uncontested policy goal. Only the British Labour Party was sceptical, fearing that it would undermine existing tax standards in the UK. By contrast, in the 1990s, with the exception of the trade union movement, there was widespread consensus among political elites that tax decisions are a national matter and that tax competition among EU members was beneficial. Also the centre-left parties, which traditionally supported high taxes on corporate profits, argued that modern social democrats recognize the benefits of corporate tax cuts: they were considered to raise profitability, support incentives to invest and thus stimulate economic activity.

The Commission's reform plans correspond with the ideational shifts that had occurred among political and socio-economic leaders. It shows that the extent to which a particular set of economic ideas is institutionalized among the member states is crucial and influences European reform objectives. It is unlikely that tax harmonization with minimum standards is perceived as an appropriate solution when low corporate taxes and competition serve as ideals in the member states. Hence, the dominance of a certain set of economic ideas constrains the solutions available to policymakers at the supranational level.

The analysis shows that the Commission has a crucial stake and can shape Europe's official tax agenda. It can frame the reform to mediate between opponents and by timing the reform accordingly. Nonetheless, the heterogeneous composition of the Council, combined with the unanimity procedure that applies in many economic fields, make an interventionist tax approach highly unlikely. Even a market-liberal solution such as the Code of Conduct was not easy to push through. A more interventionist approach would require more horse-trading or a broader consensus, which is unlikely in a Union of 28 with diverse economic, political and cultural backgrounds.

Hanna Lierse is currently a fellow at the Minda de Gunzburg Centre for European Studies at Harvard University. During her stay, she will examine the rise and the transformation of wealth taxation in Europe since the nineteenth century, and gauge redistributive implications. She has published articles pivoting around European integration, the political economy, and particularly linked to issues of taxation, welfare and redistribution, including: 'Trade Liberalization and the Global Expansion of Modern Taxes', *Review of International Political Economy* 23(2) (2016) (with Carina Schmitt und Laura Seelkopf); and 'Capital Markets and Tax Policy-Making: A Comparative Analysis of European Tax Reforms since the Crisis', *Comparative European Politics*, published online first: January 2015 (with Laura Seelkopf).

Notes

1. It is possible to identify two main conduits through which the European Union can influence national tax systems. First, through positive integration, which means that the member states jointly issue new policies at the supranational level. Secondly, through negative integration, which refers to the fact that the construction of the common market exerts an influence on the national tax system by increasing tax competition.

2. For an overview, see John Douglas Wilson, 'Theories of Tax Competition', *National Tax Journal* 52(2) (1999): 269–304; Philipp Genschel and Peter Schwarz, 'Tax Competition: A Literature Review', *Socio-Economic Review* 9 (2011), 339–70.

3. Hugh J. Ault and Brian J. Arnold, *Comparative Income Taxation: A Structural Analysis* (The Hague, 2004).

4. European Commission, *Taxation Trends in the European Union* (Luxembourg, 2013), 36.

5. The role of the European Court of Justice (ECJ) has also become more relevant for national tax matters. The ECJ has increasingly intervened in tax issues since the 1990s. See Uhl, Susanne (2007) 'Steuerstaatlichkeit in Europa: Über die Transformation der Steuersysteme Europäischer Mitgliedstaaten, deren Bedeutung für die nationale Steuerautonomie und die steuerpolitische Verfasstheit Europas', Dissertation, Jacobs University Bremen. More and more ECJ decisions have overruled national tax laws, asserting their incompatibility with the EU's 'four freedoms'.

6. Cathie Jo Martin, *Shifting the Burden: The Struggle over Growth and Corporate Taxation* (Chicago, 1991); Charles E. McLure and George R. Zodrow, 'The Study and Practice of Income Policy', in *Modern Public Finance*, ed. John M. Quigley and Eugene Smolensky, (Cambridge, MA, 1994), 165–209; Hanna Lierse, *The Evolution of the European Economic Governance System: Monetary and Business Tax Cooperation* (Baden-Baden, 2011).

7. Hanna Lierse, 'European Taxation during the Crisis: Does Politics Matter?', *Journal of Public Policy* 32 (2012): 207–30.

8. OECD, 'Tax Policy Reform and Economic Growth', *OECD Tax Policy Studies* 20 (2010).

9. Neill Nugent, *The Government and Politics of the European Union* (Basingstoke, 2006).

10. Neill Nugent, 'The Leadership Capacity of the European Commission', *Journal of European Public Policy* 2(4) (1995): 603–23.

11. European Communities, 'Proposal for a Council Concerning the Harmonization of System of Company Taxation and of Withholding Taxes on Dividends', *Bulletin of the European Communities* (COM/1975/392), Supplement 10/75 (Brussels, 23 July 1975).

12. Ibid., Art. 3.

13. See also Lierse, *Evolution*.

14. Werner Plan, 'Report to the Council and the Commission on the Realization by Stages of Economic and Monetary Union in the Community' (Luxembourg, Commission of the European Communities, 8 October 1970); 'Resolution of the Council on the Achievement by Stages of Economic and Monetary Union in the Community', *Official Journal C 38* (18 April 1972), 3–4.

15. Nicole Leuchtweis, 'Deutsche Europapolitik zwischen Aufbruchstimmung und Weltwirtschaftskrise: Willy Brandt und Helmut Schmidt', in *Deutsche Europapolitik: von Adenauer bis Merkel*, ed. Gisela Müller-Brandeck-Bocquet et al. (Wiesbaden, 2002), 67–199.

16. Lierse, *Evolution*.

17. Chris Gifford, *The Making of Euroscpetic Britain* (Aldershot, 2008); Helen Parr, *Britain's Policy towards the European Community: Harold Wilson and Britain's World Role, 1964–1967* (London, 2006).

18. Confederation of British Industry, Annual Report 1973 (London, 1973), 12; quotation in: Confederation of British Industry, Annual Report 1975 (London, 1975), 10.

19. Parr, *Britain's Policy*.

20. Trade Union Congress, Annual Congress Reports, Manchester 1973, Modern Records Centre, University Library, University of Warwick.

21. Stenographischer Bericht Deutscher Bundestag, 7. Wahlperiode, 100. Sitzung, Bonn, 17 May 1974, 6593B, in: http://dip21.bundestag.de/dip21/btp/07/07100.pdf. The translation is by the author.

22. European Union, 'Towards Tax Co-ordination in the European Union: A Package to Tackle Harmful Tax Competition', Communication from the Commission to the Council (COM/1997/495) (Brussels, 1 October 1997).

23. European Communities, 'Guidelines on Company Taxation', Communication to Parliament and Council from Commission of the European Communities (SEC/90/601) (Brussels, 20 April 1990), 11.

24. European Union, 'Towards Tax Co-ordination'.

25. Ibid., 2.

26. Ibid.

27. Harmful tax measures can include legislative provisions, regulations and administrative procedures, which provide for a significantly lower effective level of taxation or zero taxation compared to the rate that is normally applied in the member state. It is the objective to abolish special measures that discriminate by being granted only to certain corporations and can be regarded as a form of state aid.

28. Duncan Watts, *Britain and the European Union: An Uneasy Partnership* (Sheffield, 2000); Alistair Jones, *Britain and the European Union* (Edinburgh, 2007).

29. 'EU tax stand puts UK in conflict with Germany', *Financial Times*, 24 November 1998.

30. Confederation of British Industry, *"News", January 1999* (London, 1999).

31. 'Waigel will die Steueroasen austrocknen: Der Bundesfinanzminister drängt die EU Staaten zu klaren Absprachen/Abwerbung von Unternehmen soll gestoppt werden', *Süddeutsche Zeitung*, 18 September 1997.

32. Tony Blair and Gerhard Schröder, *Europe: The Third Way/Die Neue Mitte*, Friedrich Ebert Foundation, South Africa Office, Working Documents, no. 2 (1998).

33. ETUC Resolutions. Brussels: European Trade Union Congress, 1995–96.

Bibliography

Ault, Hugh J., and Brian J. Arnold, *Comparative Income Taxation: A Structural Analysis* (The Hague, 2004).

European Commission, *Taxation Trends in the European Union* (Luxembourg, 2013).

Genschel, Philipp, and Peter Schwarz, 'Tax Competition: A Literature Review', *Socio-Economic Review* 9 (2011): 339–70.

Gifford, Chris, *The Making of Eurosceptic Britain* (Aldershot, 2008).

Jones, Alistair, *Britain and the European Union* (Edinburgh, 2007).

Leuchtweis, Nicole, 'Deutsche Europapolitik zwischen Aufbruchstimmung und Weltwirtschaftskrise: Willy Brandt und Helmut Schmidt', in *Deutsche Europapolitik: von Adenauer bis Merkel*, ed. Gisela Müller-Brandeck-Bocquet et al. (Wiesbaden, 2002), 67–199.

Lierse, Hanna, *The Evolution of the European Economic Governance System: Monetary and Business Tax Cooperation* (Baden-Baden, 2011).

———, 'European Taxation during the Crisis: Does Politics Matter?', *Journal of Public Policy* 32 (2012): 207–30.

Martin, Cathie Jo, *Shifting the Burden: The Struggle over Growth and Corporate Taxation* (Chicago, 1991).

McLure, Charles E., and George R. Zodrow, 'The Study and Practice of Income Policy', in *Modern Public Finance*, ed. John M. Quigley and Eugene Smolensky (Cambridge, MA, 1994), 165–209.

Nugent, Neill, 'The Leadership Capacity of the European Commission', *Journal of European Public Policy* 2(4) (1995): 603–23.

———, *The Government and Politics of the European Union* (Basingstoke, 2006).

OECD, 'Tax Policy Reform and Economic Growth', *OECD Tax Policy Studies* 20 (2010).

Parr, Helen, *Britain's Policy towards the European Community: Harold Wilson and Britain's World Role, 1964–1967* (London, 2006).

Uhl, Susanne, 'Steuerstaatlichkeit in Europa: Über die Transformation der Steuersysteme Europäischer Mitgliedstaaten, deren Bedeutung für die nationale Steuerautonomie und die steuerpolitische Verfasstheit Europas', Dissertation, (Jacobs University Bremen 2007)

Watts, Duncan, *Britain and the European Union: An Uneasy Partnership* (Sheffield, 2000).

Wilson, John Douglas, 'Theories of Tax Competition', *National Tax Journal* 52(2) (1999): 269–304.

CHAPTER 8

The European Community and the Rise of a New Educational Order (1976–1986)

SIMONE PAOLI

Introduction

At the Council of Europe's Standing Conference of European Ministers of Education, which was held in Helsinki in 1987, the European commissioner for social affairs, employment and education, Manuel Marín, summarized the activities of the European Community (EC) in the field of education in 1985 and 1986, so emphasizing a historic shift:

> [W]hereas in the previous period, attention had focused strongly on the links between education and social policy, especially in developing measures to combat growing unemployment amongst young people, a new and greater emphasis has been given to the contribution of education and training to the task of modernising the economies, of exploiting the potential of the new technologies.[1]

The present chapter, which is part of a wider research project on the history of the education policies of the European Community from the late 1950s to the early 1990s,[2] analyses the reasons why, and the ways in which, the EC institutions changed their approach to both vocational and higher education.

The main argument is that, in the mid-1980s, the European Community's conception of education underwent a significant transformation. From the late 1960s to the early 1980s, education policies at the

---

Notes for this section begin on page 147.

EC level were conceived of primarily as an instrument for promoting social mobility, enhancing social inclusion and cohesion, and protecting the most vulnerable in society. Since the mid-1980s education policies at the level of the European Community have increasingly been intended as means of serving the interests of the individual, contributing to the modernization of the economy and improving the competitiveness of enterprises.

This change, which was due to a series of political initiatives taken by deputies in the European Parliament, members of the European Commission, ministers of education and, last but not least, leaders of organizations representing business interests, was highly influential in the development of education debates, legislation and programmes in all European Union (EU) member states.

The Long Social Democratic Decade (1968–1984)

Although education was formally recognized as a legitimate area of EU responsibility in the Maastricht Treaty in 1992, the European Community began to deal with education issues much earlier, between the late 1960s and the early 1970s.[3]

The shift of labour from manufacturing to services, the technological transformation of secondary industry and the establishment of the European customs union contributed to a change and an increase in the level of qualifications and competences required by European employers. As a consequence, in the late 1960s and the early 1970s, authoritative members of the European Commission, the Council of Ministers and the European Parliament, supported by representatives of both trade unions and private companies – especially in France and Italy – began to advocate the adoption of education policies at the Community level in order to complement the implementation of a modern labour market on a European scale.

In the same period, the emergence of student movements in all the major EC countries ushered in a period of ferment and reform in higher education which, according to the French minister of education, Olivier Guichard, and the leadership of the Conference of European Rectors, needed to be managed in a coordinated manner.[4] In addition, struck and worried by the student and youth movements' hostile indifference to the EC and its purely mercantile purposes, prominent members of the European Commission, including President Jean Rey and vice-presidents Lionello Levi Sandri and Sicco Mansholt, and prominent members of the European Parliament, including the president of the Parliamentary Committee on Political Affairs, Carlo Scarascia Mugnozza, realized that a European Community concerned primarily with traders and farmers was no longer satisfactory and that it should acquire a stronger cultural – and educational – profile.[5]

After five years of paralysing disagreements over the content of cooperation in the field of education and the form that such cooperation should take, the EC member states eventually agreed on a Resolution defining the broad outline of future areas of cooperation and the principles that should underpin them. On the basis of a communication written by the newly established Directorate for Education and Training under the supervision of European commissioner for research, science and education, Ralf Dahrendorf,[6] in 1974 the EC ministers of education adopted the resolution on cooperation in the field of education. With this resolution, the ministers agreed to lay down the areas of action in which cooperation was possible. They committed themselves to: improving relations between European education systems; providing up-to-date documentation and statistics on education; increasing cooperation between institutions of higher education; encouraging recognition of academic diplomas and periods of study; supporting mobility of teachers, students and researchers; promoting better facilities for education and training of migrant workers and their children; and enhancing equal opportunity for free access to all forms of education. In addition, the ministers set out two major principles on which such cooperation should be based. First, cooperation in the field of education, while reflecting the progressive harmonization of economic and social policies in the European Community, had to be adapted to the specific objectives and requirements of this field; on no account, therefore, should education be regarded merely as a component of economic life. Secondly, cooperation had to make allowances for the traditions of each country and the diversity of their respective education systems and policies; harmonization of these systems or policies, consequently, could not be considered an end in itself.[7]

This resolution paved the way for the adoption of the first Community action programme in the field of education, which was formally adopted by the ministers of education of the EC member states in 1976. This action programme confirmed all the priority areas for cooperation that were stated in the 1974 resolution on the cooperation in the field of education. However, the resolution comprising an action programme in the field of education was innovative in two main respects. On one hand, the ministers established an explicit connection between the EC education action programme and the EC social action programme; accordingly, the education actions most closely concerned with social issues – such as better facilities for the education and training of migrant workers and their children – were given special emphasis.[8] On the other hand, in the wake of the economic recession and the consequent rise in unemployment rates experienced by all EC member states after the 1973 oil shock, the ministers of education committed themselves to taking measures within the framework of basic education and initial vocational training in order to prepare young people for work, facilitate their transition from study to working life and increase their chances of finding employment. In addition, they made a commitment to provide, in the context of continuing education and training, complementary courses to improve young workers' and young unemployed persons' chances of finding employment.[9]

In compliance with these commitments, between the mid-1970s and the early 1980s, education policies at the European level were developed in close relationship with the Community social strategy. Apart from promoting European cooperation in higher education through joint programmes of study, the EC prioritized education measures linked to social concerns, including the education and training of migrant workers and their children, and the transition of young people from school to working life.[10]

At the suggestion of the European commissioner for social affairs, Patrick Hillery, in 1977 the ministers for social affairs of the EC member states adopted a directive on the education of the children of migrant workers. Strongly supported by Italian representatives in the Council of Ministers,[11] the Socialist Group in the European Parliament and the newly established Standing Committee on Migrant Workers of the European Trade Union Confederation (ETUC), the directive required the EC member states to take appropriate measures to ensure that free tuition to facilitate initial reception was offered in their territory to the children of EC migrant workers, including, in particular, the teaching of the official language of the host state. The directive also required the member states to take appropriate measures to promote, in cooperation with countries of origin and in coordination with normal education, teaching of the mother tongue and the culture of the country of origin for the children of EC migrant workers. The aim was to encourage educational and social integration of such children without breaking the relationship with their respective countries and to combat the school failure that tended to affect them.[12] With a view to supporting the implementation of this directive, comparative studies were carried out and pilot projects were set up, focused on the development of new pedagogical approaches for teaching both the language of the host state and the mother tongue.

In 1976, with the support of the European commissioner for regional policy and coordination of Community funds, Antonio Giolitti, the Socialist Group in the European Parliament, and trade unions' representatives in the European Economic and Social Committee, the ministers of education of the member states of the EC adopted a resolution concerning measures to be taken to improve the preparation of young people for work and to facilitate their transition from education to working life. The aim was to provide the

EC countries with guidelines to be followed in developing national policies and pilot projects to test new methods and disseminate best practices,
especially aimed at strengthening motivation to study and work, helping
disadvantaged individuals and groups in difficulty and improving teacher
training.[13] After an extension decided upon in 1980, in 1982 a second programme concerning measures to be taken to improve the preparation of
young people for work and to facilitate their transition from education to
working life was adopted for a five-year period.[14]

While unemployment in general, and youth unemployment in particular, was increasing in all the EC member states, a majority in every
Community institution continued to believe that education should be considered primarily as an instrument of active employment policy designed to
promote social development and equal opportunities. The Confederation of
the Socialist Parties of the European Community (CSPEC), on one hand,
and the European Trade Union Confederation, on the other, played a major
role in lobbying the Community institutions to adopt education policies
with a strong social dimension. Significantly, in its common manifesto for
the elections of the European Parliament in 1979, the CSPEC put great
emphasis on education, stating that education was to be regarded as a fundamental tool for the establishment of a more human, just and inclusive
Europe. Similarly, in its first programme in the field of education and training in 1981, the ETUC highlighted that education should be seen as a crucial
means for improving the chances of disadvantaged individuals and categories, achieving equal opportunities for all and even transforming society in
favour of workers.[15] During the fourth statutory congress of the ETUC,
held in The Hague in 1982, the chairman of the European Trade Union
Committee for Education (ETUCE), Guy Georges, went as far as to say that
'we are workers who have a major responsibility in social terms.'[16]

This approach was reflected in the reorganization of the institutions
of the European Community, including the European Parliament and
the European Commission. In 1976, the European Parliament decided
to abolish the Parliamentary Committee on Cultural Affairs and Youth,
which had held responsibility for education since 1973, and to give competence for education to the newly created Parliamentary Committee on
Social Affairs, Employment and Education; in so doing, the European
Parliament intended to establish a more explicit connection between education and the fight against unemployment, especially youth unemployment.[17] Similarly, in 1981 the European Commission agreed to dismember
the Directorate-General for Research, Science and Education, which had
been established in 1973, and to transfer the department dealing with education to the new Directorate-General for Employment, Social Affairs and
Education, together with the department dealing with vocational training.

As highlighted by the director of the Education and Training Division of the Commission, Hywel Ceri Jones:

> the Commission's decision to merge in 1981 the education and training departments within a single frame of social policy, thus breaking the previous sectoral link with science and research, was a direct response to the political mood of the times. Since unemployment ... has become the central point on the agenda of the Community's domestic preoccupations, education has moved from the periphery to a more strategic location in the spectrum of Community policies.[18]

The Neoliberal Shift (1984–1986)

A fundamental change in attitudes towards education occurred in the early 1980s, when a number of authoritative members of both the European Parliament and the European Commission started to voice a criticism that, until then, had been grumbled only privately.[19]

As unemployment continued to rise and production continued to stagnate, a group of members of the European Parliament inspired by Derek Prag, an influential exponent of the European People's Party with strong links to the British business world, began to argue openly that the root cause of the socio-economic crisis in Europe was a lack of competitiveness with the United States, Japan and the so-called Asian Tigers, and that the solution was to be found in the modernization of the European economy. Modernization, in turn, implied a broad process of technological innovation and the establishment of a common market, which should be paralleled by consistent modernization of educational constructs and practices. In accordance with these ideas, the same group of European parliamentarians maintained that actions to improve the preparation and employability of disadvantaged people, which then formed the core of the Community education policies, were no longer adequate to meet the challenges facing the EC. The time had come, according to them, for the Community to shift the focus of education policies away from pursuing social aims and towards enhancing European competitiveness by fully exploiting the potential of new technologies and the forthcoming single European market.

This faction in the European Parliament was not alone in advocating a radical change in EC education policies. In the same period, in fact, a group of members of the Gaston Thorn's Commission, including the commissioner for employment, social affairs and employment, Ivor Richard, the commissioner for industrial market, industrial innovation, customs union, the environment, consumer protection and nuclear safety, Karl-Heinz Narjes, and the commissioner for industrial affairs and energy, Étienne Davignon, produced a series of documents advocating a radical reform of EC education policies. In their view, a crucial aim of the European Community should be to help European workers to adapt to the rapid pace of technological change, new patterns of work, growing international competition and the completion of a single market in Europe. In this perspective, it was argued that the EC should stop using education as an instrument of social policy and begin to use it as an instrument of economic policy – and competition policy in particular.[20]

Apart from British Socialist Richard, all these politicians, namely Luxembourg Liberal Thorn, German Christian Democrat Narjes and Belgian Liberal Davignon, had in common their membership of conservative parties and the Trilateral Commission, a discussion group formed by American banker David Rockefeller in 1973, and maintained close relationships with the business community. Étienne Davignon, in particular, acted as a sort of liaison between the European Commission and an important part of the European business world which, in the same period, was beginning to strengthen its channels of representation and involvement in the EC and, contextually, to call into doubt the effectiveness of education policies developed at the Community level up to then.

Before being appointed chairman of the executive committee of the Bilderberg Group, an annual meeting of top Western multinationals' executives and political leaders initiated in 1954, Davignon, together with the chief executive of Volvo, Pehr Gustaf Gyllenhammar, inspired a group of top businessmen to establish the European Round Table of Industrialists (ERT). The aim of this organization, set up in 1983, was to lobby the European Community to promote policies more favourable to business interests, not least education policies oriented towards enhancing competitiveness and meeting market needs. As remarked by the chairman of Nokia and chairman of the Employment Working Group of the ERT, Kari Kairamo, top businessmen in Europe considered education a key factor in improving the competitiveness of European enterprises and economies, and the European Community as a strategic actor in this domain: '[H]aving an abundance of natural resources is no longer necessarily the factor that determines a country's competitiveness; to an ever-increasing degree, such competitiveness is founded on intellectual resources and the employment potential they contain'.[21] The increasing awareness of the importance of education as a competitive factor was also demonstrated by the fact that the ERT, since its inception, had focused on education as one of the six crucial issues or strategic areas for the whole of Europe, and had established a Standing Working Group for Education.

The changes in the approach to education that emerged in significant sectors of both the European Parliament and the European Commission, and in powerful segments of the European business community in the early

1980s, went hand in hand with a parallel transformation in the education policies of major EC countries, including the United Kingdom and France.[22]

After the Great Debate on education, launched by prime minister James Callaghan in 1976, there was a tendency in the United Kingdom to blame the education system for failing to meet the needs of industry and contributing to the country's decline as a trading power. When Margaret Thatcher was elected prime minister in 1979, therefore, large sectors of public opinion were ready to welcome the drastic reforms in the British education system initiated by secretaries of state for education and science, Keith Joseph and Kenneth Baker.[23] Despite resistance from militant trade unions, local authorities and leftist academics, between 1985 and 1988 laws were adopted that introduced more centralization, selectivity, privatization and involvement of private companies in the British education system, the aim being to put education more in line with employers' needs.[24]

Despite differences in the political composition of their respective governments, a tendency similar to that in the United Kingdom was present in France after Alain Savary's resignation from the post of minister of education, and the parallel collapse of the socialist–communist coalition government in 1984. While Savary was concerned primarily with education's social mission, his successor, Jean-Pierre Chevènement, came into line with the new Laurent Fabius government, whose main aim was the modernization of France. Within this strategy, education, together with scientific research and vocational training, should contribute primarily to enhancing productivity and, in so doing, improving the international competitiveness of the French economy.[25]

The European Councils in Fontainebleau in 1984 and in Milan in 1985 gave a decisive boost to education policies at the Community level.[26] With a view to establishing a 'people's Europe' and, more importantly, to creating a single market and a technological economy and society in the European Community, in fact, more emphasis than ever before was put on the need for the Community to provide the necessary human resources to ensure that the potential of the internal market and technological changes were exploited to the full.[27]

The man who, initially, was assigned the task of submitting proposals for such a strategy was Peter Sutherland, commissioner for competition, social affairs and education in the first Jacques Delors Commission. Like Davignon, Sutherland was an international businessman and a conservative politician with close relationships with the Bilderberg Group, the Trilateral Commission and the ERT. Like Davignon, in addition, he was convinced that:

> in recent years education and vocational training have too often been considered merely as means to help young persons avoid unemployment and to provide them with qualifications for jobs. Only recently did we begin to put

the debate on education and vocational training systems in a global context ...
The aims are to end the serious shortage of qualified human resources required
by European industry ... and to give Europe the means to remain on an equal
footing with Japan and the United States in the field of industrial innovation
and development.[28]

On the basis of these convictions, in 1985 Sutherland and his cabinet proposed two programmes on higher education that marked a watershed in the
history of Community education policies and, to a certain extent, in the
history of West European education policies: the programme for cooperation between universities and enterprises regarding training in the field of
technology (COMETT), which was adopted in 1986, and the EC action
scheme for the mobility of university students (ERASMUS), which was
adopted in 1987.[29]

COMETT was expected to promote closer relations between higher
education and industry, thereby helping to provide European companies
with workers with the kind of knowledge, competence and mentality that
business needed. As remarked by the director of the Education and Training
Division of the European Commission, Hywel Ceri Jones, COMETT in
particular should establish more structured relations between the world of
universities and that of industry, and in so doing, overcome the skills deficit
that was facing the EC member states: '[W]hat is the nature of the skills
deficit in the EC? The real issues are not ones of quantity, but of quality:
issues of quality about the kind of education and training that we should be
providing through our universities in cooperation with the world of industry
defined in the very broad sense'.[30]

At the same time, contrary to what is largely believed, ERASMUS was
not primarily intended as a way to establish and foster a common identity in Europe. As highlighted by the head of the Erasmus Bureau, Alan
Smith, ERASMUS was considered by its own proponents as 'an essential
component in helping to raise the awareness of interdependence within the
Community, thereby contributing to the completion and consolidation of
the internal market, which will be the key to ensuring EC competitiveness
on the world stage'.[31]

Conclusion

In the second half of the 1980s, a number of members of the European
Commission, including the successors to Sutherland, Manuel Marín and
Vasso Papandreou, political groups in the European Parliament, especially the
Rainbow Group, the Communist and Allies Group and part of the Socialist
Group, and the ETUC and its representatives in the European Economic

and Social Committee and in the Social Dialogue made attempts to resist various aspects of the education policies initiated by the EC in the mid-1980s. However, none of these forces managed to significantly change the widespread idea that education should be conceived of primarily as a component of the competitive strategy of the EC and European companies, and to revert to the idea of education as an instrument to solve social problems and transform European societies into being more inclusive and equitable.

As a result of this failure, as highlighted by two French sociologists, Christian Laval and Louis Weber, in the last three decades the European Community has contributed greatly, together with other important international organizations such as the World Trade Organization, the World Bank and the Organisation for Economic Cooperation and Development, to the rise and consolidation of a new world educational order, characterized by:

> a model consistent with free trade rules, the strategies of multinational corporations and the ideologies that underpin them. Education is merely regarded as a factor of production affecting productivity, capacity to attract capital, competitiveness ... Cuts in public spending on education, introduction of market mechanisms and values, and emphasis on the economic aims of education are the complementary aspects of the educational reform supported by the guardians of orthodoxy.[32]

Simone Paoli is professor of History and Political Science at the International Studies Institute (ISI) in Florence, and post-doctorate fellow at the Department of Political Science, Law and International Studies of the University of Padua. He has published volumes, articles and essays on the history of the European integration, with an emphasis on cultural and social dimensions. These include *Il sogno di Erasmo: La questione educativa nel processo di integrazione europea* [The Erasmus' Dream: The Educational Issue in the European Integration Process], Milan 2010.

Notes

1. European Commission, 'Activities of the Commission of the EC in the Fields of Education and Training during 1985 and 1986'. A contribution to the standing conference of the European ministers of education held in Helsinki from 5 to 7 May (Luxembourg, 1987), 92.

2. The main results of the research were published in a monograph: Simone Paoli, *Il Sogno di Erasmo: La questione educativa nel processo di integrazione europea* (Milan, 2010).

3. Simone Paoli, 'La politica comunitaria in materia di istruzione nel corso degli anni sessanta', in *Lo spazio sociale europeo: Atti del convegno internazionale di studi, Fiesole, 10–11 ottobre 2003*, ed. Laura Leonardi and Antonio Varsori (Florence, 2005), 57–75; idem, 'Alle radici della politica educativa europea, 1968–1974', *Ventunesimo Secolo* 9 (2006), 199–228; idem, 'La nascita di una dimensione educativa comunitaria: Tra interessi nazionali e istanze di movimento, 1969–1976', in *Alle origini del presente: L'Europa occidentale nella crisi degli anni Settanta*, ed. Antonio Varsori (Milan, 2006), 251–73; idem, 'Building a European Cultural and Educational

Model: Another Face of the integration process, 1969–1974', in *Beyond the Customs Union: The European Community's Quest for Deepening, Widening and Completion, 1969–1975*, ed. Jan van der Harst (Brussels, 2007), 251–73.

4. Simone Paoli, 'Between Sovereignty Dilemmas and Cultural Strategies: France and the Birth of the Community Education Policy, 1968–1974', in *The Road to a United Europe: Interpretations of the Process of European Integration*, ed. Morten Rasmussen and Ann-Christina L. Knudsen (Brussels, 2009), 319–33.

5. Simone Paoli, 'The Influence of Protest Movements on the European Integration Process: An Interpretation of the 1972 Paris Summit', in *Europe in the International Arena during the 1970s: Entering a Different World*, ed. Antonio Varsori and Guia Migani (Brussels, 2011), 253–77.

6. European Commission, 'Education in the European Community: Communication to the Council', *Bulletin of the European Communities* 3 (1974), 23–37.

7. Council of Ministers of the EC, 'Resolution of the ministers of education meeting within the Council of 6 June 1974 on cooperation in the field of education', *Official Journal of the European Communities* C 98 (1974).

8. Council of Ministers of the EC, 'Council Resolution of 21 January 1974 concerning a social action programme', *Official Journal of the European Communities* C 13 (1974).

9. Council of Ministers of the EC, 'Resolution of the Council and of the ministers of education meeting within the Council of 9 February 1976 comprising an action programme in the field of education', *Official Journal of the European Communities* C 38 (1976).

10. Anne Corbett, *Universities and the Europe of Knowledge: Ideas, Institutions and Policy Entrepreneurship in EU Higher Education Policy, 1955–2005* (New York, 2005), 25–59; Steve Bainbridge and Julie Murray, *An Age of Learning: Vocational Training Policy at European Level* (Luxembourg, 2000), 7; Andreas Moschonas, *Education and Training in the EU* (Aldershot, 1998), 95–97; Guy Neave, *The EEC and Education* (Stoke-on-Trent, 1984), 16–17.

11. Simone Paoli, 'La costruzione di una politica europea dell'istruzione. Il ruolo dell'Italia (1957–1976)', *Annali della Fondazione Ugo La Malfa* 19 (2004), 218–19; idem, 'L'isolamento creativo: Ragioni, caratteri, esiti del contributo italiano allo sviluppo di una dimensione educativa comunitaria, 1961–1975', in *L'Italia e la dimensione sociale nell'integrazione europea*, ed. Luciano Tosi (Padova, 2008), 227–30.

12. Council of Ministers of the EC, 'Council Directive of 25 July 1977 on the education of the children of migrant workers', *Official Journal of the European Communities* L 199 (1977).

13. Council of Ministers of the EC, 'Resolution of the Council and of the ministers of education meeting within the Council of 13 December 1976 concerning measures to be taken to improve the preparation of young people for work and to facilitate their transition from education to working life', *Official Journal of the European Communities* C 308 (1976).

14. Council of Ministers of the EC, 'Resolution of the Council and of the ministers of education meeting within the Council of 19 July 1982 concerning measures to be taken to improve the preparation of young people for work and to facilitate their transition from education to working life,' *Official Journal of the European Communities* C 193 (1982).

15. Simone Paoli, 'Il sindacato europeo, la crisi economica e il nuovo ordine educativo', in *Fra mercato comune e globalizzazione: le forze sociali europee e la fine dell'età dell'oro*, ed. Ilaria Del Biondo, Lorenzo Mechi and Francesco Petrini (Milan, 2010), 151–78.

16. Fourth Statutory Congress of the ETUC. Report of Proceedings, 19–23 April 1982, The Hague, ETUC Fond, 3382, Historical Archives of the International Institute of Social History, Amsterdam (Netherlands).

17. Simone Paoli, 'La forza di due debolezze: Il ruolo del Parlamento europeo nella nascita di una politica comunitaria dell'istruzione (1957–1976)', in *Sfide del mercato e identità europea: Le politiche di educazione e formazione professionale nell'Europa comunitaria*, ed. Antonio Varsori (Milan, 2006), 42–43.

18. Hywel Ceri Jones, 'L'éducation et la Communauté européenne', *Revue d'action sociale* 2 (1984), 16 (author's translation).

19. Simone Paoli, 'Formazione e ricerca: la storia e il futuro', in *Legittimare l'Europa: Diritti sociali e crescita economica*, ed. Luciano Barca and Maurizio Franzini (Bologna, 2005), 307–16.

20. Etienne Davignon, 'Préface. Communauté européenne et industrie', in *L'après 1993: Nouvelle donne sur l'échiquier industriel européen*, ed. Jeanne-Pierre Husson and Yves André Perez (Paris, 1993), 5–11; Karl-Heinz Narjes, 'Europe's Technological Challenge: A View from the European Commission', *Science and Public Policy* 6 (1988): 395–402.

21. Kari Kairamo, 'Education and the European Competitiveness Factor', *Cahiers de Bruges* 46 (1988): 211.

22. Eurydice, *Two Decades of Reform in Higher Education in Europe: 1980 Onwards* (Brussels, 2000), 174; Eurydice, *A Decade of Reforms at Compulsory Education Level in the EU: 1984–1994* (Brussels, 1997), 7.

23. Margaret Thatcher, *The Downing Street Years* (New York, 1993), 590–99.

24. Henry Miller and Mark Ginsburg, 'Restructuring Education and the State in England', in *Understanding Educational Reform in Global Context: Economy, Ideology and the State*, ed. Mark Ginsburg (New York and London, 1991), 49–77.

25. Jean-Pierre Chevènement, Hervé Hamon and Patrick Rotman, *Le pari sur l'intelligence* (Paris, 1985), 267; Laurent Fabius, *Le cœur de futur* (Paris, 1985), 52–54.

26. Luce Pépin, *The History of European Cooperation in Education and Training: Europe in the Making – An Example* (Luxembourg, 2006), 99–100.

27. Jacques Delors, *Mémoires* (Paris, 2004), 103–37.

28. Peter Sutherland, 'Extrait d'un discours sur la politique d'éducation dans la Communauté prononcé lors d'une réunion de la commission de la Jeunesse, de la Culture, de l'Éducation, de l'Information et des Sports du Parlement européen', 25 April 1985, Brussels, IP(85) 167, Historical Archives of the Council of Ministers of the EU, Brussels (author's translation).

29. Hywel Ceri Jones, 'COMETT and ERASMUS: Two Flagships for Higher Education in the EC', *Wirtschaftspolitische Blätter* 35 (1988): 680–89. These two programmes on higher education, which received the lion's share of EC resources devoted to education and vocational training, were followed, between 1987 and 1990, by minor programmes on initial and continuing vocational education and training, including an action programme for the vocational training of young people and their preparation for adult and working life (PETRA) and an action programme for the development of continuing vocational training in the EC (FORCE).

30. Hywel Ceri Jones, 'New Perspectives for EC Action: The COMETT and ERASMUS Programmes', in *Mutations technologiques et identité européenne: l'apport des universités*, ed. Ladislav Cerych (Paris, 1986), 94.

31. Alan Smith, 'ERASMUS: An Investment in the Future of the Community', *Social Europe* 3 (1987): 43.

32. Christian Laval and Louis Weber, *Le nouvel ordre éducatif mondial: OMC, Banque mondiale, OCDE, Commission européenne* (Paris, 2002), 113 (author's translation).

Bibliography

Bainbridge, Steve, and Julie Murray, *An Age of Learning: Vocational Training Policy at European Level* (Luxembourg, 2000).

Chevènement, Jean-Pierre, Hervé Hamon and Patrick Rotman, *Le pari sur l'intelligence* (Paris, 1985).

Corbett, Anne, *Universities and the Europe of Knowledge: Ideas, Institutions and Policy Entrepreneurship in EU Higher Education Policy, 1955–2005* (New York, 2005).

Davignon, Etienne, 'Préface. Communauté européenne et industrie', in *L'après 1993: Nouvelle donne sur l'échiquier industriel européen*, ed. Jeanne-Pierre Husson and Yves André Perez (Paris, 1993), 5–11.

Delors, Jacques, *Mémoires* (Paris, 2004).

European Commission, 'Activities of the Commission of the EC in the Fields of Education and Training during 1985 and 1986'. A contribution to the standing conference of the European ministers of education held in Helsinki from 5 to 7 May (Luxembourg, 1987).

———, 'Education in the European Community: Communication to the Council', *Bulletin of the European Communities* 3 (1974): 23–37.

Eurydice, *A Decade of Reforms at Compulsory Education Level in the EU: 1984–1994* (Brussels, ———, *Two Decades of Reform in Higher Education in Europe: 1980 Onwards* (Brussels, 2000).

Fabius, Laurent, *Le cœur de futur* (Paris, 1985).

Jones, Hywel Ceri, 'L'éducation et la Communauté européenne', *Revue d'action sociale* 2 (1984): 14–36.

———, 'New Perspectives for EC Action: The COMETT and ERASMUS Programmes', in *Mutations technologiques et identité européenne: l'apport des universités*, ed. Ladislav Cerych (Paris, 1986), 84–116.

———, 'COMETT and ERASMUS: Two Flagships for Higher Education in the EC', *Wirtschaftspolitische Blätter* 35 (1988): 680–89.

Kairamo, Kari, 'Education and the European Competitiveness Factor', *Cahiers de Bruges* 46 (1988): 199–214.

Laval, Christian, and Louis Weber, *Le nouvel ordre éducatif mondial: OMC, Banque mondiale, OCDE, Commission européenne* (Paris, 2002).

Miller, Henry, and Mark Ginsburg, 'Restructuring Education and the State in England', in *Understanding Educational Reform in Global Context: Economy, Ideology and the State*, ed. Mark Ginsburg (New York and London, 1991), 49–77.

Moschonas, Andreas, *Education and Training in the EU* (Aldershot, 1998).

Narjes, Karl-Heinz, 'Europe's Technological Challenge: A View from the European Commission', *Science and Public Policy* 6 (1988): 395–402.

Neave, Guy, *The EEC and Education* (Stoke-on-Trent, 1984).

Paoli, Simone, 'La costruzione di una politica europea dell'istruzione: Il ruolo dell'Italia (1957–1976)', *Annali della Fondazione Ugo La Malfa* 19 (2004): 187–220.

———, 'Formazione e ricerca: la storia e il futuro', in *Legittimare l'Europa: Diritti sociali e crescita economica*, ed. Luciano Barca and Maurizio Franzini (Bologna, 2005), 307–29.

———, 'La politica comunitaria in materia di istruzione nel corso degli anni sessanta', in *Lo spazio sociale europeo: Atti del convegno internazionale di studi, Fiesole, 10–11 ottobre 2003*, ed. Laura Leonardi and Antonio Varsori (Florence, 2005), 57–75.

———, 'Alle radici della politica educativa europea, 1968–1974', *Ventunesimo Secolo* 9 (2006): 199–228.

———, 'La forza di due debolezze: Il ruolo del Parlamento europeo nella nascita di una politica comunitaria dell'istruzione (1957–1976)', in *Sfide del mercato e identità europea: Le politiche di educazione e formazione professionale nell'Europa comunitaria*, ed. Antonio Varsori (Milan, 2006), 11–52.

———, 'La nascita di una dimensione educativa comunitaria: Tra interessi nazionali e istanze di movimento, 1969–1976', in *Alle origini del presente: L'Europa occidentale nella crisi degli anni Settanta*, ed. Antonio Varsori (Milan, 2006), 221–50.

———, 'Building a European Cultural and Educational Model: Another Face of the Integration Process, 1969–1974', in *Beyond the Customs Union: The European Community's*

Quest for Deepening, Widening and Completion, 1969–1975, ed. Jan van der Harst (Brussels, 2007), 251–73.

————, 'L'isolamento creativo: Ragioni, caratteri, esiti del contributo italiano allo sviluppo di una dimensione educativa comunitaria, 1961–1975', in *L'Italia e la dimensione sociale nell'integrazione europea*, ed. Luciano Tosi (Padova, 2008), 199–232.

————, 'Between Sovereignty Dilemmas and Cultural Strategies: France and the Birth of the Community Education Policy, 1968–1974', in *The Road to a United Europe: Interpretations of the Process of European Integration*, ed. Morten Rasmussen and Ann-Christina L. Knudsen (Brussels, 2009), 319–33.

————, 'Il sindacato europeo, la crisi economica e il nuovo ordine educativo', in *Fra mercato comune e globalizzazione: le forze sociali europee e la fine dell'età dell'oro*, ed. Ilaria Del Biondo, Lorenzo Mechi and Francesco Petrini (Milan, 2010), 151–78.

————, *Il Sogno di Erasmo: La questione educativa nel processo di integrazione europea* (Milan, 2010).

————, 'The Influence of Protest Movements on the European Integration Process: An Interpretation of the 1972 Paris Summit', in *Europe in the International Arena during the 1970s: Entering a Different World*, ed. Antonio Varsori and Guia Migani (Brussels, 2011), 253–77.

Pépin, Luce, *The History of European Cooperation in Education and Training: Europe in the Making – An Example* (Luxembourg, 2006).

Smith, Alan, 'ERASMUS: An Investment in the Future of the Community', *Social Europe* 3 (1987): 38–49.

Thatcher, Margaret, *The Downing Street Years* (New York, 1993).

CHAPTER 9

Project–Based Learning from the Late 1960s to the Early 1980s

A Case Study from Lansing and Bremen

ANNA WELLNER

Introduction

During the twentieth century – and especially its second half – higher educa-tion changed in many countries across the globe. Thus far, however, little critical attention has been paid to aspects of changing curricula and the development of new programmes and even disciplines. This is surprising because the quest for a 'relevant curriculum' was an important aspect of the international student protests of the 1960s and 1970s.[1] Protesters claimed that science was often exploited to support industrial, technological and military developments.[2] They demanded more academic liberty and a teaching style that would do more than merely 'provide [them] with the skills and knowl-edge base necessary to fit into the existing social structure'.[3]

   One international academic innovation resulting from these complaints in the late 1960s and early 1970s was the initiation of project-based learning. Students engaged in social projects outside the walls of the ivory tower. They tutored children, provided financial counselling to low-income families and analysed the environmental conditions of nearby communities. While these projects were also aimed at applying academic theories to real-world issues and at reflecting possible future job practices, they sought especially to stim-ulate the students' political consciousness. The early initiators hoped that the engaged students, as representatives of their universities, would contribute to the betterment of society.

In what follows, the development of project-based learning will be depicted by focusing on two case studies: the University of Bremen in Germany, and Michigan State University (MSU) in Lansing, United States.[4] The project method has been a vital element of academic affairs at both institutions. Since its initiation more than forty years ago, it has changed enormously due to shifts in student needs and desires, changing university conditions, and new local and federal education and science policies. In Bremen, its reformatory mission became highly contested and evermore regulated from the late 1970s. In Lansing, project-based learning caused less debate. However, its central scope was adjusted to further students' career perspectives.

It is the aim of this chapter to show that academic objectives might change considerably over time even though their formal structure remains the same, as in the case of project-based learning. The reasons lie not so much in reconsiderations of desirable pedagogical concepts, but often in pragmatic adjustments to changing political and institutional demands.

The factors that led to the initiation of project-based learning at MSU and the University of Bremen are comprehensible only in light of the very different situations at the respective institutions. In this chapter, these conditions are depicted briefly, before we turn to the initiation of project-based learning in more detail. Finally, the changes in project-based learning and the reasons for them are examined.

University of Bremen and Michigan State University

The history of project-based learning in Bremen is inextricably linked to the history of the university itself. This institution of higher education in the north of Germany was founded in 1971.[5] Bremen was only one of many new universities to be established at that time to meet the growing student population. The young institutions were also seen as answer to a perceived crisis in higher education.[6] Among other themes, student protestors and liberal education policy officials alike criticized science that was conducted in 'Einsamkeit und Freiheit' (loneliness and freedom) – in other words, detached from societal concerns.[7] Also, they disapproved of the traditional way of teaching, namely, the transmission of a body of knowledge regardless of its worth to the learner.[8]

Existing institutions of higher education were often seen as resistant to reform. Critics hoped that new institutions could implement change more easily. In Bremen, the university senate responsible for establishing the new institution decided that the university's aim was to conduct 'dynamic and critical science' that contributed to the development of society.[9] To accomplish that task, the senate decided to focus on reforming academic learning, especially in teacher training.[10] Traditional seminars did not seem able to achieve reform. Thus, the senate decided early on in the planning process to implement project-based learning as the predominant teaching method.[11]

As in Bremen, the history of project-based learning at MSU cannot be understood without a general knowledge of the university's history. During the twentieth century, MSU, 'America's pioneer land-grant college',[12] turned from an agricultural institution into one of the Big Ten internationally known, top research universities.[13] Mainly under the auspices of its president, John A. Hannah, MSU engaged in national and international research projects. One of the most famous, although also most contested, is MSU's engagement in Vietnam. In 1955, the Michigan State University Group (MSUG), the largest technical assistance project abroad initiated by the 'nation-building' programme of the Eisenhower administration, provided technical assistance, supported public administration, trained security personnel and wrote the South Vietnamese constitution.[14] With the (financial) help of the American government and initiatives such as MSUG, Ngo Dinh Diem, a former Vietnamese graduate research assistant at MSU, became the first president of South Vietnam in 1955.[15] The MSUG terminated in June 1962 when Diem's dictatorial politics finally led to the termination of the project group's work.[16] The case became widely known when *Ramparts* magazine published an article in 1966 linking MSUG to CIA operations.[17] MSUG definitely marked a change in the direction of the university's endeavours. While big research and international projects continued, protest at home grew stronger. Students and young faculty members criticized MSU's overseas projects and its pretended neutral support of governmental affairs.[18] In their views, MSU played an important part in helping to expand the 'hyperactive … American Empire'.[19] As a consequence, students at MSU started to develop their own educational programmes during the 1960s. Project-based learning became a central element. In the next section we look in detail at the development of the project-method at the two universities.

Project-Based Learning: The Initial Period

Project-based learning in Bremen and Lansing started at around the same time in answer to a perceived crisis in higher education. In Bremen, the university senate chose project-based learning as a new method to successfully reform academic teaching. Unfortunately, neither the senate nor any of its subordinate planning committees had much experience with this kind of technique. Only a little literature on the subject was available in Germany, and the number of examples at institutes of higher education in other countries was even fewer.[20] Thus, it took a considerable time for Bremen University to determine what project-based learning actually was before it could be implemented. In 1970, the planning committee on teacher education defined it as 'problem-oriented, job-oriented, interdisciplinary, and socially relevant'.[21]

Accordingly, academic studies were arranged in three phases. At the beginning, students attended different courses that all focused on introducing them to the social, political and economic conditions of their future profession. Then, two project phases followed, each covering three terms. Students could choose from projects that analysed specific problems of the teaching profession, such as education policy issues or philosophy of educational science. However, they could also select a project that covered societal problems in general. All the projects applied theories appropriated from a variety of disciplines to analyse the respective problems.[22] Furthermore, students had to develop their own teaching units and test them in schools at the end of each phase. Also, they had to hand in papers to be marked.[23] Taken together, project-based learning in Bremen aimed at fostering autonomous, critical, democratic and creative thinking, as well as communicative, cooperative and solidarity-oriented behaviour.[24] The planning committee conceptualized project-based learning in Bremen to provide a relevant teaching experience. Another goal was to offer projects that helped students to develop political consciousness.[25]

While project-based learning in Bremen was defined before it was actually executed, in Lansing it was executed long before it was considered to be an academic method. While activists protested in favour of university reforms during the 1960s, civic and political engagement of students and faculty members grew stronger. Already in 1963, the Student Education Corps was launched at MSU. Student volunteers helped teachers out in socially deprived areas by tutoring classes or individual students.[26] Another volunteer effort was conducted between 1965 and 1968. Within the framework of the Civil Rights Movement, MSU students went to Rust College in Holly Springs, Mississippi each summer to give tutorials on voter registration.[27] At the end of the 1960s, volunteering efforts at MSU had become so popular that several students decided to operate a central bureau that would bring the different initiatives together. On 22 November 1967, the Board of Trustees approved the establishment of the 'Office of Volunteer Programs', which was later renamed the 'Center for Service-Learning and Civic Engagement' (CSLCE, hereinafter 'the centre').[28] It was one of the first university-based centres to coordinate volunteer efforts in the country,[29] and, in contrast to the university senate and the planning committees in Bremen, it was originally student run.[30]

In Lansing, volunteer efforts were initially aimed at effecting social change.[31] However, educational benefits also played an important role at MSU: '[T]he volunteer programs give practical meaning and application to the lessons of the classroom. ... In addition, the somewhat abstract world of the classroom takes on new value as course content is seen as necessary and practical in a real-world setting'.[32]

At the beginning, however, the design of the projects was fairly simple. They were usually organized in the fields of education, recreation and correction.[33] Students gave tutorial assistance to children from schools in the community,[34] helped to build community gardens,[35] and provided photography courses for children.[36] The centre's role lay in matching the volunteer's interest with community needs. The academic component of the projects was only marginal. The centre offered orientation sessions that would give general information about the volunteer projects.[37] It also advertised university seminars related to the volunteer efforts. A famous example is the seminar entitled 'Volunteer Leadership Training', in which '[t]he content of the course focused on general leadership techniques, group dynamics, social problems, and most importantly, the methods of individual initiative in meeting the needs of our society'.[38]

In Bremen, as well as in Lansing, the initiation of project-based learning depended not only on the respective committee or centre. Often, political support led to more acceptance of academic innovation. In the case of Bremen, the German Science Council (*Wissenschaftsrat*) favoured the establishment of new universities.[39] In addition, the Federal Assistant Professors Council (*Bundesassistentenkonferenz*) encouraged the idea of implementing project-based learning.[40] On a more local level, the planning commission could initially count on the minister of education of the Bremen Senate, Moritz Thape, who argued in favour of reforms in Bremen in general and of project-based learning in particular.[41] All of these agents saw the need to change higher education to respond to the ever-increasing number of critics. Also in Lansing political support and national recognition have been important. The *Michigan State Journal* quoted the most important incidences in an article of 1970:

> Mrs Richard M. Nixon, the nation's First Lady, honoured MSU volunteers in March when she included Lansing on her list of sites to see college volunteers in action benefitting the community. The MSU volunteer effort was selected as one of four 1969 finalists for the Lane Bryant Volunteer Awards, annually recognizing outstanding individual or organization voluntary service on the community, state or national level. James R. Tanck, first director of the MSU volunteer office, accepted an offer from President Nixon, based on his MSU

service, to join the White House's Office of Youth Affairs to head the National Program for Voluntary Action.[42]

The interest in MSU volunteering, especially by top-ranking politicians, did not stem merely from a deep inner conviction of the usefulness of student volunteering. Similar to the situation in Bremen, the new projects seemed to offer an answer to the tumult on campus. They were 'constructive efforts to change and improve the world'.[43] Thus, politicians could counteract the predominantly negative news coverage of student protests and prove that they were still in control of educational matters.

Project-based learning in Bremen and Michigan had several similarities. They had started at almost the same time, and aimed at providing relevant teaching experience that was related to current societal issues and that furthered political awareness. However, the organizational structure was completely different. In Bremen, university leaders conceptualized project-based learning as a central teaching tool. In Lansing, the student-run centre was only one of numerous academic endeavours. These different concepts probably help to explain why it has been easier for the latter to implement change. It was simply less at the centre of attention than the former. Project-based learning changed dramatically at both institutions. Again, education policies played a decisive role in the matter. This time, however, they acted less in favour of initial concepts. The final section will now elaborate on this development.

Project-Based Learning – Contested and Regulated

The first major change in the constitution of early projects lay in the minimization of political engagement at both institutions. Creating political awareness and fostering social change were simply illusionary educational goals. In Lansing, students became frustrated when they realized their inability to change the social conditions of the children they took care of during their projects.[44] Gail Woods, a social work major involved in fieldwork at an elementary school, said: 'The hardest thing about this is that I like to see change, and with these kids it's very hard to see any'.[45] The situation in Bremen was similar. Some students were disappointed by the lack of scientific proficiency of their academic education. Wilfried Müller, former president of the University of Bremen and a student at that time, later recalled in an article: '[S]ome courses taught more political agitation than science'.[46]

The negative criticism endangered project-based learning. Although nationally known and praised, the centre in Lansing always struggled for financial support.[47] It could not afford to offer faulty projects. Apart from reacting to the criticisms expressed by students, that might have been an additional reason for director John H. Cauley, Jr. to tie the projects more closely to the academic affairs of the university.[48] Four major changes were implemented in the early 1970s: the orientation sessions were restructured 'to give the new volunteer as much information as possible for effectively carrying out a volunteer assignment'.[49] Moreover, the duration of the projects was prolonged to enhance the quality of the service experience.[50] To further minimize the risk of misconception, experienced volunteers offered leadership to new ones.[51]

In Bremen, the criticism of the political agenda of project-based learning resulted in profound controversy within and outside the university. Although members of the university senate and the different planning committees agreed on reforming higher education in Bremen in general, they had different ideas on how to achieve that reform.[52] Controversies about the conception of project-based learning resulted in a series of debate in 1970. Even some members of the different university groups considered the ideas of the planning committee to be too provocative and dismissed the concept.[53] The news media reported on the case, creating the long-lived image of the University of Bremen as a '*rote Kaderschmiede*' (socialist hotbed).[54] Project-based learning was always inextricably linked to that image. Though already contested at this early stage, project-based learning was still very common during the 1970s.[55] However, the aspired coherent project structure never existed.[56] Faculty lacked the necessary experience and sometimes the willingness to conceptualize projects.[57] Thus, more traditional seminars were offered.[58]

From the end of the 1970s, the project method was less often implemented in Bremen. This shift stemmed essentially from an increase in government regulation of higher education. In 1976, the Framework Act for Higher Education (*Hochschulrahmengesetz*) centralized its functions.[59] Technically, it left much room for individual institutions to experiment. Practically, innovative ideas could be executed only if compatible with the act. More importantly, from 1979 teacher exams were also federally organized,[60] and thus it became increasingly difficult to arrange reformatory learning concepts and impossible to provide other forms of exams.[61] As a result, project-based learning simply became less feasible. The new policies, together with a general hiring freeze in the teaching profession at that time, led to a shift in direction at the University of Bremen. From the early 1980s, the former emphasis on teaching shifted towards further engagement in research. Bremen became part of the German Research Foundation (*Deutsche Forschungsgemeinschaft*).[62] Again, project-based learning was affected by this shift in direction. In 1977, the famous project 'Contaminant loads and its proof in the workplace and in the Unterweser region' [Schadstoffbelastung und –nachweis am Arbeitsplatz und in der Region Unterweser – SAIU] received international recognition at a conference in Bremen.[63] Alexander Wittkowsky, then-president of the university, praised the project as a manifestation of the university's successful research endeavours, completely neglecting the importance that project-based learning used to have as an innovative teaching method.[64]

In Lansing, project-based learning was less contested. During the first half of the 1970s, however, the centre experienced a decrease in interest on the part of students.[65] Lower job prospects and the general economic crisis affected the student generation. Career training became fashionable. The centre adhered to the new demands. In 1976, its newsletter addressed future volunteers accordingly:

> You are ... very different from the student activist of the '60s who volunteered to change the social conditions of the world. ... Volunteering gives you a chance to explore the career you've chosen, to get some experience on the job, and to test in a 'real life' situation some of the theories you are learning in class.[66]

During the 1980s, the shift from serving the public good altruistically to stimulating career development became even more important to the centre. This time, federal and regional politics accounted for that change. In December 1984 the Governor's Commission on the Future of Higher Education in Michigan issued its report entitled 'Putting our Minds Together: New Directions for Michigan Higher Education'.[67] Resembling the federal report 'A Nation at Risk' of 1983, the rhetoric of the governor's commission also inextricably linked higher education to economic success. James K. Robinson, chairman of the commission, mentioned the scope of the report in his introductory letter: 'The emphasis throughout is on the vital partnership between our higher education system and our economic well-being. One cannot flourish without the other'.[68] Consequently, the commission suggested that Michigan's education system should help to provide 'greater access to relevant training programs and career choices' for its students.[69] Cecil Mackey, then-president at MSU, welcomed the report and its suggestions.[70] The times when political support for the centre's community service was guaranteed were long gone. Faced with decreasing funds from the early 1980s,[71] it was only reasonable to arrange the centre's mission according to the new wind in higher education.

Conclusion

Project-based learning was initiated internationally at different universities to answer a perceived crisis in higher education in the late 1960s and early 1970s. The projects aimed at constituting an academic method that applied scientific knowledge to societal and professional issues. Moreover, initially, project-based learning also aimed at stimulating the students' political consciousness. The early initiators hoped that the engaged students, as representatives of their universities, would contribute to the betterment of society – this, especially in the case of Bremen, led to a series of debates. The reform of higher education became thoroughly contested and, with it, the project method. Education policies further regulated the academic innovation. Though project-based learning never entirely vanished in Bremen, it was either associated with a politically motivated reform that had failed or received a totally new image as a useful research tool.

In Lansing, on the other hand, the project method began as mere volunteer service that was just one of many university endeavours. Though not as contested as in Bremen, initial attempts to achieve social change were soon discouraged, too. While project-based learning became more sophisticated over the years, changes in student needs and the demands from education policies further challenged the implementation of projects. In the end, it was directed almost solely at furthering students' career prospects to accord with political demands.

By comparing the two case studies from Bremen and Lansing, the chapter has tried to show that although project-based learning has been persistent for over forty years, its pedagogical objectives have changed considerably. The change in direction was not caused by reconsiderations of desirable learning outcomes, but often resulted from pragmatic adjustments to new trends in education and science policy as well as to institutional restrictions. The case of project-based learning exemplifies that the longevity of academic programmes during the last third of the twentieth century depended increasingly on their ability to secure money and prestige, and, thus, to respond to institutional and political demands. Therefore, the history of project-based learning shows that the process of transferring market-like efforts to the field of higher education – referred to as 'academic capitalism'[72] – also applied to academic teaching and learning.

Today, project-based learning is receiving renewed appreciation at both universities. The University of Bremen prides itself on belonging to a small number of German institutions of higher education that have been rated by the German Science Council as 'excellent'.[73] Its concept of the future includes ideas closely related to those of project-based learning.[74] In Lansing, community service gained renewed appreciation during the 1990s,[75] and in the academic year of 2010/11, nearly eighteen thousand students were accommodated through the CSLCE – roughly half of all the undergraduate students.[76]

Anna Wellner (née Groeben) holds a diploma from the University of Passau in Intercultural Business and Language Studies. From 2010 to 2015, Anna Wellner has been employed as teaching and research assistant at the University of Hamburg, Chair for North American, Carribean and Atlantic History. She is currently employed with the Project Management Agency of the German Centre for Aeronautics and Space Research (DLR-PT). Anna has scientific and teaching interests that focus on the history of science and higher education from the late eighteenth to the early twenty-first century. Her current research investigates the development of service-learning in US higher education, applying theories from the sociology of science to historical analysis. In 2012, together with Sarah Lentz and Claudia Schnurmann, she contributed the article 'Universities' to *Oxford Bibliographies in Atlantic History*, ed. Trevor Burnard (New York).

Notes

1. See CSLCE 'The Volunteer Action Effort at Michigan State University: A Report on the Initial Year of the M.S.U. Office of Volunteer Programs', 1968, 35–36; Julie A. Reuben, 'Reforming the University: Student Protests and the Demand for a "Relevant" Curriculum', in *Student Protest: The Sixties and After*, ed. Gerard J. DeGroot (London and New York, 1998), 153–68; Kenneth Heineman, *Campus Wars: The Peace Movement at American State Universities in the Vietnam Era* (New York and London, 1993), 2.

2. Heineman, *Campus Wars*, 78.

3. Timothy K. Stanton, Dwight E. Giles Jr. and Nadinne I. Cruz (eds), *Service-Learning: A Movement's Pioneers Reflect on its Origins, Practice, and Future* (San Francisco, 1999), 17–18.

4. In 2008, Michigan State University celebrated the 40th anniversary of the 'Center for Service-Learning and Civic Engagement' (CSLCE). Many of the centre's historical documents have not yet been officially archived. The author of this chapter gained access to the centre's private archive. In this chapter, the unarchived sources are cited according to the original document's title, adding the centre's name. Many thanks to Karen McKnight Casey, director of the CSLCE until June 2013, and Nicole Springer, associate director of the CSLCE, for providing this material.

5. Birte Gräfing, *Tradition Reform: Die Universität Bremen 1971–2001* (Bremen, 2012), 45.

6. Ibid., 18; Wilfried Rudloff, 'Die Gründerjahre des bundesdeutschen Hochschulwesens: Leitbilder neuer Hochschulen zwischen Wissenschaftspolitik, Studienreform und Gesellschaftspolitik', in *Zwischen Idee und Zweckorientierung: Vorbilder und Motive von Hochschulreformen seit 1945*, ed. Andreas Franzmann and Barbara Wolbring (Berlin, 2007), 79–80.

7. Rudloff, 'Die Gründerjahre', 80.

8. 'Protokoll der Diskussion zum Projektstudium', 40. Sitzung des Gründungssenats für die Universität Bremen vom 8. November 1970, 9.00 Uhr bis 9. November 1970 – 13.00 Uhr, Gründungssenat, 1/GS – 606, Universitätsarchiv, Universität Bremen, Bremen.

9. 'Eine dynamische und kritische Wissenschaft', Anlage 41/2, 41. Sitzung des Gründungssenats für die Universität Bremen 19. Dezember 1970, 11 Uhr bis zum 21. Dezember 1970, 17.30 Uhr, Gründungssenat, 1/GS – 606, Universitätsarchiv, Universität Bremen, Bremen.

10. Gräfing, *Tradition Reform*, 201.

11. 'Protokoll der Diskussion zum Projektstudium', 40.

12. David A. Thomas, *Michigan State College: John Hannah and the Creation of a World History, 1926–1969* (East Lansing, 2008), vii.

13. Ibid., xiv.

14. John Ernst, 'Forging a Fateful Alliance: The Role of Michigan State University in the Development of America's Vietnam Policy', *Michigan Historical Review* 19(2) (1993): 49–50; Heineman, *Campus Wars*, 22, 47; Thomas, *Michigan State College*, 227.

15. Heineman, *Campus Wars*, 46–47; Ernst, 'Forging a Fateful Alliance', 56–7.

16. Heineman, *Campus Wars*, 47; Ernst, 'Forging a Fateful Alliance', 50, 62.

17. Heineman, *Campus Wars*, 49; Thomas, *Michigan State College*, 229.

18. Thomas, *Michigan State College*, 232, 418.

19. Marge Piercy and Peter Henig, 'MSU – Expansionist University in an Imperialist State', in *The Paper*, 16 January 1968, 4, Box 2645, Folder 8, Grapevine Journal Collection, U.A.12.7.3, Michigan State University Archives & Historical Collections, East Lansing, Michigan.

20. 'Protokoll der Diskussion zum Projektstudium', 40.

21. 'Problemorientiert – fächerübergreifend integrativ – berufsbezogenen [*sic*] – und gesellschaftlich relevant', Informationsabteilung, 'Vorlage der Planungskommission Lehrerbildung für den Gründungssenat der Universität Bremen: Zum Projektstudium der Universität Bremen', 1975, 7/D, n°77, Universitätsarchiv, Universität Bremen, Bremen.

22. Thomas von der Vring, *Hochschulreform in Bremen: Bericht des Rektors über die Gründung und Aufbau der Universität Bremen während seiner Amtszeit von 1970–1974* (Frankfurt and Cologne, 1975), 80–82; Wiltrud Ulrike Drechsel and Bodo Voigt, 'Projektstudium in der Lehrerausbildung – Erfahrungen und Vorschläge', in *Reform-Ruinen: Bremen, Oldenburg, Roskilde*, ed. Wolfgang Nitsch (Hamburg, 1982), 139; Informationsabteilung, 'Vorlage der Planungskommission Lehrerbildung für den Gründungssenat der Universität Bremen: Zum Projektstudium der Universität Bremen', 1975, 7/D, n°77, Universitätsarchiv, Universität Bremen, Bremen; Gräfing, *Tradition Reform*, 204–5.

23. Informationsabteilung, 'Vorlage der Planungskommission'; Von der Vring, *Hochschulreform*, 80–82; C. Noack and F. Schmithals, 'Projektstudium an der Universität Bremen: zur Entwicklung in den naturwissenschaftlichen Studiengängen', in *Projektstudium in den Naturwissenschaften: Berichte vom Symposium, Project-Orientation in Higher Education for Science and Science-Based Professions. Bremen, 23.–26. März 1976*, ed. Friedemann Schmithals and Malcolm G. Cornwall (Hamburg, 1977), 41.

24. Bundesassistentenkonferenz, *Materialien zum Projektstudium* (Bremen, im November 1973), 62, 7/D, n° 338, Universitätsarchiv, Universität Bremen, Bremen.

25. See ibid., 64.

26. Seer Student Education Corps, 'Sketch and Perspective', n.d., Box F.D., Folder 5, Center for Service-Learning Records U.A. 7.15, Michigan State University Archives & Historical Collections, East Lansing, Michigan.

27. John Duley, 'The Origin and Execution of the MSU/Rust College STEP Project'. My reflections on it, n.d., CSLCE.

28. CSLCE, '1968–1988 Office of Volunteer Programs Service-Learning Center. Student Affairs and Services', 1968–88, 7, 9.

29. CSLCE, 'Annual Report, Office of Volunteer Programs', 1968–69, 1.

30. CSLCE, 'Annual Report, Office of Volunteer Programs', n.d., 2.

31. CSLCE, 'Volunteer Action Effort', 9.

32. Ibid., 27.

33. Mike Wagoner, 'MSU Volunteers. Campus Agency to Provide Help May Also Innovative New Programs', *The Michigan State Journal*, 20 August 1971, Box 1490, Folder 8,

SLC 1971–75, U.A. 8.1.1. Media Communications, Michigan State University Archives & Historical Collections, East Lansing, Michigan.

34. CSLCE, '1968–1988 Office of Volunteer Programs', 12–13.

35. CSLCE, 'Annual Report of the Office of Volunteer Programs', January–July 1968, 11.

36. Ibid.

37. CSLCE, 'Volunteer Action Effort', 89.

38. CSLCE, 'Annual Report, Office of Volunteer Programs', 1968–69, 4.

39. Rudloff, 'Die Gründerjahre', 77–78.

40. Anlage 41/2, 41. Sitzung des Gründungssenats für die Universität Bremen 19. Dezember 1970, 11 Uhr bis zum 21. Dezember 1970, 17.30 Uhr, Gründungssenat, 1/GS – 606, Universitätsarchiv, Universität Bremen, Bremen.

41. Mitteilungen der Pressestelle des Senats der Freien Hansestadt Bremen 2. Juli 1970, Gründungssenat, 1/GS – 623, Universitätsarchiv, Universität Bremen, Bremen.

42. Mike Wagoner, 'Student Volunteerism Big Business at MSU', in *The Michigan State Journal*, 26 May 1970, Box 1490, Folder 7, SLC 1967–70, U.A. 8.1.1. Media Communications, Michigan State University Archives & Historical Collections, East Lansing, Michigan.

43. 'Campus Wreckers Still in Minority', *The Michigan State Journal*, 17 September 1970, Box 1490, Folder 7, SLC 1967–70, U.A. 8.1.1. Media Communications, Michigan State University Archives & Historical Collections, East Lansing, Michigan.

44. Marion Nowak, 'The Volunteer in Action and Some Personal Views', in *Michigan State News*, 23 November 1969, Box 1490, Folder 7, SLC 1967–70, U.A. 8.1.1. Media Communications, Michigan State University Archives & Historical Collections, East Lansing, Michigan.

45. Ibid.

46. 'In manchen Fächern wurde mehr politische Agitation gelehrt als wissenschaftlich gearbeitet', Marion Schmidt, 'Hochschulmanager des Jahres: Wilfried Müller – der Wunderheiler von der Weser', in *Financial Times Deutschland*, 4 December 2012.

47. John E. Peterson, 'He's a Do-gooder's Samaritan', in *The Detroit News*, 1 November 1971, Box 1490, Folder 8, SLC 1971–75, U.A. 8.1.1. Media Communications, Michigan State University Archives & Historical Collections, East Lansing, Michigan; CSLCE, 'Service-Learning Center Annual Report,' 1980–81.

48. Wagoner, 'Student Volunteerism'.

49. CSLCE, 'Summary Annual Report Office of Volunteer Programs', 1970–71, 2; cf. Barbara Fary, 'Bureau Alters Orientation', in *Michigan State News*, 5 April 1971, Box 1490, Folder 8, SLC 1971–75, U.A. 8.1.1. Media Communications, Michigan State University Archives & Historical Collections, East Lansing, Michigan; Barbara McIntosh, News Release. News Bureau MSU, Department of Information Services, 17 March 1970, Box 1490, Folder 7, SLC 1967–70, U.A. 8.1.1. Media Communications, Michigan State University Archives & Historical Collections, East Lansing, Michigan.

50. 'Volunteer Opportunities for 1972', Box 1490, Folder 8, SLC 1971–75, U.A. 8.1.1. Media Communications, Michigan State University Archives & Historical Collections, East Lansing, Michigan; Fary, 'Bureau Alters Orientation'; Ray Anderson, 'Office Lacks Student Volunteers', in *Michigan State News*, 30 July 1971, Box 1490, Folder 8, SLC 1971–75, U.A. 8.1.1. Media Communications, Michigan State University Archives & Historical Collections, East Lansing, Michigan.

51. CSLCE, 'Annual Report, Office of Volunteer Programs', 1973–1974, 5.

52. 'Protokoll der Diskussion zum Projektstudium', 40; Jörn Schützenmeister, *Professionalisierung und Polyvalenz in der Lehrerausbildung* (Marburg, 2002), 250.

53. 'Protokoll der Diskussion zum Projektstudium,' 40; Anlage 40/3, 40. Sitzung des Gründungssenats für die Universität Bremen vom 8. November 1970, 9.00 Uhr bis 9. November 1970 – 13.00 Uhr, Gründungssenat, 1/GS – 606, Universitätsarchiv, Universität

Bremen, Bremen; 41. Sitzung des Gründungssenats für die Universität Bremen 19. Dezember 1970, 11 Uhr bis zum 21. Dezember 1970, 17.30 Uhr, Gründungssenat, 1/GS – 606, Universitätsarchiv, Universität Bremen, Bremen.

54. Rudloff, 'Die Gründerjahre', 98–99; Schmidt, 'Hochschulmanager des Jahres'; Gräfing, *Tradition Reform*, 15.

55. Noack and Schmithals, 'Projektstudium an der Universität Bremen', 40.

56. Von der Vring, *Hochschulreform*, 79.

57. Gräfing, *Tradition Reform*, 202; Schützenmeister, *Professionalisierung und Polyvalenz*, 250–51; Noack and Schmithals, 'Projektstudium an der Universität Bremen', 39.

58. Noack and Schmithals, 'Projektstudium an der Universität Bremen', 40.

59. Ulrich Teichler, 'Hochschulen: Die Verknüpfung von Bildung und Forschung', in *Handbuch Bildungsforschung*, ed. Rudolf Tippelt and Bernhard Schmidt (Wiesbaden, 2010), 428.

60. Schützenmeister, *Professionalisierung und Polyvalenz*, 242–43.

61. Ibid., 244.

62. (Peter) Maaß an 1. Senator für Bildung, Wissenschaft und Kunst z.Hd. Herrn Ditt, Betr.: Deutsche Forschungsgemeinschaft, Bremen, den 28. Februar 1975, 1/AS – 291, AS III/326, Universitätsarchiv, Universität Bremen, Bremen; Gräfing, *Tradition Reform*, 250, 252.

63. Gräfing, *Tradition Reform*, 207.

64. Ibid.

65. Anderson, 'Office Lacks Student Volunteers'; 'Volunteers Needed for MSU Bureau', in *The Michigan State Journal*, 25 September 1971, Box 1490, Folder 8, SLC 1971–75, U.A. 8.1.1. Media Communications, Michigan State University Archives & Historical Collections, East Lansing, Michigan; 'Unit Seeks Volunteers', in *Michigan State News*, 3 August 1973, Box 1490, Folder 8, SLC 1971–75, U.A. 8.1.1. Media Communications, Michigan State University Archives & Historical Collections, East Lansing, Michigan; 'Volunteer Bureau Lists Available Opportunities', in *Michigan State News*, 16 November 1972, Box 1490, Folder 8, SLC 1971–75, U.A. 8.1.1. Media Communications, Michigan State University Archives & Historical Collections, East Lansing, Michigan.

66. Jane Smith, 'Dimensions', in *MSU Volunteer*, December 1976, CSLCE.

67. The Governor's Commission on the Future of Higher Education in Michigan, 'Putting our Minds Together: New Directions for Michigan Higher Education. Final Report', December 1984, Box 1876, Folder 59, Commission on the Future of Higher Education 1983–86, U.A. 8.1.1. Media Communications, Michigan State University Archives & Historical Collections, East Lansing, Michigan.

68. Ibid.

69. Ibid.

70. Cecil Mackey, President Michigan State University, Statement on 'Putting our Minds Together: New Directions for Michigan Higher Education', 13 December 1984, Box 1876, Folder 59, Commission on the Future of Higher Education 1983–86, U.A. 8.1.1. Media Communications, Michigan State University Archives & Historical Collections, East Lansing, Michigan.

71. CSLCE, 'Service-Learning Center Annual Report', 1980–81.

72. Sheila Slaughter and Larry L. Leslie, *Academic Capitalism: Politics, Policies, and the Entrepreneurial University* (Baltimore, MD, 1997), 8.

73. See: http://www.bmbf.de/de/1321.php (accessed 28 March 2017).

74. Wilfried Müller, *Ambitioniert und agil: Antrag zur Einrichtung und Förderung eines Zukunftskonzepts zum projektbezogenen Ausbau der universitären Spitzenforschung*, Bremen, 26 August 2011, 2; available at: http://www.uni-bremen.de/fileadmin/user_upload/univer-sitaet/Exzellenzinitiative/Antrag_ExIni/Universitaet_Bremen_-_Zukunftskonzept_oA.pdf (accessed 28 March 2017).

75. CSLCE, 'Service-Learning Center. Annual Report', 1992–93.

76. See: http://www.servicelearning.msu.edu/about/history; and http://www.msu.edu/about/thisismsu/facts.html (accessed 28 March 2017).

Bibliography

Drechsel, Wiltrud Ulrike, and Bodo Voigt, 'Projektstudium in der Lehrerausbildung: Erfahrungen und Vorschläge', in *Reform-Ruinen: Bremen, Oldenburg, Roskilde*, ed. Wolfgang Nitsch (Hamburg, 1982), 113–47.

Ernst, John, 'Forging a Fateful Alliance: The Role of Michigan State University in the Development of America's Vietnam Policy', *Michigan Historical Review* 19(2) (1993): 49–50.

Gräfing, Birte, *Tradition Reform: Die Universität Bremen 1971–2001* (Bremen, 2012).

Heineman, Kenneth, *Campus Wars: The Peace Movement at American State Universities in the Vietnam Era* (New York and London, 1993).

Noack, C., and F. Schmithals, 'Projektstudium an der Universität Bremen: zur Entwicklung in den naturwissenschaftlichen Studiengängen', in *Projektstudium in den Naturwissenschaften: Berichte vom Symposium, Project-Orientation in Higher Education for Science and Science-Based Professions. Bremen, 23–26 März 1976*, ed. Friedemann Schmithals and Malcolm G. Cornwall (Hamburg, 1977), 41.

Reuben, Julie A., 'Reforming the University: Student Protests and the Demand for a "Relevant" Curriculum', in *Student Protest: The Sixties and After*, ed. Gerard J. DeGroot (London and New York, 1998), 153–68.

Rudloff, Wilfried, 'Die Gründerjahre des bundesdeutschen Hochschulwesens: Leitbilder neuer Hochschulen zwischen Wissenschaftspolitik, Studienreform und Gesellschaftspolitik', in *Zwischen Idee und Zweckorientierung: Vorbilder und Motive von Hochschulreformen seit 1945*, ed. Andreas Franzmann and Barbara Wolbring (Berlin, 2007), 77–101.

Schützenmeister, Jörn, *Professionalisierung und Polyvalenz in der Lehrerausbildung* (Marburg, 2002).

Slaughter, Sheila, and Larry L. Leslie, *Academic Capitalism: Politics, Policies, and the Entrepreneurial University* (Baltimore, MD, 1997).

Stanton, Timothy K., Dwight E. Giles Jr. and Nadinne I. Cruz (eds), *Service-Learning: A Movement's Pioneers Reflect on its Origins, Practice, and Future* (San Francisco, 1999).

Teichler, Ulrich, 'Hochschulen: Die Verknüpfung von Bildung und Forschung', in *Handbuch Bildungsforschung*, ed. Rudolf Tippelt and Bernhard Schmidt (Wiesbaden, 2010), 421–44.

Thomas, David A., *Michigan State College: John Hannah and the Creation of a World History, 1926–1969* (East Lansing, 2008).

Vring, Thomas von der, *Hochschulreform in Bremen: Bericht des Rektors über die Gründung und Aufbau der Universität Bremen während seiner Amtszeit von 1970–1974* (Frankfurt and Cologne, 1975).

Part III

REGULATORY TRANSITIONS IN ENTERPRISE PRACTICES

CHAPTER 10

Technological Advance, Transatlantic Trade, External Equilibrium

American Financial Assistance to the Italian Nuclear Power Programmes from the 1960s through to the First Oil Crisis

SIMONE SELVA

Introduction

After the implementation of the Marshall Plan in the late 1940s and through the following financial and economic assistance programmes promoted under the umbrella of US governments, NATO, and the international economic institutions born out of the 1944 Bretton Woods conference, foreign economic assistance was a vital component of the American stabilization policies towards the West European partners and other industrial democracies. A variety of issues at the end of the Second World War contributed to it: among others, the post-war strength of the US dollar against other currencies, the dollar scarcity plaguing most European economies, and the much-needed rescue of war-torn European societies, as well as a widespread perception of the Soviet threat as a by-product of economic scarcity. All of these aspects of the post-war era made the foreign aid programmes of US governments, and American economic assistance in general, the best way of achieving political stabilization all across Western Europe. During the second half of the 1950s the International Bank for Reconstruction and Development (IBRD) and the International Monetary Fund (IMF) began pairing off with Washington's official foreign assistance programmes through either infrastructural or balance of payments aid. From the early 1960s through to the first oil crisis, when the international system – led by the United States, and revolving around the dollar as laid down at Bretton Woods – collapsed, the post-war US foreign aid policy, that had aimed to promote economic recovery and extend or strengthen American political influence on the allies, faded away. With the historical downturn of dwindling US balance of payments from around 1958, through to the progressive shrinking in the US balance of trade that eventually turned into deficit in 1971, American foreign aid programmes proved to be outdated and unsuccessful in strengthening transatlantic political and economic bonds with European partner economies.

Through a case study of American economic support of Italy's nuclear power policies and programmes until the start of the first oil crisis, this chapter explores the attempt by the United States to replace direct foreign aid – drawing on federal funds approved by the US Congress, typical of the post-war era – with the promotion of continued economic bonds, either in the trade or the financial field, based on resources coming from private or federal banks, such as the Export Import Bank of the United States, or the Bretton Woods international economic institutions, mostly the IBRD. In the framework of increasingly transnational exchange in consumer goods and flows in capital, US promotion of new energy sources such as nuclear power aimed to help Italy both in coping with the energy crisis, and in preventing her from further economic doldrums and political instability. In such a manner, during the 1970s US foreign assistance programmes made the removal of controls on international capital movements and trade the pillar of a foreign aid policy that, consistently with the past, used economic aid to tackle the internal political stability of Italy and to support her continued transatlantic foreign policy.[1] As a matter of fact, owing to the economic meltdown and political uncertainty that hit Italy during the 1970s, the economic assistance to Rome's energy policy demonstrates that American policymakers wished to stimulate trade exchanges in raw materials, capital-intensive instrumental goods and energy products, with the aim both to strengthen the productivity of Italian industry, which was at that time under severe strain due to the oil price hikes, and to promote domestic growth. The latter target, in turn, was an essential step to warrant the internal stability of Italy and to keep her under the US sphere of influence. Therefore, through the case study of technology exchanges, and the financial flows to finance them, we can establish a linkage between the framework of unfettered international trade and capital flows germane to the deregulation arising during this decade, and the possibility to recast bilateral political bonds on the part of the United States.

American assistance to the Italian nuclear power programmes tightened existing political bonds between the two countries, promoting unfettered transatlantic trade and financial relations. In fact, notwithstanding its collapse and final demise by the late 1970s, US nuclear assistance met a long-standing Italian call on Washington and the Western community to finance the ambitious nuclear power programmes that ENEL, the state-owned concern for energy production and distribution born out of the 1962 nationalization of the Italian energy sector, had planned for construction and operation since the very late 1960s. This story demonstrates that in the twentieth-century history of US foreign economic relations, foreign aid was a successful way to shape and to push forward American foreign policy: in fact, though the US government discontinued nuclear assistance to Rome at the start of the 1980s, it let bilateral relations between the two countries get through a decade of economic doldrums and political turmoil.

Finally, through the case study of Italy we investigate the extent to which the search for alternative energy sources to oil affected a number of very different areas. Ranging from the pace of industrial modernization to the stability of the foreign exchange equilibrium, through to the interplay between the development of energy policies and the involvement of capital markets to finance them, the debate and implementation of nuclear production for civilian uses sheds light on a variety of topics. Before delving into reconstruction it is worth looking briefly at the details of these varying objectives. From the viewpoint of international economic relations, one leading and consolidated interpretation of US energy policy in the period makes the argument that Washington, while considering energy diversification policies to be essential in coping with the oil crisis, supported a slow and constant oil price rise by the OPEC oil-exporting countries in order to retain negotiating heft with them and to bolster American hegemony over the West European oil-importing industrial nations. According to the most authoritative works on the subject, the United States favoured oil price hikes to strengthen its worldwide economic prominence and to stimulate the development of alternative energy policies.[2] By contrast, researching US support for the Italian nuclear power programmes during the 1970s helps us to understand Washington's commitment to easing the industrial democracies off dependence on the non-Western oil-producing countries as a way of ensuring stable economic and political relations within the Western community. The case study of nuclear power sheds light on the US search for promoting an oil import substitution energy policy across its European partners, with the aim both to resurrect their balance of trade, which had been hit hard by the first oil crisis, and to make technological trade and commercial partnership with the United States grow larger. In this respect, the turn towards the nuclear sector showcases the twofold economic and political stabilization strategy towards Italy: it was both to ease off the strains of peaking oil prices on the Italian foreign trade, and to strengthen American involvement in Italian internal affairs through the financial, industrial and diplomatic bonds that bilateral negotiations on American and IBRD assistance to this industrial field stimulated.

We shall also argue that the search for alternative energy policies by the West European countries linked the stabilization of transatlantic commercial bonds to the trajectories of technological development across the Old Continent. In doing so, we closely follow the relatively recent literature on the impact of the early American economic assistance programmes on the recovery of Europe. From Eichengreen to Behrman, these scholarly works stress the extent to which, from shortly after the end of the Second World War, Washington aimed to combine the reorganization of domestic European markets through industrial upgrade and the reintegration of the European economy within the post-war system of transatlantic economic and political cooperation.[3] During both the reconstruction of the late 1940s and the economic upswing of the 1950s, as well as over the course of the gloomy early 1970s, the dual impact of American economic aid to Europe took place in the framework of a US strategy aimed to make foreign economic assistance a power lever to extend and to consolidate American political influence across Western Europe. During both periods, the United States linked support of industrial upgrade to the shaping of US–European trade bonds to respectively build up and reorganize American political-economic hegemony over Western Europe, and on a global scale. In fact, during the early 1950s the supra-national integration of the West European economies within the framework of the European integration process was linked to an industrial modernization based on the import of average capital-intensive instrumental goods from dollar markets. Likewise, the case study of Italy in the 1970s demonstrates that the development of nuclear production programmes based on American technology was an excellent gateway to advance a capital-intensive leap forward in the Italian energy-producing and mechanical industries. In turn, as this chapter will show, the development of nuclear power was to reduce the strains imposed by the fourfold oil price rise on the competitiveness of Italian manufactured goods in both domestic and foreign markets, thus propping up internal economic expansion. Therefore, the United States played a crucial role both in the process of Italian industrial modernization, and in the reorganization of Italy's foreign economic relations.

This chapter will also highlight how US support for the Italian nuclear power projects in order to ease the country's dependence on foreign oil supplies following the first oil shock triggered an uneven financing issue. Unlike the economic assistance programmes of previous decades, declining

Congress appropriations for foreign assistance brought the role of domestic and international capital markets substantially into the picture.

American nuclear assistance to Italy during the 1970s is an exemplary case to assess the level of capital markets deregulation and trade liberalization typical of the period; the efforts of the American government to finance ENEL's import requirements and investments, and American companies' and banks' involvement in the business of nuclear power, help to situate the decade as a significant leap forward in the late twentieth-century ascendancy of economic neoliberalism in forging the system of international economic relations.[4]

We shall limit our reconstruction to the first oil shock because it was during the period from the deterioration of the Bretton Woods fixed exchange rate system in the late 1960s through to the first oil crisis that the economic targets of technological advance, transatlantic trade cooperation and the remaking of European manufacturers' competitiveness on foreign markets were intended by the United States to make economic and financial assistance a glue to secure only the internal stability of the country. By contrast, as some recent historical research has stressed, from 1975 through to the second oil crisis, the United States provided financial assistance to target the country's balance of payments problems and industrial upgrade both to recast Italy's domestic growth and political stand, and to tackle political issues pertaining to the country's foreign policy. In particular, during the second half of the decade the Americans aimed to prevent Rome from changing its international political status. To date, historians have linked the US energy and economic assistance programmes and the American objective of keeping Italy from falling under the sway of the Middle East oil-producing countries, as well as from veering any further to the political left.[5]

American Nuclear Assistance before the 1970s: From European Integration to Transatlantic Commerce and Technological Transfer

In his thorough reconstruction, Gunnar Skogmar has convincingly maintained that the United States supported the first stage of European nuclear cooperation as a way of launching the process of European economic integration as early as the mid-1950s, most notably through full support for the establishment of Euratom.[6] Notwithstanding Washington's early active role in making the nuclear industry a bulkhead of the European integration process, it was only during the second half of the 1960s that American policymakers linked it to the strengthening of trade and industrial bonds between the US and West European economies. At the end of the 1950s the IBRD, at the forefront in financing a number of early nuclear power programmes in the least-developed West European countries in accordance with US government policy, had failed to consider such a support as a way of bridging transatlantic economic cooperation and promoting trade exchanges between the United States and the EEC countries. In the Italian case, for example, in the very late 1950s the IBRD clearly framed its funding of the first nuclear power station against the backdrop of the development assistance programmes launched to promote the building of basic infrastructures across the least-developed countries. Notwithstanding the Italian government's call to establish a link between that nuclear power programme and the recasting of stable trade exchanges between Rome and Washington, the IBRD did not pay much attention to the impact of nuclear power on industrial modernization and exports.[7] It was only by the second half of the 1960s that the United States turned to the nuclear sector for civilian production purposes to advance European industrial upgrade and to promote transatlantic trade cooperation with its European partners. Furthermore, on the eve of the 1970s, Washington aimed to protect its European allies' balance of payments and terms of trade, increasingly under pressure due to rising prices on the international commodities markets. A number of reasons account for this turn. On one hand, it is worth mentioning the Johnson administration's deep concerns about the harmful implications for transatlantic relations of a long-standing technological gap between the United States and Western Europe. This gap induced Washington to facilitate technological transfer to prevent restrictive business practices and protectionist trade reactions by the Europeans, a mighty scenario that would in turn be harmful to the US political heft over the Old Continent.[8] On the other hand, what made the US government focus on the development of nuclear production capabilities for civilian purposes across Western Europe was the financial impact of the oil price rise that occurred in the late 1960s on the balance of payments of European partners. Although the exceptional stability of crude petroleum prices lasted until 1970,[9] in the wake of the Arab–Israeli War and the closure of the Suez Canal oil prices peaked, and the decision of the Middle East oil-producing countries not to accept any more payments in sterling made the international oil market an essentially dollar-denominated trade system.[10] This wave of events, soon followed by the Deutschmark revaluation, at the same time eroded both oil prices and the Bretton Woods fixed exchange rate system. In the United Kingdom, soon after the 1967 sterling devaluation, an earlier increase in nominal oil prices on international markets was aggravated by the decision of the British oil companies operating in the Middle East oil fields to impose a surcharge on import prices.[11] This sequence of events, combined with substantially decreasing production costs in the assembly of nuclear power plants,[12] fully explains the American move to make Europeans go nuclear in the very late 1960s. The US government's attitude to relaxing its security control policy on the transfer of nuclear technology, tightly enforced throughout the 1960s, offers us an opportunity to track this American move.

This unilateral US control policy was eased when the International Atomic Energy Agency (IAEA), an agency of the United Nations, took over responsibility for disseminating technical information involved in the use of nuclear energy for peaceful uses. In particular, the IAEA was charged with sharing information on technology required to implement the nuclear power programmes set up by the West European countries during the 1960s. From 1968, this agency also became the administrator of the Nuclear Non-Proliferation Treaty (NPT). As such, the IAEA was supposed to implement safeguards and conduct inspections.[13] Notwithstanding this transfer of responsibility from the US government to the IAEA, by the beginning of the 1970s Washington was still keeping sensitive uranium enrichment technology under its full control. The change in US policy on uranium enrichment-related technologies in the early 1970s marked a step towards sharing technical know-how and industrial expertise on nuclear power with West European partners. As early as 1969, President Nixon directed a 'wider study of the feasibility of alternative ownership arrangements for US enriched uranium production facilities to investigate the national security implications of public and private ownership'.[14] More importantly, the following year the US administration directed another review to specifically determine whether any kind of security classification of uranium enrichment technology, either gaseous diffusion technology or the centrifugal process, was still needed.[15]

From the turn of the decade to the devaluation of the dollar, Nixon considered both declassifying technical information on nuclear technology and engaging in trade exchange of high added-value components with West European partners. In 1971 the White House set up an ad hoc inter-ministerial group chaired by the Department of State to investigate the peaceful application of atomic energy. In establishing this committee, Washington aimed to promote international technical cooperation with the other advanced industrial nations, as well as to review American export controls on the interchange of nuclear technologies and equipment.[16] On the eve of the oil crisis, the US government moved to relax restrictions on 'the transfer to other countries of highly enriched uranium for the fuelling of nuclear power reactors' in light of 'current and prospective demand for highly enriched uranium'.[17] Therefore, prior to the oil crisis American policymakers had already linked the removal of controls on the transfer of sensitive nuclear technology to the objective of extending commercial bonds between the United States and its partner economies, and to strengthen broad American influence over Europe.

A Flywheel to Technological Advance, Trade Cooperation and External Equilibrium: Nuclear Power Programmes in the late 1960s

The US financial assistance programme for Italy enables us to track this trend in American international energy policy from the late 1960s into the 1970s. The United States and the international economic institutions set up at the 1944 Bretton Woods conference had showed interest in Italian energy matters as early as the late 1950s. In 1959 the World Bank approved a loan to finance the first nuclear power station built in Italy under its umbrella. During the implementation of that early IBRD assistance project, which involved both the financing of technological imports and the training of personnel, the 1962 nationalization of the Italian electricity industry triggered a substantial capital outflow leaving the sector on the verge of potential financial constraints.[18] The IBRD and the US Treasury reacted to the establishment of ENEL by anticipating the future retrenchment from financing the Italian nuclear programme. Notwithstanding this fierce reaction, over the second half of the 1960s the American commitment to advancing the Italian nuclear sector gained momentum, enhancing the transfer of American technology and the involvement of US companies in Italian industrial affairs and foreign trade. In 1967 an Italian–American industrial partnership between Ansaldo Meccanica Nucleare (AMN), a firm controlled by the state shareholding specializing in the mechanical sectors (IRI), and General Electric (GE), a leading American company, established Fabbricazioni Nucleari (FN) to produce the highly specialized and capital-intensive components required for thermonuclear power plants.[19] On the other hand, for its part the World Bank did not discontinue its 1959 financial assistance programme until the second half of the 1970s.[20] Against this backdrop of American-financed transfer of technology and know-how, the Italian industry increased its participation in European industrial consortia and trade exchanges. In the late 1960s a firm controlled by the state hydrocarbon agency (ENI) received an order to build a fuel-processing reactor, which led to a partnership with the French Commissariat à l'Energie Atomique.[21]

Thus American assistance to the Italian nuclear power programme set in motion technological transfer, rising competitiveness on foreign markets and a corollary increase in trade exchange and commercial relations in the sector, at both European and transatlantic levels. In this respect, the Italian case is exemplary of a consistent and worldwide American policy. By the late 1960s, in the Portuguese colonies the Export–Import Bank of the United States financed the development of Portugal's energy sector to bolster commercial bonds between European colonies and US manufacturers.[22] In the Middle East, the US government itself launched a significant

financial assistance package to promote the export to Iran of uranium enrichment technology and of several highly value-added industrial components,
which thereafter expanded further over the course of the 1970s.[23] In the
Mediterranean basin, Washington enhanced a number of technology trans-
fer-based economic assistance programmes to help the Greek government
build nuclear reactors to produce power for domestic use.[24] Therefore, right
before the first energy crisis, the Italian case sheds light on a much broader
American move to make the nuclear sector a flywheel to promote both
international trade and domestic industrial advancement in developing and
industrializing countries. By the early 1970s a variety of funding institutions
had replaced US Congress appropriations, but the transfer of technology
in the framework of American international nuclear policy contributed to
strengthen American global influence and to expand freely floating transnational flows in goods and capital.

This American turn gained further sway in light of the early 1970s energy
crisis and the ensuing international economic downturn. The evolution of
American policy towards Italy offers us a good opportunity to examine the
development of US international energy policies in the 1970s as a step over
in the process of increasingly unregulated and expanding international trade
and capital movements.

American Assistance in the Making, and Italy's Betting on the Nuclear Option after the End of Bretton Woods

While the Nixon administration reviewed the control policy on nuclear
technology dissemination and transfer to friendly nations, IRI, ENI and
the Italian government set in motion Italy's nuclear programme for the
1970s to develop the very objectives underpinning American financial
assistance to the Europeans. In fact, the Italian nuclear power programme
was supposed to enhance industrial cooperation and trade partnership with
European and American allies through technological advance. The programme also aimed to convert petroleum-powered facilities into nuclear-
powered industrial premises in order to shape an import-substituting
alternative energy policy. In turn, this move was supposed to cut the oil
import bill, reduce the energy costs of Italian manufacturers and improve
their competitiveness on foreign markets.

From the start, the programme, launched in 1971, involved both
public entities and private industrial groups, all operating under American
licences. That year, IRI and ENI created two consortia led by the two
state shareholdings, respectively. They were to produce recent generation
nuclear power reactors and fuel processing production cycles. The two

state entities linked their commitment to convert some of their production chains to nuclear power programmes to joining European and international consortia. According to the Italians, participation in international cooperation initiatives would be conducive to importing nuclear technology and exporting power reactors and components.[25] Over the next two years, Italy joined three European collaborative initiatives. The first was EURODIF, a French-led group including Italy, Belgium, Spain and Iran, to build a gaseous diffusion plant to enrich uranium.[26] Then, the Italian firm NIRA and the French Commissariat à l'Energie Atomique signed a memorandum of understanding to develop research on the production of recent generation fast nuclear reactors. In a third instance, ENEL, the French EDF and others started collaboration to build up recent generation fast nuclear reactors. Finally, ENI became involved in ACE, an international consortium to develop centrifuge technology to enrich uranium.[27] In all these cases, the attempt to catch up technologically as a condition of entering trade exchanges with other European countries and the United States underpinned the Italian effort.

Following the 1973 fourfold rise in the price of crude petroleum, the West European countries pushed forward their energy diversification policies by implementing extensive nuclear power programmes. The US government was well aware of how crucial it was to help the Europeans and the Italians finance those programmes to develop technological advance and competitiveness on foreign markets. According to the Defense Intelligence Agency of the US Department of Defense, notwithstanding a significant advance in manufacturing most of the equipment and facilities needed to produce nuclear power, 'the small size of the European countries and their correspondingly small financial base has been a major impediment to the growth of their nuclear power programs'.[28] From 1973, following dollar devaluation and the beginning of the oil crisis, Washington undertook consistent support for the Italian nuclear power programme. In so doing, the United States took advantage of both dollar devaluation, and the recent American relaxation on the control of exchange of nuclear technology information and equipment transfer: dollar devaluation made the export of American technology cheaper for European importers, whereas relaxation on the control of equipment transfer let American firms export a larger array of products.

In December 1973 ENEL announced the placing of two procurement contracts with two consortia, one of private firms led by Fiat and one headed by AMN. They were to put into production two nuclear power plants, each with a capacity of 1,000 MW for an expected total cost of up to USD 1 billion.[29] These two contracts were the hallmark of an intensive and short-lived period of bilateral negotiations on the scale of American financial support to these ambitious Italian programmes. Right before the announcement of ENEL, American foreign technology and trade policies had definitely turned to support West European countries' nuclear plans. Furthermore, although as late as summer 1972 the Department of State still bound the transfer to friendly nations of highly enriched uranium to the ratification of NPT,[30] by 1973 the United States considered technology dissemination and the selling to European partners of capital-intensive nuclear equipment to be of the utmost importance to strengthen transatlantic political and economic relations.[31] The White House thus paired easing of American control over nuclear technology with supplying highly enriched uranium.[32] On the other hand, in the course of 1973 the US administration showed an increasing commitment to financing technological exports to let American industry take advantage of exchanges of technological equipment. Using the Italian case for reference, in autumn 1973 the US Department of Commerce directed a detailed review of the export opportunities that the ongoing Italian labour-saving industrial restructuring could offer to American manufacturers.[33] In this respect, ENEL's import programmes to erect the two nuclear power plants was an excellent opportunity for US exporters: the Italian state entity expected that '20 per cent of total investments, according to engineers of the nuclear section, will comprise special equipment, components and instrumentation to be imported from the US'.[34]

The implementation of ENEL's nuclear power programme occurred even as the country had to cope with the most hard-hitting balance of payment crisis to date.[35] Following the first oil shock, from the 1973 Italian lira devaluation to the beginning of ENEL's nuclear power programme and throughout the first half of 1974, the Central Bank of Italy both repeatedly intervened on foreign exchange markets to support the Italian import industries, and resorted to the country's net official assets to finance the balance of payments deficit.[36] This policy led the Italian monetary authorities to finance domestic investments by combining a number of monetary policy measures. The government devised three ways to reach this target: it resorted to direct industrial investments by the state; it borrowed bonds from the securities market; and it forced the domestic capital market to impede capital outflows. The way in which Rome financed ENEL's programme is a case in point: from the summer of 1973 to the first semester of 1974, the Central Bank forced the Italian commercial banks to divert their flexible-rate short-term investments towards medium- and long-term fixed-interest securities. This policy of selective credit control was supposed to make the Italian commercial banks purchase bonds issued by ENEL, IRI and ENI to finance capital-intensive investments.[37]

Concluding Remarks

Drawing on the Italian case, it is quite clear that the United States offered its support to promote the development of nuclear power for peaceful uses across Western Europe from as early as the 1960s to promote European economic integration and transatlantic trade. However, it was only from the rise of oil prices and the deterioration of international monetary stability to the dollar devaluation that American assistance to finance the development of nuclear production was linked to promoting technological advance and competitiveness across Western Europe. These goals were pursued by expanding commercial bonds between the two continents. The full American support for the Italian nuclear power programme during the early 1970s further demonstrates these US objectives. It also sheds light on the link between Italy's dependence on foreign oil and the impact of the oil crisis on industrial competitiveness and balance of payments. In this perspective, the search for import substitution energy policies through nuclear power helps us to track how the US financial assistance was intended to promote energy policies that were an alternative to foreign oil supply. Against this backdrop the United States channelled technological transfer to resurrect its European allies' competitiveness and to cope with the strains of the oil shock on balances of payments. In this framework, the case of nuclear assistance to Italy sheds light on the link between the US international energy policy, American technological transfer, and the strengthening of transatlantic economic bonds, in turn a prerequisite to bolster American business and political involvement in European affairs during the critical decade of the 1970s. If we keep an eye on the story of American nuclear energy policy from the late 1950s through to the first oil crisis, two things clearly emerge: first, the increasing involvement of private and international financial institutions in the shaping and financing of American foreign aid programmes; and second, that nuclear assistance took place alongside a staggering expansion of transnational flows in both capital and goods typical of the time frame from the 1960s to the first half of the 1970s, and within a framework of broad state retrenchment and unfettered transnational markets.

Simone Selva is currently a research fellow in the History of International Economic Relations at the Università degli studi di Napoli 'L'Orientale'. He is the author of *Supra-national Integration and Domestic Economic Growth: The United States and Italy in the Western Bloc Rearmament Programs, 1945–1955* (Brussels, New York, Oxford and Frankfurt, 2012), as well as of *Before the Neoliberal Turn: The Rise of Energy Finance and the Limits to US Foreign Economic Policy* (London, 2017)

Notes

1. The removal of barriers and preferences on international trade and on capital movements led the US trade negotiations with the EEC well in advance of the first oil crisis. For this firm American stance, see for reference the US government documents located in RG56, General Records of the Department of the Treasury, Office of the Assistant Secretary for International Affairs, Office of the Deputy Assistant Secretary for International Monetary Affairs, Briefing Books 1971–1980, b. 1, National Archives and Records Administration, College Park, Maryland (hereinafter NARA).

2. Simon Bromley, *American Hegemony and World Oil: Industry, the State System, and the World Economy* (University Park, PA, 1991); G. John Ikenberry, *Reasons of State: Oil Politics and the Capacities of American Government* (Ithaca, NY, 1988). Some fresh new and authoritative studies making this point have recently appeared: see David Painter, 'Oil and the American Century', *Journal of American History* 99(1) (June 2012): 24–39; Timothy Mitchell, *Carbon Democracy: Political Power in the Age of Oil* (London, 2011); Kenneth A. Rodman, *Sanctity versus Sovereignty: The United States and the Nationalization of Natural Resource Investments* (New York, 1988). For a more traditional interpretation of the oil price hikes as a unilateral initiative of the OPEC countries, see Fiona Venn, *The Oil Crisis* (London, 2002).

3. Greg Behrman, *The Most Noble Adventure: The Marshall Plan and the Time when America Helped Save Europe* (New York, 2007); Barry Eichengreen, *The European Economy since 1945: Coordinated Capitalism and Beyond* (Princeton, NJ, 2007). Recently some more monographs have followed this approach: see Francesca Fauri and Paolo Tedeschi (eds), *Novel Outlooks on the Marshall Plan: American Aid and European Re-Industrialization* (Brussels, 2011); Simone Selva, *Supra-national Integration and Domestic Economic Growth* (Brussels, 2012); David Ellwood, *The Shock of America: Europe and the Challenge of the Century* (Oxford, 2012).

4. For a rather different interpretation about the meaning of the 1970s in the history of trade liberalization and transnational capital movements, see Giuseppe La Barca, *International Trade in the 1970s: The US, the EC and the Growing Pressure of Protectionism* (London, 2013). According to this study, most industrial economies reacted to the recession by significantly withdrawing from the process of international economic integration to drift into their respective national markets.

5. Mario Del Pero, 'The US and the Crises in Southern Europe', in *Europe in the International Arena in the 1970s*, ed. Antonio Varsori and Guia Migani (Brussels, 2011), 301–16; Silvio Labbate, 'Italy and the Development of European Energy Policy: From the Dawn of the Integration Process to the 1973 Oil Crisis', *International History Review* 20(1) (2013): 67–93; Umberto Gentiloni Silveri, *L'Italia sospesa: La crisi degli anni Settanta vista da Washington* (Turin, 2009); Olav Njolstad, 'The Carter Administration and Italy: Keeping the Communists Out of Power without Interfering', *Journal of Cold War Studies* 3 (2002): 56–94; Irwin Wall, 'L'amministrazione Carter e l'Eurocomunismo', *Ricerche di Storia Politica* 2 (2006): 181–96; Alessandro Brogi, *Confronting America: The Cold War between the United States and the Communists in France and Italy* (Chapel Hill, NC, 2011), 335ff. The latest studies that appeared on US nuclear policy towards Italy took a much broader approach to the subject by exploring technological and cultural cooperation in the field: see for instance Elisabetta Bini and Igor Londero (eds), *Nuclear Italy: An International History of Italy's Nuclear Policies during the Cold War* (Trieste, 2017).

6. Gunnar Skogmar, *The United States and the Nuclear Dimension of European Integration* (Basingstoke and New York, 2004).

7. Remarks by Mr. C. Allardice, adviser on atomic energy to the World Bank before the European Conference for Industrial Management, Stresa, Italy, 11–14 May 1959, in Country Operational Files – Italy, Fold. Nuclear Power Project-Italy-Loan 235-Negotiations-Vol. 3, World Bank Group Archive, Washington DC (hereinafter WBGA).

8. In this respect, see the Report of the Interdepartmental Committee on the Technological Gap, 27 December 1967, in Declassified Documents and Reference System: http://www.gale.com/primary-sources (hereinafter DDRS).

9. IMF, 'Petroleum Average Crude Prices 1950–2011', *International Financial Statistics (IFS)*, available at: http://data.imf.org/TimeSeries?key=61409989 (accessed 26 March 2017).

10. Barry Eichengreen, *Exorbitant Privilege: The Rise and Fall of the Dollar* (Oxford, 2011), 57.

11. Memorandum by the Minister of Power, 'Oil Prices: Devaluation and Surcharge', 19 December 1967, in Cabinet Papers, The National Archives, Kew, Richmond (hereinafter TNA).

12. The World Bank Assistant Director to the Engineering Project Department to the President of ENEL, 23 February 1967, Country Operational File-Italy, fold. Italy-General-Nuclear Power Mission-correspondence 01, WBGA.

13. US Defense Intelligence Agency, Directorate for Scientific and Technical Intelligence, 'Nuclear Energy Programs – Western Europe', September 1975, in Digital National Security Archive: http://nsarchive.gwu.edu/publications/dnsa.html (hereinafter DNSA).

14. National Security Council (NSC), National Security Study Memorandum (NSSM) n. 56, 'Uranium Enrichment Facilities', 14 May 1969, National Security Study Memoranda Collection (NSSMC), b. H-207, Nixon Presidential Library, Yorba Linda, CA (hereinafter NPL).

15. NSSM 101, 'Review of Security Requirements Regarding Uranium Enrichment Technology', 14 September 1970, NSSMC, b. H-207, NPL.

16. NSC, NSSM 120, 'United States Policy on Peaceful Applications of Atomic Energy', 19 February 1971, NSSMC, b. H-207, NPL.

17. NSC, NSSM 150, 'US Policy on Transfer of Highly Enriched Uranium', 13 March 1972, NSSMC, b. H-207, NPL.

18. See, for example, G. Torelli (IBRD), Office Memorandum, 'Italy-Loan 235-Italy-SENN Project', 17 February 1964, in Country Operational File – Italy, fold. Italy Nuclear Power Project – Administration 01, WBGA.

19. AMN, 'Note sul bilancio 1972', in Archivio pratiche degli uffici (numerazione nera), Ispettorato, Relazioni ordinate per numero, 1973, pratiche dal n. 16, p. 25, Historical Archive IRI, Rome (hereinafter ASIRI).

20. See the documentation in Country Operational File – Italy, fold. Nuclear Power Project Italy – Loan 0235, Correspondence Volume 1, WBGA.

21. 'Osservazioni sul terzo piano quinquennale del CNEN (1971–75)', in Archivio Generale, Pratiche societarie, Simea Società italiana meridionale energia atomica, rapporti IRI-ENI (AGPSSimea. Rapporti IRI-ENI), ASIRI.

22. J. Connelly to the President, 'Memorandum for the President', 27 April 1971, in RG56, Records of the Secretary of the Treasury George Schultz 1971–1974, b. 7 (Secretary of State c-1974 to Council of International Economic Policy), fold. GBC-Memoranda for the President 1971, NARA.

23. Department of Defense, Joint Chiefs of Staff to the Secretary of State, 'US–Iran Nuclear Cooperation Agreement', 16 May 1978, DDRS.

24. RG59, Bureau of Near Eastern and South Asia Affairs, Office of Greece Affairs, Records Relating to Greece 1963–1974, b. 16, NARA.

25. Finmeccanica, 'Riassetto del settore nucleare nazionale', February 1971, 4–6, AGPS Simea. Rapporti IRI-ENI, ASIRI.

26. US Defense Intelligence Agency, Directorate for Scientific and Technical Intelligence, 'Nuclear Energy Programs – Western Europe', September 1975, 5–6, DNSA.

27. Ministero degli Affari Esteri, 'Possibili temi di collaborazione tra Stati Uniti e Italia nel settore nucleare', undated (likely 1973), Aldo Moro Papers (hereafter AMP), Ministry for Foreign Affairs series, b.160, fold. 242, National Archives Italy, Rome (hereinafter ACS).

28. Defense Intelligence Agency, Directorate for Scientific and Technical Intelligence, 'Nuclear Energy Programs Western Europe', September 1975, DNSA, 15.

29. American Embassy in Rome (AmEmbassyR) to Secretary of State, 'Government of Italy (GOI) plans to place orders for two nuclear power plants', December 1973, RG59, Central Foreign Policy Files (CFPF), telegrams 1.1.1973–12.31.1973, NARA: http://aad. archives.gov/aad/series-description.jsp?s=4073&cat=all&bc=sl.

30. R .Curran (active Executive Secretary), Memorandum for Henry Kissinger, 'Highly enriched uranium for power reactors (NSSM 150), 24 August 1972, DNSA.

31. H. Kissinger, National Security Decision Memorandum (NSDM) n. 255, 'Security and other aspects of the growth and dissemination of nuclear power industries', 3 June 1974, National Security Council Institutional Files, b. H-208, NPL.

32. H. Kissinger, NSDM 235, 'NSSM 150, US Policy on Transfer of Highly Enriched Uranium for Fueling Power Reactors', 4 October 1973, NPL.

33. AmEmbassyR to Secretary of State, 'Fiscal year 1974 – commercial objectives', 23 September 1973, RG59, CFPF, NARA: http://aad.archives.gov/aad.

34. AmEmbassyR to Secretary of State, 'GOI plans to place orders for two nuclear power plants', 11 December 1973, RG59, CFPF, NARA: http://aad.archives.gov/aad.

35. From 1973 to 1974 the worsening of the balance of payments turned into a rocky drop in the current account position of the country. For an overview, see IMF Balance of Payments Division of Bureau of Statistics, *Balance of Payments Statistics* 32 Yearbook, part 1 (Washington DC, 1981), 251–55.

36. AmEmbassyR to Secretary of State, 'Italian Exchange Market developments', 20 December 1973, RG59, CFPF, NARA: http://aad.archives.gov/aad; Memo from the Under Secretary of the Treasury (Bennett) to Secretary of the Treasury Simon, 'Your Meeting with Minister Duisenberg', 9 May 1974, *FRUS 1969–1976, Vol. XXXI, Foreign Economic Policy 1973–1976*, (Washington DC, 2009), 270.

37. AmEmbassyR to Secretary of State, 'New credit measure', 18 December 1973, RG59, CFPF, NARA: http://aad.archives.gov/aad.

Bibliography

Behrman, Greg, *The Most Noble Adventure: The Marshall Plan and the Time when America Helped Save Europe* (New York, 2007).

Elisabetta Bini and Igor Londero (eds), *Nuclear Italy: An International History of Italy's Nuclear Policies during the Cold War* (Trieste, 2017).

Brogi, Alessandro, *Confronting America: The Cold War between the United States and the Communists in France and Italy* (Chapel Hill, NC, 2011).

Bromley, Simon, *American Hegemony and World Oil: Industry, the State System, and the World Economy* (University Park, PA, 1991).

Del Pero, Mario, 'The US and the Crises in Southern Europe', in *Europe in the International Arena in the 1970s*, ed. Antonio Varsori and Guia Migani (Brussels, 2011), 301–16.

Eichengreen, Barry, *The European Economy since 1945: Coordinated Capitalism and Beyond* (Princeton, NJ, 2007).

———, *Exorbitant Privilege: The Rise and Fall of the Dollar* (Oxford, 2011).

Ellwood, David, *The Shock of America: Europe and the Challenge of the Century* (Oxford, 2012).

Fauri, Francesca, and Paolo Tedeschi (eds), *Novel Outlooks on the Marshall Plan: American Aid and European Re-Industrialization* (Brussels, 2011).

Ikenberry, G. John, *Reasons of State: Oil Politics and the Capacities of American Government* (Ithaca, NY, 1988).

La Barca, Giuseppe, *International Trade in the 1970s: The US, the EC and the Growing Pressure of Protectionism* (London, 2013).

Labbate, Silvio, 'Italy and the Development of European Energy Policy: From the Dawn of the Integration Process to the 1973 Oil Crisis', *International History Review* 20(1) (2013): 67–93.

Mitchell, Timothy, *Carbon Democracy: Political Power in the Age of Oil* (London, 2011).

Njolstad, Olav, 'The Carter Administration and Italy: Keeping the Communists Out of Power without Interfering', *Journal of Cold War Studies* 3 (2002): 56–94.

Painter, David, 'Oil and the American Century', *Journal of American History* 99(1) (June 2012): 24–39.

Rodman, Kenneth A., *Sanctity versus Sovereignty: The United States and the Nationalization of Natural Resource Investments* (New York, 1988).

Selva, Simone, *Supra-national Integration and Domestic Economic Growth* (Brussels, 2012).

Silveri, Umberto Gentiloni, *L'Italia sospesa: La crisi degli anni Settanta vista da Washington* (Turin, 2009).

Skogmar, Gunnar, *The United States and the Nuclear Dimension of European Integration* (Basingstoke and New York, 2004).

US Office of the Historian, *Foreign Relations of the United States (FRUS), FRUS 1969–1976, Vol. XXXI, Foreign Economic Policy 1973–1976*, (Washington, DC, 2009)

Venn, Fiona, *The Oil Crisis* (London, 2002).

Wall, Irwin, 'L'amministrazione Carter e l'Eurocomunismo', *Ricerche di Storia Politica* 2 (2006): 181–96.

CHAPTER 11

Capital Hits the Road

Regulating Multinational Corporations during the Long 1970s

FRANCESCO PETRINI

Introduction

On 27 February 1997 the Renault CEO, Louis Schweitzer, announced to the press – without prior consultation with the representatives of the 4,500 workers concerned – the closure of the Belgian production plant in Vilvoorde. As the European Industrial Relations Observatory (EIRO) stated: '[T]he decision ignored all legal rules and procedures concerning factory closures. This includes ILO and OECD procedures as well as national codes of conduct, and European Union and national legislation on collective redundancies and works council rights'.[1] The rules and procedures the EIRO alluded to were the offspring of a heated debate on the regulation of multinational corporation (MNC)[2] activities that started in the late 1960s. In those years international trade union organizations and Third World countries were, for different reasons, the driving forces behind a series of proposals for the regulation of the activities of MNCs. These proposals constituted an attempt to regulate, at an international level, the geographical restructuring of manufacturing. This chapter investigates those efforts, focusing on the dialectic between international trade union organizations and business circles, and is based mainly on primary sources from these societal actors. The first section sketches out the premises and context of the story;

Notes for this section begin on page 195.

the second section narrates the core of it, the struggle to regulate MNC activities; and the final section draws some conclusions.

Democracy at Work, Capital on Strike

A push from below towards enlarging the confines of democracy was at the heart of 'the long 1970s', the period opened by the 'failed world revolution' of 1968 and closed by the monetarist counter-revolution.[3] This phenomenon developed along many dimensions, from international relations (the struggle of postcolonial states for equal sovereignty and economic redistribution) to schools and factories, and spread throughout the globe. In the advanced capitalist countries, in the wake of two decades of sustained economic growth, citizens mobilized en masse to demand not only a larger slice of the cake, but also a bigger say in the organization of their jobs. Far from being a mere by-product of the student protests, the high level of industrial conflict of the late 1960s was closely linked to the generalized condition of full employment that allowed workers to demand a radical revision of the balance between capital and labour.[4] In the process they achieved much, in terms of both wages and control over work organization. In conjunction with the worsening of the competition between the major capitalist centres,[5] this produced a substantial compression of profits.[6]

    This situation prompted a reaction from capitalists, aimed at reconstituting the conditions for profitability. On the ideological plane, business circles engaged in a struggle for the definition of a new hegemonic balance, founded on the ideology of the self-regulating market and a conception of macroeconomic policy that assumed the fight against inflation as its guiding star, relegating full employment to the role of a dependent variable.[7] On the material plane, capital became more flexible, increasingly turning to finance in search of higher profits;[8] on the factory floor, employers undertook a process of reorganization based on the intensification of automation and the adoption of lean manufacturing, with the aim of curtailing workers' bargaining power, a power that was further eroded by the increasing reliance on immigrant labour. This was accompanied, outside the factory, by a centrifugal movement, with the transfer of production lines or of entire plants to areas with a cheaper and/or more docile manpower. As Prem Shankar Jha points out, the answer to the profit squeeze produced by a strong unionism was the migration of capital, 'both within and, with increasing unification of world product markets, out of the country'.[9] In summary, as noted by Beverly Silver, the reaction of capital was to 'go on strike': 'an increasingly mobile capital "voted with its feet" … by intensifying and deepening the geographical relocation of productive capital'.[10]

To be sure, one might object that in fact the shift of manufacturing from the advanced capitalist countries to the developing ones occurred in large numbers only after the late 1970s. In previous years, direct investments to less developed countries, although accelerating, had still been outnumbered by those within the developed world.[11] Moreover, as Silver states, concluding her analysis of workers' mobilization in the automotive industry, in the long term the strategy of relocation proved powerless to restore the level of profits, ultimately producing a mere shift of conflict from one geographical area to another. However, regarding the effects on the bargaining power of workers in the countries of mature capitalism, there is little doubt that that the strategy met business's original expectations. As Silver writes: 'By the early 1980s labour movements in Western Europe ... were generally on the defensive'.[12] At that time the dismissed factory workers in the West would certainly not have been much relieved if they had known that the flight of factories that had left them jobless would, in a few years, bring the same conflicts that saw them defeated to the regions of new expansion. What is more, from the standpoint of Western workers, the fact that the bulk of the investments were not heading towards developing countries but remained within the industrialized world did not do much to relieve the pressure on their bargaining power. The existence of a plurality of production sites within the same company was itself sufficient to weaken labour's bargaining power, regardless of whether these plants were located in countries with low labour costs. For example, in response to the strike wave that hit the Ford factories in Britain in the late 1960s, the management threatened to move production lines not to Asia or Latin America but to the existing Ford establishments in Belgium and Germany. As summarized by a conference brief of the Trades Union Congress (TUC): 'In many companies the existence of alternative sources of supply gives management scope to threaten to switch products to other locations'.[13]

The (failed) Democratization of Multinational Corporations

From the early 1960s the International Trade Secretariats (ITS), the unions' transnational industry organizations, took note of these developments. In September 1963 the Central Committee of the International Metalworkers' Federation (IMF), at the urging of Walter Reuther, leader of the United Auto Workers, the main US auto union, decided to focus its approaching world conference on the problems posed by the growth 'in size and power of giant international corporations'.[14] As stated in the preparatory document, only an internationally coordinated industrial action could effectively protect the rights of workers against companies that were acting above national

borders. The IMF's action led to the formation in 1966 of the first two
world company works councils, at Ford and General Electric. But, as soon
became apparent, this attempt at transnational bargaining, while relatively
easier in sectors characterized by a high concentration of capital, was much
harder to realize in more fragmented areas. Furthermore, the International
Confederation of Free Trade Unions (ICFTU), the major non–communist
international trade union organization, did not want to leave the initiative
to the ITS in such a delicate matter. Thus, as an alternative to (and in competition with) the bargaining approach of the ITS, the ICFTU chose to
focus on political action, pushing for the creation of an international legislative framework to regulate multinational activities. In July 1969, the ninth
ICFTU World Congress passed a resolution accusing multinational companies of undermining, by arbitrarily transferring production facilities from one
country to another, 'established industrial relations systems; restrict[ing] the
right of the workers to organise in defence of their interests … limit[ing] their
right to enter into coordinated collective bargaining …; [and] exploit[ing]
international labour cost differentials in order to boost profits'.[15]

To counterbalance these threats, it was necessary, according to the
ICFTU, to establish a form of democratic control of corporate decision
making at every level, 'so as to advance the democratisation of multinational corporations'. In this perspective the ICFTU presented a request to
the United Nations (UN) to organize a conference with the goal of drawing
up a code of conduct for multinationals' activities.

The rising tide of hostility towards multinationals did not escape the
attention of the business community. The political and cultural climate of
the time did not allow for a static defence of the status quo. Thus from the
internal debate of the International Chamber of Commerce (ICC) emerged
the idea of taking the initiative and trying to govern a process that threatened
to assume alarming proportions if left to the initiative of the trade unions
and the developing countries. Thus the ICC adopted, in November 1972,
the 'Guidelines for International Private Investors and Governments', a non-
binding set of directions to be followed in relations between corporations
and governments. The ICC document, falling far short of the demands of
the unions and of developing countries, clearly indicated the employers'
preference for a voluntary approach and for non-legislative measures in order
to preserve multinationals' freedom of action.

In the wake of the outrage caused by the revelations about the involvement of the US multinational ITT in the attempted coup in Chile in
October 1970,[16] in July 1972 the UN Economic and Social Council passed
a resolution establishing the 'Group of Eminent Persons' (GEP), with the
task of submitting 'recommendations for appropriate international action'
on the MNC issue.[17] The GEP was composed of twenty members from

different backgrounds (nine were from government circles, six from academy and five from public or private enterprises), but none from the international trade union movement.[18] This provoked a reaction on the part of the ICFTU, which decided, together with the Christian-oriented World Confederation of Labour, to boycott the GEP's work. Therefore in the hearings held by the group in late 1973 only two unionists were interviewed: Albertino Mazetti, of the communist World Federation of Trade Unions, and Nathaniel Goldfinger of the American AFL/CIO (which had recently left the ICFTU). In contrast, the employers were represented by an impressive array of prominent personalities, such as: Emilio (Pete) Collado, vice-president of Standard Oil of New Jersey and president of the OECD Business and Industry Advisory Committee (BIAC); Ernest Woodroofe and Gerrit Klijnstra, chairmen of Unilever; Jacques Maisonrouge, president of IBM; Thomas Murphy, vice-president of General Motors; Gianni Agnelli, chairman of Fiat; Gerrit Wagner, chairman of Shell; and Renato Lombardi, president of the ICC. In his statement, Agnelli prefigured the strategy to be followed by business in subsequent years:

> [A] binding multilateral agreement ... in the form of a 'GATT for investment' does not seem practical at the moment. Instead, the idea of developing a *voluntary* code on the rights and responsibilities of the multinational corporations seems to be an attractive one. The 'Guidelines for Foreign Investment', drafted by the International Chamber of Commerce, represents a good beginning.[19]

At the end of 1973 the GEP published an interim report characterized as 'blatantly unbalanced' by the ICFTU due to its total disregard for labour relations in the home countries of multinationals.[20] However, after the non-communist unions were admitted to informal consultations in early 1974,[21] the climate changed and the GEP final report was greeted with favour by the unions: 'Despite its composition, the United Nations Group seems to have taken note of most of the criticisms that have been levelled at multinational corporations'.[22] The unions still had reservations about parts of the report, but their doubts were amply compensated by the explicit reference contained therein to the need for a comprehensive agreement with the force of an international treaty and machinery for enforcement. This was in consonance with the appeal issued jointly by the ICFTU and the International Trade Secretariats calling for the establishment of 'a new international agency under United Nations auspices ... for the control of multinational company activities'.[23] The employers criticized the report as biased because of its 'disproportionate emphasis on the presumed disadvantages' of the activities of MNCs, and reiterated their preference for the adoption of a non-binding code of conduct along the lines of that adopted by the ICC.[24]

The concrete result of the GEP's works was the establishment of the UN Centre on Transnational Corporations and the Intergovernmental

Panel on Transnational Corporations, a negotiating forum on issues related to MNCs. They were judged by the ICFTU to be only a first step towards a binding agreement, 'a sort of GATT',[25] to govern the multinational phenomenon. On the contrary, for the employers these developments represented the embryo of a dangerous system of public control of the market, and they deemed it necessary to pre-empt unwelcome developments. The OECD, with its membership restricted to developed countries, seemed the perfect alternative to the universal, turbulent UN agencies. As affirmed in a memo sent by the Business and Industry Advisory Committee (BIAC, the officially recognized organization representing business interests to OECD) to the OECD Council:

> We believe that the OECD is uniquely equipped to carry out such investigations [on MNC activities], having within its membership the countries where two-thirds of international investment takes place. As most of the member nations are the home and the host of multinational enterprises, *there is a greater likelihood of the OECD finding a common approach and reaching balanced conclusions, considering not only malpractices but also benefits conferred by multinational corporations*. The EEC [European Economic Community], by contrast, comprises too narrow a range of countries, and the UN is a forum where there is too great a divergence of approach and interests.[26]

The assumption was that within the West-dominated OECD it would be possible to negotiate an agreement more in line with business views than what was expected to come from the UN, where the influence of the Third World and the socialist countries was strong.

It is impossible here to go into the details of the debate within the OECD. Suffice to say that in June 1976, after eighteen months of negotiations, at a speed that contrasts sharply with the snail's pace of the work of the UN intergovernmental panel, the OECD Council approved the 'Guidelines for Multinational Companies'. Basically these were a series of recommendations of a non-binding nature and without legal force, which established standards of conduct for multinationals' operations on the territories of OECD member states, in many ways foreshadowing what later became known as 'corporate social responsibility'. As stated by one of the most informed observers of the debate on multinationals:

> There can be little doubt that the OECD Guidelines were consciously written as a model which the United Nations, it was hoped, could be persuaded to copy, rather than simply to pursue the more ambitious plans for compulsory regulations which were born of the climate of political confrontation that characterised the first half of the 1970s.[27]

This was also ICFTU's opinion according to which the OECD document was a 'set of voluntary and at least partially vague recommendations', which constituted 'a pre-emptive strike in view of further action by other international organizations'.[28] In a sense this view was confirmed by Emil van Lennep, OECD secretary general, who affirmed that 'the consensus reached in the OECD represents a joint philosophy and common approach on the part of a group of countries accounting for most international investment. This should have an influence even beyond the OECD area'.[29] And it did have an influence: the negotiations on a UN code of conduct quickly turned towards the adoption of a voluntary instrument, despite the ICFTU's protests.[30] Similarly, in November 1977 the ILO approved the 'Tripartite Declaration of Principles Concerning Multinational Enterprises and Social Policy', which, although politically significant because directly signed by social forces, had no legal force and was judged 'vague and open to considerable interpretation'.[31]

From the unions' standpoint, the multinational debate seemed lost in 'endless corridors of technocratic tergiversation and indecision'.[32] However, the European Community, with its legislative powers and supranational character, seemed to offer a promising alternative. In the early 1970s the European trade union movement had opened talks with the EC Commission on the MNC issue. In February 1973 the European adherents to the ICFTU had decided to set up their own, autonomous regional organization: the European Trade Union Confederation (ETUC). One of the main reasons underlying this move was the desire to act more effectively on the MNC matter.[33] Moreover, le '*défi américain*', the challenge posed by the expansion of the US corporations on European soil, dominated the European public debate of the time. Responding to these solicitations, in November 1973 the commissioner for industry and technology, Altiero Spinelli, issued a programme of action on multinationals. The commission's document, which aimed fundamentally at strengthening the internationalization of European corporations, responded to unions' requests by making workers' protection one of its key priorities. To this end it considered it essential to 'encourage' the establishment of a 'trade union counterweight'.[34] Not surprisingly, this part of the commission's proposals met the strong hostility of business organizations, which expressed 'anxiety' about the 'heavy measure of dirigisme' that the implementation of the commission's programme would imply.[35] Despite these fears, in February 1975, as a first step towards the implementation of the Spinelli programme, the EC Council adopted a directive on mass dismissals, setting some limitations on employers' room for manoeuvre. In February 1977 the council adopted another directive on the safeguarding of employees' rights in the event of a relocation of business activities to other member states.

The unions considered these measures only partially satisfactory as long as they did not address the fundamental problem posed by the decision-making structure of MNCs: the difficulty of identifying a valid interlocutor of workers' representatives. Thus on several occasions the ETUC demanded the establishment of a system of information and consultation for the employees of MNCs, through 'binding provision', because 'it will not suffice merely to introduce recommendations or a procedural code with no legal obligation'.[36] The focus on information and consultation, espousing neither the confrontational model of the Southern European unions nor the more collaborative German codetermination, allowed the ETUC to find an acceptable compromise between the different national industrial relations traditions.

In fact, the EC Commission's work stalled till the late 1970s, because of the contrast between the two commissioners in charge: Etienne Davignon for Industry and Henk Vredeling for Social Affairs. The first, a prominent figure in the world of business, thought that the OECD's non-compulsory guidelines provided a sufficient regulatory framework, while Vredeling, a long-time member of the Dutch Labour Party, was much more in tune with the unions' ideas.[37]

The worsening economic conditions at the end of the 1970s represented a powerful incentive for the trade unions to renew their pressure. On 24 October 1980 the commission finally approved the 'Vredeling initiative', a proposal for the adoption of a directive on information and consultation of employees in MNCs. The commission scheme demanded that MNCs' decisions on key issues such as investment planning and diversification would be subject to advance consultation of employee representatives of European subsidiaries.[38] The Vredeling initiative broke with the legal fiction according to which each national subsidiary acted independently and treated the MNCs as single legal entities, allowing workers to directly address the MNC's headquarters in case the local management was unable to provide satisfactory information. If the MNC's headquarters was located outside the EC, then the parent company, or its single largest subsidiary inside the EC, was asked to designate an 'agent' inside the EC to inform and consult with workers' representatives. Moreover, the draft directive established a sort of extraterritoriality of its effects, explicitly covering companies with headquarters beyond EC borders.[39]

The unions welcomed the proposed directive. ETUC stressed that the commission proposal could be 'regarded politically as the successful outcome of the trade unions' efforts', and that it represented a 'needed complement' to the non-binding codes of conduct already adopted or under discussion.[40] Ernst Piehl, ETUC general secretary, affirmed: 'The most positive feature is the *compulsory* [emphasis in the original] character that the EEC has chosen as the first – and thus far the only – international institution, in order to assert workers' rights'.[41]

Business organizations reacted strongly. The Union of Industries of the European Community (UNICE), protested in February 1981 against the imposition of what it saw as a rigid, 'unacceptable' system.[42] UNICE confirmed its support for a voluntary approach like that adopted by the OECD and the ILO, stressing that there was no need for EC legislation and criticizing in detail the proposed directive. US-based MNCs, affected by the extraterritorial character of the proposal, protested vehemently. The National Foreign Trade Council in New York and the American Chamber of Commerce in Brussels declared that the adoption of the Vredeling proposal would have a negative effect on US investment in Europe.[43] The International Chamber of Commerce expressed 'strong opposition' to the commission proposal on the grounds that it would have a depressing effect on foreign direct investment in the EC and that it would introduce the idea of management/labour negotiations beyond the national level, a concept – it was stressed – 'not accepted in the ILO tripartite declaration and the OECD Guidelines'.[44]

We cannot go into the details of a debate that lasted nearly six years. Suffice it to recall that, after being emptied of most of its innovative capacity with the amendments introduced at the end of 1982 by the centre-right majority of the European Parliament, the attempt to adopt binding European legislation on the consultation of workers was finally dismissed by the EEC Council of ministers in May 1986.[45]

Conclusion

In sum, the discussions on a UN code of conduct for multinationals dragged on for years without leading to any tangible result. The non-binding OECD guidelines were considered by the trade unions to be only a first step towards a more stringent form of protection of worker rights, but the second step was never advanced. Finally, in 1994, the EU Council adopted a directive on the information and consultation of employees establishing the European works councils, but only on a voluntary basis, renouncing any ambition to uniform and binding regulation. Therefore, the mountain of a decade of international debates on MNC regulation gave birth to the proverbial mouse. Why?

A first factor that helps to explain the outcome is the internal divisions and rivalries of the labour movement and its consequent difficulties in acting transnationally.[46] It still holds true what the Dutch trade unionist Eddo Fimmen wrote in 1924: '[T]he workers have international organisations; hold international congresses; pass numerous and high-sounding resolutions. None the less, they continue to restrict their activities to national arenas'. By contrast, employers 'do not hold congresses; they do not pass pious resolutions about international class solidarity. Nevertheless, they think and act

internationally, for they are well aware that their interests can best be promoted in this way'.[47]

Second, the unions' choice of international organizations as the main
battleground on which to engage MNC power seemed to have been a poor
one: 'Indeed from a corporate standpoint the best way to escape regulation
from such outmoded national agencies as the Internal Revenue Service and
the Anti-Trust Division is to shift the burden to an international agency
with broad unenforceable powers and a modest budget'.[48]

Of course, a leap in the scale of trade union action seemed inescapable:
'Trade union leaders are negotiating in a labour market which is organized
nationally or locally; management are now operating in a product market,
and a capital market, which is organised internationally'.[49] Moreover, the
emphasis on the international level allowed the international confederations
to strengthen their role within the labour movement. At the same time,
the involvement of the United Nations seemed to provide an opportunity to reconcile the otherwise divergent demands of Western workers and
developing countries. On the unions' part, however, there was no adequate
assessment of the risks involved in entrusting the fate of the debate on
multinationals to the treacherous currents of organizations in which the
democratic push from below is often attenuated by the prevalence of 'high
politics'.

Conversely, on the business side there was a deep awareness of the possibilities that the international arena opened up for the defence of employers' positions, as confirmed by the words of a senior executive of a British
multinational: '[T]he business lobby should attempt to proceed internationally (at the pace of the slowest nation) rather than nationally (under
socialist pressure)'.[50] The radicalization of Western democracies pushed the
employers to think that 'the popular world was slipping out of control and
that it required international effort by men in responsible positions to call
the establishment to order'.[51] In this perspective the international space,
dominated by a technocratic logic and heavily influenced by a transnational
network of relationships between elites, and in particular some international
organizations in which these trends were stronger, offered the best opportunities for the affirmation of business's viewpoint.

Capital has always enjoyed a freedom of movement from which labour
is precluded: 'unlike other commodities, labour power has to go home
every night'.[52] In the era of embedded liberalism, this asymmetry was partially reduced. From the late 1960s, capitalism proceeded to reform itself
towards forms of greater flexibility, in a sort of 'Great Transformation' in
reverse that paved the way for the neoliberal restructuring of the following
decade. The failure of attempts to build a binding international legal framework to regulate MNC activities contributed to this development.

Francesco Petrini is permanent researcher in History of International Relations at the Department of Political Science, Law and International Studies of the University of Padua, Italy. He has published essays on European integration history, Italy's economic and social history, and history of the oil industry. His latest book is *Imperi del profitto: Multinazionali petrolifere e governi nel XX secolo* [Empires of profit: Oil multinationals and governments in the twentieth century] (Milan, 2015).

Notes

1. See: http://www.eurofound.europa.eu/eiro/1997/03/feature/be9703202f.htm (accessed 1 March 2017).

2. 'A firm which has the power to *coordinate* and *control* operations in more than one country' – Peter Dicken, 'Economic Globalization: Corporations', in *The Blackwell Companion to Globalization*, ed. George Ritzer (Oxford, 2007), 292.

3. Giovanni Arrighi, Terence K. Hopkins and Immanuel Wallerstein, *Antisystemic Movements* (London, 1989), 97.

4. On 1968 as a workers revolt, see Gerd-Rainer Horn, *The Spirit of 68: Rebellion in Western Europe and North America, 1956–1976* (Oxford, 2007); Francesco Petrini, 'Il '68 e la crisi dell'età dell'oro', in *Annali dell'Istituto Ugo La Malfa* XXII (2007): 47–71.

5. Robert Brenner, 'The Economics of Global Turbulence. Uneven Development and the Long Downturn: The Advanced Capitalist Economies from Boom to Stagnation, 1950–1998', *New Left Review* 1(229) (1998): 1–265.

6. Philip Armstrong, Andrew Glyn and John Harrison, *Capitalism Since 1945* (Oxford, 1991), 169–207. For an interpretation of the crisis that combines the horizontal (between enterprises) and vertical (between capital and labour) conflicts, see Giovanni Arrighi, *Adam Smith in Beijing: Lineages of the 21st Century* (London, 2009), 116–39.

7. Serge Halimi, *Le grand bond en arrière* (Marseille, 2012).

8. On financialization and its role in systemic cycles of accumulation, see Giovanni Arrighi, *The Long Twentieth Century: Money, Power and the Origins of Our Times* (London, 2010).

9. Prem S. Jha, *The Twilight of the Nation State: Globalisation, Chaos, and War* (London, 2006), 77.

10. Beverly J. Silver, *Forces of Labor: Workers' Movements and Globalization since 1870* (Cambridge, 2003), 163. Of course, social conflict was not the only reason driving the relocation of manufacture. As highlighted by the literature, there are many motivations behind the decision to relocate (for example, the search for raw materials or the need to surmount customs barriers). See Geoffrey Jones, *Multinationals and Global Capitalism* (Oxford, 2005), 16–42. However, in my view, the main rationale motivating the increased pace of globalization from the late 1960s was the workers' unrest in the advanced capitalist countries.

11. John H. Dunning and Sarianna M. Lundan, *Multinational Enterprises and the Global Economy* (Chelthenam, 2008), 31–32.

12. Silver, *Forces of Labor*, 53.

13. TUC Conference on international companies, *International Companies and British Trade Union Experience*, 21 October 1970, MSS.292D/340.9/1, Modern Records Centre (MRC), University of Warwick, Archive of the Trades Union Congress (ATUC).

14. International Metalworkers' Federation 38, V^th World Automotive conference, October 1963, International Institute of Social History (IISH), Amsterdam.

15. Ninth World Congress, Brussels, 2–8 July 1969, *Resolution on MNCs and Conglomerates*, IISH, Archive of the ICFTU (AICFTU) 1358, ICFTU.

16. On the 1970 attempted coup, see Kristian C. Gustafson, 'Reexamining the Record: CIA Machinations in Chile in 1970', *Studies in Intelligence* 3 (2003): 35–49. On the ITT involvement, see US Senate Committee on Foreign Relations, Subcommittee on Multinational Corporations, 93rd Congress, 1st Session, '*The International Telephone and Telegraph Company and Chile, 1970–1971*' (Washington, DC, 1973).

17. UN Economic and Social Council, Resolution 1721 (LIII), 28 July 1972, *UN Yearbook 1972*, 242–44, available at: http://unyearbook.un.org/ (accessed 1 March 2017).

18. There was only one former unionist: Hans Matthoefer, minister in the West German government, former head of the IG Metall department for trade union education.

19. UN Department of Economic and Social Affairs, 'Summary of the Hearings before the Group of Eminent Persons' (New York, 1974), 149–50, italics added.

20. According to the ICFTU, only six lines out of one hundred pages were dedicated to matters directly related to trade unions concerns – Rebecca Gumbrell-McCormick, 'Facing New Challenges: The International Confederation of Free Trade Unions 1974–1990s', in *The International Confederation of Free Trade Unions*, ed. Anthony Carew et al. (Bern, 2000), 388.

21. ICFTU/ITS Working Party on MNCs (WP), 'Report on activities since the last meeting', 17 May 1974, IISH, AICFTU 1360.

22. TUC, 'International companies', private and confidential, 10 July 1974, MRC, ATUC, MSS.292D/340.9/4.

23. WP, 'National and international legislation required to bring the activities of MNCs under social control', 28 May 1974, IISH, AICFTU 1360.

24. ICC Executive Committee, 'Multinational enterprises and their role in economic development', Hamburg, 10 June 1974, MRC, Archive of the Confederation of British Industry (ACBI), MSS.200/C/3/INT/16/1.

25. Charter of trade union demands for the legislative control of MNCs, 12 August 1975, IISH, AICFTU 1362.

26. BIAC, 'Multinational enterprises', November 1974, MRC, ACBI, MSS.200/C/3/INT/14/57 (italics added by author). For its part, the ICFTU defined the OECD as 'the international lobby of the industrialised economies, leaning heavily on the philosophy of free enterprise and a free functioning of the market forces' (WP, 'Socialising the transnational corporation: The trade union response to the transnational challenge', September 1979, IISH, AICFTU 1369).

27. John Robinson, *Multinationals and Political Control* (Aldershot, 1983), 117.

28. WP, 'Socialising the transnational corporation', September 1979, IISH, AICFTU 1369.

29. 'Foreword to the OECD Guidelines', Paris, June 1976, cit. in Robinson, *Multinationals*, 117–18. A similar position was taken by the US government – see Vernie Oliveiro, 'The United States, Multinational Enterprises, and the Politics of Globalization', in *The Shock of the Global: The 1970s in Perspective*, ed. Niall Ferguson et al. (Cambridge, MA, 2010), 149.

30. Tagi Sagafi-Nejad, *The UN and Transnational Corporations* (Bloomington, IN, 2008).

31. G. Hamilton, 'Initiatives Undertaken by International Organisations in the Field of Employee Information and Consultation in Multinational Undertakings (ILO, OECD, UN)', in *Employee Consultation and Information in Multinational Corporations*, ed. Jacques Vandamme (London, 1986), 107.

32. WP, 'National and international legislation required to bring the activities of MNCs under social control', 28 May 1974, IISH, ICFTU 1360.

33. Bernhard Ebbinghaus and Jelle Visser, 'European Union Organizations', in *Trade Unions in Western Europe since 1945*, ed. Bernhard Ebbinghaus and Jelle Visser (Basingstoke, 2000), 775.

34. 'Multinational Undertakings and the Community', Communication of the European Commission to the Council, 7 November 1973, in *Bulletin of the EC*, Supplement 15/73, 10.

35. CBI Memorandum, 'MNCs', 21 November 1973; and UNICE, *Compte rendu de la réunion du 16 novembre 1973*, 27 November 1973, MRC, ACBI, MSS/200/C/3/INT/16/9.

36. ETUC, 'Demands for company-law regulations for multinational Konzerne', Brussels, March 1976, IISH, ETUC 738. See also: ETUC, Executive Committee, Resolution, 6 February 1975, IISH, ETUC 738; ETUC, Second Statutory Congress, London, 22–24 April 1976, Objectives 1976–1979, chapter II: 'Democratisation of the Economy: Multinational Groups of Companies', IISH, ETUC 739.

37. Hamilton, 'Initiatives Undertaken', 95.

38. See the text of the directive in *Journal Officiel des Communautés Européennes*, 15 November 1980.

39. Robinson, *Multinationals*, 58–63.

40. ETUC, Executive Committee, 'Information on and evaluation of the Proposal of the EC Commission', 8 December 1980, IISH, ETUC 2200.

41. 'Informations sur la proposition de la Commission européenne d'une directive sur l'information et la consultation des travailleurs', 9 October 1980, IISH, ETUC 2200.

42. UNICE, 'Proposal for a Directive on employee information and consultation', *UNICE Position*, 12 February 1981, MRC, ACBI, MSS/200/C/3/INT/16/12.

43. Bennett Harrison, 'The International Movement for Prenotification of Plant Closures', *Industrial Relations* 23(3) (1984), 395–96.

44. ICC, 'Statement submitted by the Secretary General to the EEC authorities', 7 July 1981, IISH, ETUC 2223.

45. On the more recent developments, see Jeremy Waddington, *European Works Councils: A Transnational Industrial Relations Institution in the Making* (London, 2011).

46. Patrick Pasture and Johan Verberkmoes (eds), *Working-Class Internationalism and the Appeal of National Identity: Historical Debates and Current Perspectives* (Oxford, 1998).

47. Edo Fimmen, *Labour's Alternative: The United States of Europe or Europe Limited* (London, 1924), available at: http://www.globallabour.info/en/labours_alternative_by_edo_fim/; quote from chapter 5, http://www.globallabour.info/en/2006/09/chapter_5.html (accessed 1 March 2017).

48. Richard J. Barnet and Ronald E. Müller, *Global Reach: The Power of the Multinational Corporations* (New York, 1974), 373.

49. TUC Conference, 'International companies', 21 October 1970, MSS.292D/340.9/1.

50. D.E. Midgley (Company Secretary, Gascoigne Group) to CBI, 28 November 1978, MRC, ACBI, MSS.200/C/3/INT/16/10.

51. Charles S. Maier, '"Malaise": The Crisis of Capitalism in the 1970s', in *The Shock of the Global: The 1970s in Perspective*, ed. Niall Ferguson et al. (Cambridge, MA, 2010), 41.

52. David Harvey, *The Urban Experience* (Baltimore, MD, 1989), 19.

Bibliography

Armstrong, Philip, Andrew Glyn and John Harrison, *Capitalism Since 1945* (Oxford, 1991), 169–207.

Arrighi, Giovanni, *Adam Smith in Beijing: Lineages of the 21st Century* (London, 2009).

————, *The Long Twentieth Century: Money, Power and the Origins of Our Times* (London, 2010).

Arrighi, Giovanni, Terence K. Hopkins and Immanuel Wallerstein, *Antisystemic Movements* (London, 1989).

Barnet, Richard J., and Ronald E. Müller, *Global Reach: The Power of the Multinational Corporations* (New York, 1974).

Brenner, Robert, 'The Economics of Global Turbulence. Uneven Development and the Long Downturn: The Advanced Capitalist Economies from Boom to Stagnation, 1950–1998', *New Left Review* 1(229) (1998): 1–265.

Dicken, Peter, 'Economic Globalization: Corporations', in *The Blackwell Companion to Globalization*, ed. George Ritzer (Oxford, 2007), 291–306.

Dunning, John H., and Sarianna M. Lundan, *Multinational Enterprises and the Global Economy* (Cheltenham, 2008).

Ebbinghaus, Bernhard, and Jelle Visser, 'European Union Organizations', in *Trade Unions in Western Europe since 1945*, ed. Bernhard Ebbinghaus and Jelle Visser (Basingstoke, 2000), 759–802.

Fimmen, Edo, *Labour's Alternative: The United States of Europe or Europe Limited* (London, 1924).

Gumbrell-McCormick, Rebecca, 'Facing New Challenges: The International Confederation of Free Trade Unions 1974–1990s', in *The International Confederation of Free Trade Unions*, ed. Anthony Carew et al. (Bern, 2000), 341–517.

Gustafson, Kristian C., 'Reexamining the Record: CIA Machinations in Chile in 1970', *Studies in Intelligence* 3 (2003): 35–49.

Halimi, Serge, *Le grand bond en arrière* (Marseille, 2012).

Hamilton, G., 'Initiatives Undertaken by International Organisations in the Field of Employee Information and Consultation in Multinational Undertakings (ILO, OECD, UN)', in *Employee Consultation and Information in Multinational Corporations*, ed. Jacques Vandamme (London, 1986), 95–115.

Harrison, Bennett, 'The International Movement for Prenotification of Plant Closures', *Industrial Relations* 23(3) (1984): 387–409.

Harvey, David, *The Urban Experience* (Baltimore, MD, 1989).

Horn, Gerd-Rainer, *The Spirit of 68: Rebellion in Western Europe and North America, 1956–1976* (Oxford, 2007).

Jha, Prem S., *The Twilight of the Nation State: Globalisation, Chaos, and War* (London, 2006).

Jones, Geoffrey, *Multinationals and Global Capitalism* (Oxford, 2005).

Maier, Charles S., '"Malaise". The Crisis of Capitalism in the 1970s', in *The Shock of the Global: The 1970s in Perspective*, ed. Niall Ferguson et al. (Cambridge, MA, 2010), 25–48.

Oliveiro, Vernie, 'The United States, Multinational Enterprises, and the Politics of Globalization', in *The Shock of the Global: The 1970s in Perspective*, ed. Niall Ferguson et al. (Cambridge, MA, 2010), 143–55.

Pasture, Patrick, and Johan Verberkmoes (eds), *Working-Class Internationalism and the Appeal of National Identity: Historical Debates and Current Perspectives* (Oxford, 1998).

Petrini, Francesco, 'Il '68 e la crisi dell'età dell'oro', *Annali dell'Istituto Ugo La Malfa* XXII (2007): 47–71.

Robinson, John, *Multinationals and Political Control* (Aldershot, 1983).

Sagafi-Nejad, Tagi, *The UN and Transnational Corporations* (Bloomington, IN, 2008).

Silver, Beverly J., *Forces of Labor: Workers' Movements and Globalization since 1870* (Cambridge, 2003).

Waddington, Jeremy, *European Works Councils: A Transnational Industrial Relations Institution in the Making* (London, 2011).

CHAPTER 12

Marketization of the Enterprise

The Influence of Consultancy in the German Fibre Industry after the Boom

CHRISTIAN MARX

Introduction

By the end of the post-war boom, chemical enterprises in Germany were confronted with enormous economic problems. At the end of the 1960s the demand for chemical products fell and the prices of exports increased because of the appreciation of the deutschmark (DM). A few years later the cost of energy and resources rose in consequence of the oil price crisis of 1973/74. At the same time the economic framework changed due to integration in the European Economic Community (EEC) and new competitors from the United States expanding to Europe. The European fibre industry in particular faced difficulties to utilize its capacity. Because of the economic slump and the widening European market, the enterprises in the sector established a new profit strategy of geographical expansion towards the other European countries and the United States.

In the 1970s the omnipotence of multinational corporations was perceived not only in terms of the increased power of top management over the employees, but also in terms of the superiority of multinationals in conflicts with governments. Multinational corporations were regarded as monolithic and powerful antagonists of government regulation.[1] In the period of the 'economic miracle' only a lack of workforce or resources hindered expansion, and the enterprise was considered as a place of production and a superior form of organization based on lower transaction costs. Now the expansion of the enterprise was limited by weakening demand, and the external border of the organization became fluid. At the end of the Golden Age an increasing international division of labour spread, which was not limited to the differentiation of individual productive-technical operations within the factory or the division of production between several enterprises: management knowledge also became a tradable good. Robust hierarchies and rigid forms of division of labour dissolved.[2] Management experienced a kind of double rupture: first, the primacy of the production economy was abandoned in favour of market orientation and purchase patterns; and second, the institution of the enterprise became permeable, and external expert knowledge was bought on the free market.[3] Because of falling growth rates and the global shocks at the beginning of the 1970s, European managers – in the belief that they were subject to structural constraints – did not acknowledge any alternative to the expansion of international business.

In this situation the German fibre producer Vereinigte Glanzstoff-Fabriken AG (VGF) and their Dutch parent company Algemene Kunstzijde Unie (AKU) decided to merge completely. Since the 1920s the two companies had cooperated and exchanged research results. Because of the increasing international competition in the 1960s the managers thought that the companies could keep up with other chemical enterprises only by merging their capacities. Furthermore, they wanted to prevent competition between AKU and VGF on the European market.[4] The merger of AKU/VGF – creating the largest producer of synthetic fibres in Western Europe – took place in 1969, and the management engaged the US consultancy McKinsey & Company to offer a proposal on the future business structure. Thus a central managerial function was to be transferred outwards, and decision making on the firm's future was opened to external players. But the AKU/VGF managers were not convinced by McKinsey's proposal and rejected further cooperation for the time being. Only a few years later, after the first oil price crisis and an economic downturn, did the need for consultancy arise once again. In 1975 McKinsey offered new advice focusing on the market and including a reduction of overcapacity. There was a change of perspective. The market became more and more important for the organizational structure of enterprises. The disruption of Western societies in the 1970s was accompanied by a change of business structure and business philosophy, not only in the chemical industry but in industrial enterprises in general. The numerous restructurings were part of a process of radical change, a development marked by multiple crises. At the end of the 1960s, industrial managers were often associated with the economic miracle and they were proud of their skills, but the return of economic problems and increasing unemployment delegitimized management and brought to the fore the organizational knowledge of consultancies. At this time the challenges became obvious. On the basis of McKinsey's influence from the late 1960s, we shall trace this rupture and the higher status of the market and of external knowledge.[5]

The First Influence of Consultancy in the Merger of 1969

In February 1966 the VGF management issued a memo to explain the decision to merge completely. The management thought it would be necessary to integrate the two enterprises because of international business competition in the fibre market, and so proposed closer cooperation in the purchase of raw materials, production and distribution. In the 1960s VGF and AKU relinquished the purchase of resources to other enterprises and concentrated their investments on research, development and production of chemical fibres. New BASF and Bayer plants in Antwerp producing chemical base materials heightened competition, so it would have been difficult for AKU/VGF to generate any revenues in this area. Thus the profit strategy seemed to be economically reasonable. Traditional delivery relations between VGF and BASF guaranteed a price advantage for VGF, and the VGF managers intended to keep BASF out of fibre production. Negotiations on direct participation of BASF in VGF failed in 1964. Shortly afterwards AKU/VGF became aware of BASF's acquisition of Phrix AG, one of the largest fibre producers in West Germany. This increased competition in the fibre market.[6] The memorandum of 1966 aimed at strictly dividing new products between AKU and VGF; the sales companies were to remain autonomous, as the management did not expect any advantages from fusion and was afraid that the different submarkets could not be treated adequately by a single marketing organization. Furthermore, VGF managers feared losing business contacts in Germany by merging with a Dutch company, so they made a case for continuing an independent marketing and label policy.[7]

The political and economic developments proved to be crucial. The Treaties of Rome laid down the aim of a common market, which was realized gradually until the end of the 1960s. The common European market and the end of the economic miracle were fundamental to what happened to AKU/VGF subsequently. The chairman of AKU, Johannes Meynen, recommended cooperation with a third partner even before the first postwar recession of West Germany in 1966/67. In this way he intended to preserve the enterprise from the ups and downs of the synthetic fibre market. Simultaneously, the differentiation of business organization and the division of labour along national borders became less important within Europe, and industrial managers wanted to safeguard AKU/VGF from competition in the common market.[8] Therefore, in 1967, the German and the Dutch managements decided to merge their business activities. A legally binding ground for transnational mergers did not exist at the time, so it was accomplished by national law. In spring 1969 the Dutch AKU was transformed into a holding company responsible for the planning of the whole corporation, while the production plants of AKU were turned into the new Enka N.V. The German VGF with its affiliates remained legally unchanged and became a subsidiary of the new AKU holding. Then the two producing companies, Enka and VGF, were interconnected by personal union of their executive boards. In this way, the German and the Dutch parts were not only linked by capital interlocking, but also by unified management.

In contrast to the successful negotiations about the fusion of AKU and VGF, the attempt to merge with chemical enterprise De Nederlandse Staatsmijnen (DSM) failed. DSM, partially owned by the Dutch state, was engaged in the extraction of raw materials, so the company would have fit closely with the profit strategy of AKU/VGF. The German–Dutch producer of synthetic fibre negotiated for a long time with DSM, but finally political forces in the Netherlands prevented a complementary rapprochement. Consequently, the new AKU holding had to look for a new associate, and the Dutch KZO group (Koninklijke Zout-Organon N.V.) came to the fore. Both sides expected to improve their position on the world market, to enhance their access to the capital market and to diversify their risks by widening the product profile. The demand for European fibre products collapsed at the end of the 1960s, so AKU had a particular interest in broadening its supply. By the great merger of AKU and KZO in the second half of 1969, the managers intended to find a place among the top chemical enterprises in the world, and the corporation received the new name Akzo, which remained the holding company for Enka and VGF.[9]

Unlike the Dutch production site of AKU, which was already structured according to product groups with production and sales departments before 1969, the German VGF was organized in a functional way.[10] A divisional structure entails an organization along product lines or geographical regions, where each division contains all organizational functions; by contrast, a functional structure distinguishes between several sets of special tasks for the company as a whole. The agreement on the AKU/VGF merger opened the door to reconsidering the organizational structure in general. Although two national production sites persisted, with Enka and VGF, the managers considered it necessary to harmonize the organizational structure. The introduction of a divisional structure would have fundamentally changed the allocation of responsibilities in the executive board of VGF, and challenged the competencies of the managers. Here two different business cultures clashed. In reference to the economic miracle, German managers were still convinced of their strategy and wanted to continue their success story. Considering the German reservations, the German–Dutch management finally implemented a mixture of divisional and functional principles in the two sub-companies, with the result that individual product fields – filaments and fibres, technical yarn, and plastics – were responsible for development, production, sales and profitability, whereas other domains remained functionally divided. Henceforth the board meetings of VGF and Enka took place alternately at Wuppertal and at Arnhem, and also the chair of the executive board rotated between a German and a Dutch representative. In this way the managers of the chemical corporation went directly against the proposals of the prestigious US consultancy McKinsey & Company, which had called for definite allocations of power and the implementation of a strictly divisional structure. The construction of new production sites abroad and the rise of multinational corporations such as AKU (Akzo) reinforced the contingency and complexity of entrepreneurial decisions, and created an increasing demand for consultancy. In the case of AKU/VGF, in spring 1969 McKinsey was engaged to prepare the multinational merger and to advance proposals for the future organizational structure.[11]

The success of consultancy was based mainly on the establishment of a trusting customer relationship; for example, John G. McDonald, chief executive of McKinsey in Germany, had a close relationship with Hermann J. Abs, executive spokesman of Deutsche Bank, member of BASF's board of directors and chairman of VGF's supervisory board. Abs was a key figure in the German economy and could therefore pass beneficial information and contacts on to McDonald.[12] The emergence of a multidivisional business structure was one of the most significant innovations on the organizational level in the twentieth century, and consultants had an enormous impact on the diffusion of this model. McKinsey in particular carried great weight concerning the decentralization of British, French and German enterprises in the 1960s, promoting a business structure with decentralized operating subsidiaries, which were responsible for their net operating profits. In this case each subsidiary had its own purchasing and sales department.[13] BASF also awarded a contract to McKinsey. In 1969 the consultancy's study reached the conclusion that BASF was lacking an efficient management structure to achieve its growth goals, and thus proposed organizational changes.[14]

In the case of the AKU/VGF merger the managers decided to implement a mixed functional and divisional structure – in contrast to the proposals of McKinsey – and retained a residuum of self-reliance, with the consequence that McKinsey pulled out. Officially, AKU/VGF had placed two orders with McKinsey in December 1968, including the agreement to work out a proposal on the future organizational structure. The costs of the two orders were divided equally between the German and the Dutch operating companies, and the consultants presented their results in both Wuppertal and Arnhem. On one hand, the managers followed a general contemporary business trend by engaging a consultancy; on the other hand McKinsey was to act as an impartial third party between the German and Dutch business cultures.[15] The managers took note of the proposals, but they regarded the ideas as a basis for discussion rather than as instructions for implementation. At a managerial meeting of AKU/VGF, the Dutch chairman of AKU's executive board, Klaas Soesbeek, stressed to Hellmut Vits, German chairman of the VGF board, that some aspects of McKinsey's study were quite interesting, but that ultimately Vits and he should find a pragmatic and assimilable solution. Here they once more showed their self-confidence.[16]

Both the German and the Dutch managements thought that the McKinsey's plans were too strongly based on the US idea of a multidivisional business structure. The Dutch managers respected the Germans' objections. In consequence Soesbeek visited McKinsey's headquarters in the United States in spring 1969. Soesbeek's view was that the consultancy should develop a special European proposal including a tempered form of divisional structure. But McKinsey was not willing to change its advice because the idea of a multidivisional business structure was de rigueur among US business consultants. However, Vits and Soesbeek did not back down either, and declared that they would be willing to continue the dialogue only if McKinsey accepted the existing contracts. Although the German–Dutch management had initiated the engagement of consultancy – thus revealing the limits of managerial competence – both executive boards were convinced they knew better the organizational requirements of a chemical corporation. In this way, the industrial managers determined the results of consultancy a priori and aroused McKinsey's opposition. The consultants threatened to pull out if the chemical corporation did not implement their proposals to the letter. However, because of the economic recovery in 1969 and their firm belief in their course of action, the industrial managers Vits and Soesbeek concluded that they could relinquish McKinsey's advice and end the liaison.[17]

Thus the compromise between a functional and a divisional business structure at AKU in spring 1969 and the foundation of Akzo in the second half of the year was not the result of consultancy, but rather a demonstration of industrial managers' self-confidence and sense of superiority over external knowledge. They cherished the idea of a chemical corporation and did not accept proposals from an external US consultancy that had no experience in developing and producing chemical goods. Nevertheless industrial managers realized that they lacked organizational knowledge for the upcoming challenges.[18]

The Breakthrough of Market Orientation and External Consultancy: Reconstruction of Enka-Glanzstoff in the 1970s

Consultants were always called in during critical economic situations because they promised a future without crises. Even though they were hired by the management, they were supposed to act as mediator between managers and employees, and often implemented painful but necessary restructuring. Facing the darkening economic developments in the 1970s, Akzo, too, again sought McKinsey's advice. In 1971 Akzo had to take the first measures to rationalize its fibre production, and Ludwig Vaubel, chairman of VGF's executive board, even proposed revisiting McKinsey's organizational propositions of 1969, because there were still problems on the organizational level.[19] The Akzo management intended to abolish the double structure with alternating chairmen and to install a powerful managerial structure with one president at the top of Enka and VGF, but the management of Akzo, Enka and VGF could not reach agreement on the position of the two operating companies. Akzo's proposal to appoint Dieter Wendelstadt as leader of the production companies was not supported by the other VGF managers; this incident gave the impression that the management did not have enough managerial ability. Although Wendelstadt had been the chairman of the executive board of the VGF subsidiary Kuag since 1969 and a member of the VGF managing board since 1971, his colleagues disagreed with the management's proposal.[20] In 1972 the Dutch Enka and the German VGF were renamed Enka-Glanzstoff (EGS) in order to show the consistency of the Akzo fibre group, and finally the managers reached the compromise of informally appointing the co-chairman of the Akzo executive board, Leendert Huibert Meerburg, as temporary president of EGS. Considering the difficult economic situation related to the collapse of the monetary system and appreciation of the German currency, the management demonstrated a high degree of indecision and inability at this time.[21]

The structural overcapacities of West European fibre production put strong pressure on Akzo. However, other European competitors, such as Hoechst and Bayer, also suffered from the sharp decline in the fibre market. In consequence the Akzo management announced structural planning in 1972. Instead of making a linear reduction of capacities at all plants, the management proclaimed their intention to close individual production plants in Breda, Wuppertal-Barmen, Zwijnaarde and Rorschach, and to cut 5,700 jobs. The proposed job losses caused great public indignation. At once trade unions in the relevant countries organized concerted action, and the International Federation of Chemical and General Workers' Unions intervened. The controversy culminated in the occupation of the plant at Breda in the Netherlands. As a result, the Akzo managers revoked the decision on structural planning, but they did not consult the EGS executive board and caused further dissent between the different business administrations. This new dispute led to an offer by EGS top management and the chairman of the Akzo executive board, Gualtherus Kraijenhoff, to tender their resignations. But they remained in office. This impaired the reputation of Akzo and also hindered the implementation of rationalization.[22]

Because of the difficulties at managerial level, the industrial managers again called on McKinsey for help in February 1975. Max Geldens, a McKinsey consultant, presented the market trend of synthetic fibres up until 1980 based on industrial data from 1969 to 1973. Afterwards he illustrated the development of four different fibre segments: (i) fibre products with brilliant business prospects, such as industrial polyester and polyamide filaments, (ii) profitable products in a declining market, such as rayon industrial filament, (iii) products in a structural loss position, such as rayon staple and textile filament, and (iv) products with favourable market prospects, but a weak position on the part of EGS, such as acrylic and polyester staple fibres and industrial steel cord. This presentation was no simple repetition of McKinsey's proposals of 1969, which had been geared to the needs of the AKU/VGF merger and had primarily implied a divisional business structure. Instead, it contained complete market research and a new market strategy for the fibre group of Akzo: the emerging difficulties of the West European fibre industry after 1969 had depressed profitability and called for new measures; only product lines with bright market prospects should be extended and strengthened. The radical strategic alignment with the market was fairly strange to the technical staff at the managerial level.[23] In the eyes of Meerburg the valuation of McKinsey was too optimistic, so he made an impassioned plea for rapid and profound implementation of McKinsey's proposals. The new chairman of the EGS executive board, Bendert Zevenbergen, could not find any new insights in the analysis of McKinsey. He thought that McKinsey had only submitted conclusions that had already been taken by his own board and thus emphasized the correctness of his own action.[24] With McKinsey's analysis, the market became more and more important for the strategic planning of the whole corporation, even though market research and marketing had already played a major part in sales policy and investments in the 1950s and 1960s. In contrast to the assessment of Vaubel in 1970 exposing the company's turnover, now the question of profitability became the focus of attention.[25] This was a substantial change. The fixation on turnover rates was a residue of the economic miracle; these rates gave no reliable information on entrepreneurial success. Even if revenues were central economic indicators before the rupture of the 1970s, the executive board of EGS was surprised to hear about the significance of profits and different market developments from McKinsey.[26]

After the first oil price shock the managers had to take McKinsey's proposals much more seriously than they had in the years 1968 and 1969. The consultants not only strengthened the market orientation within the chemical company, but also became indispensable as analysts of the market and of organizational problems, and consultancy in general became established within the industry. The observation and assessment of the market and corresponding conclusions about strategic planning were genuine managerial functions, which were now taken out of the hands of the executive board. This basically meant that the strict external border of the enterprise became more fluid; from that time on, external knowledge had a determining influence on the company's strategy. The corporation's outward orientation towards the market and the outward perception of consultancies took on greater significance, whereas internal technical knowledge about the production process became less important. The EGS managing board officially supported McKinsey's advice to cut jobs in July 1975; this understandably aroused opposition on the employees' side. Hans Günther Zempelin, later chairman of the Enka group's executive board, confirmed in an interview that McKinsey's study was especially geared towards public criticism. The study was supposed to be objective and to justify management decisions. The structural planning of 1972 had failed because of the pressure from the public and the trade unions; now the management used McKinsey's 'neutral' analysis to enforce a staff reduction. In contrast to McKinsey, the trade unions assessed the market potential of different fibre segments more favourably, and proposed rejecting the advice. The EGS executive board intended to save 300 million DM per year by 1978 and thus was angered by the trade unions. As a consequence, it refused to enter into negotiations with a delegation of international trade unions, which were blamed for trying to use Akzo as a test case for international negotiations. The German management referred to the Works Constitution Act (*Betriebsverfassungsgesetz*), which did not allow the transfer of the works council's powers to an international committee.[27] Because of a loss of 488 million DM at EGS in 1975, the German and Dutch works councils showed more willingness to reach a compromise than the trade unions. After the Dutch works council had agreed to close down a plant at Arnhem and to cut further jobs in the Netherlands, the German general works council also entered into an agreement and compromised on interest reconciliation (*Interessenausgleich*) and a social plan (*Sozialplan*), which included the loss of nine hundred jobs in Germany.[28]

Despite all these rationalizations and job cuts, Akzo faced enormous economic problems in the second half of the 1970s. Structural change in the European fibre industry had not yet been concluded, so in the years 1976 and 1977 new restructurings were initiated and further fibre plants had to be closed down. Once again McKinsey's expertise was in demand.

The consultancy's new proposal focused on the portfolio and demanded the convergence of profit rates in the various divisions. In contrast to other divisions, the company's fibre division once more got into trouble. As a result, the management pooled Akzo's German and Dutch fibre interests in the new Enka group. In this way, Akzo ended the traditional national separation of fibre production. Subsequently the new Enka group concentrated its activities in Wuppertal and reduced its unprofitable product lines. At the same time several European fibre producers, such as Hoechst, Bayer, ICI and Akzo, arranged a structural crisis cartel at the EEC level, which was accompanied by an enormous reduction of fibre capacities in Western Europe. Because of this reduction and the economic recovery in the 1980s, the Enka group's operating results improved again. This development confirmed the predictions of the consultancy and thus indirectly reinforced the significance of external knowledge for industrial enterprises in general.[29]

Conclusion

The rupture after the post-war boom posed an enormous challenge to Western societies and was accompanied by a profound change in profit strategies and business structures at European enterprises. At the time of the economic miracle, enterprises only had to satisfy demand, but in the 1960s the wishes and intentions of the customers, as well as market orientation, became more important. The exogenous shocks of the 1970s reinforced economic contingency, and international competition increased. Industrial managers had reached the limits of their ability. Geographical expansion and diversification generated large enterprises operating in different countries and on several product markets; thus managements faced difficulties bringing them all into line. At the same time, the operations of multinational corporations were often in the hands of numerous powerful players, so even if the management had a reasonable profit strategy, it was hard to implement. Against this background, the rise of consultancies is easily comprehensible.

Although there were consultancies in Europe from the 1920s onwards, their influence assumed new significance from the 1960s onwards. With the intensified expansion of US multinationals to Europe, US consultancies entered the European market and soon offered their services to European enterprises. This coincided with the advent of new organizational problems on the part of managements. Although there was no uniform consultancy model in Europe, US consultancies had an enormous impact on the decentralization of European enterprises. German managers generally tried to keep consultants out of executive boards until the early 1970s, as they considered the engagement of consultancies to be a demonstration of their own lack of competence; they remained suspicious towards consultants. But with the challenges of the 1970s, the managements opened the door to consultancies and thus caused a fundamental change on the managerial level. Consultancies dissolved the strict hierarchies and external borders of companies, and evolved into a permanent auxiliary service to the top managements of industrial enterprises. The advice of consultancies became necessary to maintain the fiction of assurance.[30]

In the case of AKU/VGF, a broad campaign by the German and the Dutch trade unions had hindered restructuring of Akzo in the early 1970s. Based on McKinsey's authority, in 1975 the management closed down several plants and reduced fibre production. In this way US consultancies not only contributed to the diffusion of multidivisional business structures in Western Europe, but also became influential players in addition to management. The marketization of enterprises had two components: first, the entry of external players into industrial enterprises, with consultants assuming managerial functions within companies and offering their organizational knowledge as a tradable good; and second, in their reports consultants emphasized the importance of markets and profits, and persuaded companies to pursue this orientation. The relative importance of technological knowledge diminished and instead the market became the new leitmotif at all levels of the business.[31]

Consultants stressed the importance of a divisional business structure to impose a greater market orientation encompassing several product lines within one company. European enterprises wanted to profit from this organizational innovation. BASF, Bayer and Hoechst relinquished their functional separation, and Akzo finally also implemented a divisional structure based on consultant services. That way, influential consultancies such as McKinsey helped to transmit US models of business organization to Europe (although these ideas had to be assimilated to Europe's business traditions). From an organizational perspective, the restructuring of industrial enterprises was necessary because of the enormous corporate growth, both at home and abroad. The divisional structure was supposed to guarantee a close relationship to the market, because every product line had to adapt sales, distributions and investments to its special market conditions. Now the managerial overload involved in organizing a huge economic entity with numerous departments became apparent. External knowledge and the legitimacy needed to impose severe budget and job cuts became more significant. Thus external consultancies not only changed internal business structures and intensified the market orientation of individual product lines, but their advice itself became a tradable good on the market. As a consequence, the rigid borders of enterprises became more fluid, and outward orientation became more important during the 1970s.

Christian Marx is researcher at the Research Centre for Europe, Modern and Contemporary History, University of Trier. He has published essays on contemporary business and environmental history, including *Paul Reusch und die Gutehoffnungshütte: Leitung eines deutschen Großunternehmens* (Göttingen, 2013); 'Failed Solutions of the Energy Crises: Nuclear Power, Coal Conversion, and the Chemical Industry in West Germany since the 1960s', in *Historical Social Research* 39(4) (2014): 251–71; and 'Der zerplatzte Traum vom industriellen Atomzeitalter: Der misslungene Einstieg westdeutscher Chemiekonzerne in die Kernenergie während der 1960er und 70er Jahre', in *Zeitschrift für Unternehmensgeschichte* 60(1) (2015): 3–28.

Notes

1. 'Stärker als der Staat? SPIEGEL-Report über Einfluß und Arbeitsweise der multinationalen Konzerne', *Der Spiegel* 1974, no. 18 (1974), 36–54; 'Stärker als der Staat?', *Der Spiegel* 1974, no. 19 (1974), 60–77; 'Stärker als der Staat?', *Der Spiegel* 1974, no. 21 (1974), 46–62.

2. Eric Hobsbawm, *The Age of Extremes: The Short Twentieth Century* (London, 1995); Horst Kern and Michael Schumann, *Das Ende der Arbeitsteilung? Rationalisierung in der industriellen Produktion* (Munich, 1984); Morten Reitmayer and Ruth Rosenberger (eds), *Unternehmen am Ende des 'goldenen Zeitalters': Die 1970er Jahre in unternehmens- und wirtschaftshistorischer Perspektive* (Essen, 2008).

3. Klaus Dörre and Bernd Röttger (eds), *Das neue Marktregime: Konturen eines nachfordistischen Produktionsmodells* (Hamburg, 2003); Michael J. Piore and Charles F. Sabel, *The Second Industrial Divide: Possibilities for Prosperity* (New York, 1984).

4. Ludwig Vaubel, *Glanzstoff, Enka, Aku, Akzo: Unternehmensleitung im nationalen und internationalen Spannungsfeld 1929 bis 1978*, 3 vols. (Wuppertal, 1986), vol. 1; Ben Wubs, 'A Dutch Multinationals's Miracle in Post-War Germany', *Jahrbuch für Wirtschaftsgeschichte* 1 (2012): 15–41.

5. Anselm Doering-Manteuffel and Lutz Raphael, *Nach dem Boom: Perspektiven auf die Zeitgeschichte seit 1970*, 3rd, unchanged edn (Göttingen, 2012).

6. Werner Abelshauser, 'Die BASF seit der Neugründung 1952', in *Die BASF: Eine Unternehmensgeschichte*, ed. Werner Abelshauser (Munich, 2002), 525–35.

7. Vaubel, *Glanzstoff*, 132–37.

8. 'Gedanken zur möglichen Zusammenarbeit', 16.06.1967, 195-A2-53, Stiftung Rheinisch-Westfälisches Wirtschaftsarchiv zu Köln (RWWA); Vaubel, *Glanzstoff*, 141.

9. Business Report Akzo N.V. 1969, p. 17, Business Report Glanzstoff AG 1971, p. 10, Wirtschaftsarchiv Universität Köln (WAUK); Vaubel, *Glanzstoff*, 137–59.

10. Vaubel, *Glanzstoff*, 160.

11. Abelshauser, 'Neugründung', 469–78; Susanne Hilger, 'American Consultants in the German Consumer Chemical Industry: The Work of the Stanford Research Institute at Henkel in the 1960s and 1970s', *Entreprises et Histoire* 25 (2000): 46–64; Neuordnung AKU/ Glanzstoff und McKinsey, 1969, 195-B0-52, RWWA.

12. Lothar Gall, *Der Bankier Hermann Josef Abs: Eine Biographie* (Munich, 2004), 319–50; Matthias Kipping, 'American Management Consulting Companies in Western Europe, 1920– 1990: Products, Reputation, and Relationships', *Business History Review* 73 (1999): 190–220.

13. Michael Faust, 'Consultancies as Actors in Knowledge Arenas: Evidence from Germany', in *Management Consulting: Emergence and Dynamics of a Knowledge Industry*, ed.

Matthias Kipping and Lars Engwall (Oxford, 2002), 146–63; Christopher D. McKenna, *The World's Newest Profession: Management Consulting in the Twentieth Century* (Cambridge, 2006), 165–91.

14. Abelshauser, 'Neugründung', 570–84.

15. Sonderprotokoll AKU/VGF-Vorstandsbesprechung, 5.12.1968, 195-A2-38, RWWA.

16. Notiz betr. Neuordnung AKU/VGF, 4.02.1969, 195-A2-29, RWWA.

17. Notiz betr. Neuordnung AKU/VGF, 19.03.1969, 195-A2-29, RWWA; Vaubel, *Glanzstoff*, 160–66.

18. Luchien Karsten and Kees van Veen, 'Management Consultancies in the Netherlands in the 1950s and 1960s: Between Systematic Context and External Influences', in *Management Consulting: Emergence and Dynamics of a Knowledge Industry*, ed. Matthias Kipping and Lars Engwall (Oxford, 2002), 65.

19. Vaubel to Zempelin, 26.04.1971, 195-C1-26, RWWA; Business Report Akzo and VGF 1971, WAUK.

20. Vaubel, *Glanzstoff*, 183.

21. Umfimierung Glanzstoff AG in Enka Glanzstoff AG, 1972, 195-B0-54, RWWA.

22. Vaubel, *Glanzstoff*, 184–88.

23. Personal Notes of the Meeting, 24.06.1975, 195-A6-23, RWWA; Ergänzungen zum Protokoll der EGS-Vorstandssitzung, 24.02.1975, 195-B6-1-28, RWWA; Vaubel, *Glanzstoff*, 233, 241.

24. Personal Notes of the Secretary, 17.07.1975, 195-A6-22, RWWA; Personal Notes of the Meeting, 24.06.1975, 195-A6-23, RWWA.

25. Christian Kleinschmidt, 'An Americanised Company in Germany: The Vereinigte Glanzstoff Fabriken AG in the 1950s', in *The Americanisation of European Business: The Marshall Plan and the Transfer of US Management Models*, ed. Matthias Kipping and Ove Bjarnar (London and New York, 1998), 171–89; Christian Kleinschmidt, *Der produktive Blick: Wahrnehmung amerikanischer und japanischer Management- und Produktionsmethoden durch deutsche Unternehmer 1950–1985* (Berlin, 2002), 227–33; Referat Dr. Vaubel, 11.08.1970, 195-A6-23, RWWA.

26. Erklärung EG-Vorstand zur Marktstudie von McKinsey, in: informiert 35(9), 1975, pp. 1–2, 195-B0-59, RWWA.

27. Deutsche Übersetzung des Aktionärsbriefes, 24.11.1975, 195-B0-58, RWWA; Gefährdet Gewerkschafts-Strategie Arbeitsplätze?, 25.10.1975, Presseerklärung des EG-Vorstands, 26.09.1975 und 23.10.1975, 195-B0-59, RWWA.

28. Deutsche Übersetzung des Aktionärsbriefes, 24.11.1975, 195-B0-58, RWWA; Interessenausgleich und Sozialplan, 06.02.1976, 195-B0-59, RWWA; Vaubel, *Glanzstoff*, 189–91.

29. Business Report Enka Glanzstoff AG 1976, pp. 14–16, and 1977, p. 7; Business Report Akzo 1977, pp. 6–7; Christian Marx, 'A European Structural Crisis Cartel as Solution to a Sectoral Depression? The West European Fibre Industry in the 1970s and 1980s', *Jahrbuch für Wirtschaftsgeschichte* 1 (2017): 163–97; Harm G. Schröter, 'Kartelle als Kriseninstrumente in Europa nach 1970: Das Beispiel des europäischen Chemiefaserkartells', *Jahrbuch für Wirtschaftsgeschichte* 1 (2012): 87–102; Akzo faßt Chemiefaser-Unternehmen zusammen, in: Information für die Führungskräfte 4/1977, Das Zukunftsbild von Enka Glanzstoff, in: Information für die Führungskräfte 6/1977, 195-B0-58, RWWA; Zempelin an Vaubel, 02.02.1976, 195-B0-59, RWWA; Vaubel, *Glanzstoff*, 180–81, 191–92.

30. Alfred Kieser, 'Managers as Marionettes? Using Fashion Theories to Explain the Success of Consultancies', in *Management Consulting: Emergence and Dynamics of a Knowledge Industry*, ed. Matthias Kipping and Lars Engwall (Oxford, 2002), 167–83; Matthias Kipping, 'The U.S. Influence on the Evolution of Management Consultancies in Britain, France, and Germany since 1945', *Business and Economic History* 25(1) (1996): 112–23; Werner Plumpe,

'Nützliche Fiktionen? Der Wandel der Unternehmen und die Literatur der Berater', in *Unternehmen am Ende des 'goldenen Zeitalters': Die 1970er Jahre in unternehmens- und wirtschafts-historischer Perspektive*, ed. Morten Reitmayer and Ruth Rosenberger (Essen, 2008), 251–69; Helmut Raithel, 'Mut zur Selbstverleugnung', *Manager Magazin* 12 (1975): 60–64.

31. Pierre Bourdieu, *Gegenfeuer* (Konstanz, 2004); Ulrich Brinkmann, *Die unsichtbare Faust des Marktes: Betriebliche Kontrolle und Koordination im Finanzmarktkapitalismus* (Berlin, 2011), 45–77; Dieter Sauer, 'Vermarktlichung und Vernetzung der Unternehmens- und Betriebsorganisation', in *Handbuch Arbeitssoziologie*, ed. Fritz Böhle, Günter G. Voß and Günther Wachtler (Wiesbaden, 2010), 545–68.

Bibliography

Abelshauser, Werner, 'Die BASF seit der Neugründung 1952', in *Die BASF: Eine Unternehmensgeschichte*, ed. Werner Abelshauser (Munich, 2002), 359–637.

Bourdieu, Pierre, *Gegenfeuer* (Konstanz, 2004).

Brinkmann, Ulrich, *Die unsichtbare Faust des Marktes: Betriebliche Kontrolle und Koordination im Finanzmarktkapitalismus* (Berlin, 2011).

Doering-Manteuffel, Anselm, and Lutz Raphael, *Nach dem Boom: Perspektiven auf die Zeitgeschichte seit 1970*, 3rd, unchanged edn (Göttingen, 2012).

Dörre, Klaus, and Bernd Röttger (eds), *Das neue Marktregime: Konturen eines nachfordistischen Produktionsmodells* (Hamburg, 2003).

Faust, Michael, 'Consultancies as Actors in Knowledge Arenas: Evidence from Germany', in *Management Consulting: Emergence and Dynamics of a Knowledge Industry*, ed. Matthias Kipping and Lars Engwall (Oxford, 2002), 146–63.

Gall, Lothar, *Der Bankier Hermann Josef Abs: Eine Biographie* (Munich, 2004).

Hilger, Susanne, 'American Consultants in the German Consumer Chemical Industry: The Work of the Stanford Research Institute at Henkel in the 1960s and 1970s', *Entreprises et Histoire* 25 (2000): 46–64.

Hobsbawm, Eric, *The Age of Extremes: The Short Twentieth Century* (London, 1995).

Karsten, Luchien, and Kees van Veen, 'Management Consultancies in the Netherlands in the 1950s and 1960s: Between Systematic Context and External Influences', in *Management Consulting: Emergence and Dynamics of a Knowledge Industry*, ed. Matthias Kipping and Lars Engwall (Oxford, 2002), 52–69.

Kern, Horst, and Michael Schumann, *Das Ende der Arbeitsteilung? Rationalisierung in der industriellen Produktion* (Munich, 1984).

Kieser, Alfred, 'Managers as Marionettes? Using Fashion Theories to Explain the Success of Consultancies', in *Management Consulting: Emergence and Dynamics of a Knowledge Industry*, ed. Matthias Kipping and Lars Engwall (Oxford, 2002), 167–83.

Kipping, Matthias, 'The U.S. Influence on the Evolution of Management Consultancies in Britain, France, and Germany since 1945', *Business and Economic History* 25(1) (1996): 112–23.

_____, 'American Management Consulting Companies in Western Europe, 1920–1990: Products, Reputation, and Relationships', *Business History Review* 73 (1999): 190–220.

Kleinschmidt, Christian, 'An Americanised Company in Germany: The Vereinigte Glanzstoff Fabriken AG in the 1950s', in *The Americanisation of European Business: The Marshall Plan and the Transfer of US Management Models*, ed. Matthias Kipping and Ove Bjarnar (London and New York, 1998), 171–89.

_____, *Der produktive Blick: Wahrnehmung amerikanischer und japanischer Management- und Produktionsmethoden durch deutsche Unternehmer 1950–1985* (Berlin, 2002).

Marx, Christian, 'A European Structural Crisis Cartel as Solution to a Sectoral Depression? The West European Fibre Industry in the 1970s and 1980s', *Jahrbuch für Wirtschaftsgeschichte* 1 (2017): 163–97.

McKenna, Christopher D., *The World's Newest Profession: Management Consulting in the Twentieth Century* (Cambridge, 2006).

Piore, Michael J., and Charles F. Sabel, *The Second Industrial Divide: Possibilities for Prosperity* (New York, 1984).

Plumpe, Werner, 'Nützliche Fiktionen? Der Wandel der Unternehmen und die Literatur der Berater', in *Unternehmen am Ende des 'goldenen Zeitalters': Die 1970er Jahre in unternehmens- und wirtschaftshistorischer Perspektive*, ed. Morten Reitmayer and Ruth Rosenberger (Essen, 2008), 251–69.

Raithel, Helmut, 'Mut zur Selbstverleugnung', *Manager Magazin* 12 (1975): 60–64.

Reitmayer, Morten, and Ruth Rosenberger (eds), *Unternehmen am Ende des 'goldenen Zeitalters': Die 1970er Jahre in unternehmens- und wirtschaftshistorischer Perspektive* (Essen, 2008).

Sauer, Dieter, 'Vermarktlichung und Vernetzung der Unternehmens- und Betriebsorganisation', in *Handbuch Arbeitssoziologie*, ed. Fritz Böhle, Günter G. Voß and Günther Wachtler (Wiesbaden, 2010), 545–68.

Schröter, Harm G., 'Kartelle als Kriseninstrumente in Europa nach 1970: Das Beispiel des europäischen Chemiefaserkartells', *Jahrbuch für Wirtschaftsgeschichte* 1 (2012): 87–102.

Vaubel, Ludwig, *Glanzstoff, Enka, Aku, Akzo: Unternehmensleitung im nationalen und internationalen Spannungsfeld 1929 bis 1978*, 3 vols (Wuppertal, 1986), vol. 1.

Wubs, Ben, 'A Dutch Multinationals's Miracle in Post-War Germany', *Jahrbuch für Wirtschaftsgeschichte* 1 (2012): 15–41.

CHAPTER 13

From Mutual Society to Public Corporation

The Case of the Halifax Building Society

Matthew Hollow

Introduction

In most historical accounts of the UK building society movement, the
late 1980s and early 1990s have been presented as the key years in terms
of the movement's commercial development and structural modernization. According to such accounts, it was in this period that the sector was
transformed from a 'somewhat sleepy' and conservative financial industry,
offering steady rates of interest to homebuyers and small-time savers, into a
commercially competitive and fully integrated member of the UK financial
sector, providing a full range of financial services and payment facilities to its
customers.[1] Organizationally, too, it has been suggested that these years were
crucial in the managerial modernization of the movement, with the spate of
conversions from mutual ownership to public limited company (plc) status
that took place in the early 1990s being taken as proof of the extent to which
the movement embraced the market-oriented, corporatist mentality of the
era.[2] Similarly, this increasingly commercially oriented outlook has also been
taken as evidence of how far profit maximization and commercial expansion
came to replace stability and reliability as the chief priorities for managers of
UK building societies.[3]

From a historiographical perspective, such interpretations accord closely with the more general historical depiction of the 1980s as a decade of widespread financial liberalization and legislative deregulation in which neoliberal free-market economic theories came to the fore, eroding, and eventually superseding, the supposed 'welfarist consensus' that had dominated in post-1945 Europe.[4] Typically, these sorts of accounts are built around historical narratives that privilege and emphasize political developments at the legislative level, with changes in the regulation of financial markets commonly identified as being the key causal factor in explaining the organizational and structural changes that took place in industries such as the UK building society sector at this time.[5] On top of this, it is often the case that the 1980s – and to a lesser extent the 1990s – are presented and pinpointed as decades of radical upheaval and profound change in which many of the beliefs and assumptions of the previous decades, especially those related to finance and banking, were simply swept away and replaced.[6]

The aim of this chapter is to reassess the validity of such assumptions by looking back to the 1970s and analysing how far the sorts of organizational and structural changes so commonly associated with the 1980s really did differ from what had come before. The analysis will be centred on the Halifax Building Society – the largest building society in the United Kingdom at this time – and the organizational changes that occurred within it during the 1970s. Particular attention will be paid to the organization's managerial culture and how this changed over this period. Consideration will also be given to the structural transformations that took place within the Halifax during the 1970s, and the extent to which these were influenced by technological innovations. Ultimately, the intention is to use the example of the Halifax Building Society as a case study through which to assess how far the neoliberal reforms of the 1980s had their origins in the structural and organizational changes that took place in the financial sector during the 1970s. As such, this chapter not only provides a fresh insight into the transformations that took place in the UK building society movement during the latter years of the twentieth century, but also contributes to ongoing debates about how best to categorize and define the 1970s.

Origins and Development

The UK Building Society Sector

In historical terms, the story of the UK building society can be said to have first begun with the expansion of the Friendly Society movement in the eighteenth century.[7] Set up in response to the changing needs of the UK's rapidly expanding urban and working–class population, these mutual associations provided a diverse range of financial benefits to their members, including: provision for sickness or infirmity, support in case of the death of a family member, burial costs, and money towards the cost of new furniture.[8] In almost all cases, the money for these services would be provided by the members themselves, who would contribute small sums to a central pot on a regular basis (on the assumption that, should they ever need assistance or support, there would be money there to support them).

From these mutual friendly societies emerged the idea of forming local building clubs and associations with the specific aim of providing houses for their members.[9] In terms of their structure and size, these early building societies generally had between twenty and thirty members, each of whom paid a regular subscription fee to be part of the society. When sufficient money had been collected, the society then purchased some land and began building a new house for one of their members to live in.[10] Once all members of the society had been allotted a new house in this way, the society then disbanded.[11] The first-known building society of this sort is believed to be the Birmingham-based Ketley's Building Society, which was formed in 1775.[12]

Although these terminating building societies proved popular amongst working–class Britons, they were not without their problems: first, many members had to wait years before they were actually able to obtain a house; second, in the event of anyone leaving the society, it proved particularly difficult to attract new members as they necessarily had to make (often quite significant) back payments to put them on an equal footing with the other members; and third, many societies were run in such an amateurish way that there often ended up being insufficient funds to actually provide all members with a new house.[13]

Largely as a result of these problems, a new type of building society increasingly came to the fore in the UK during the nineteenth century – the permanent building society. Unlike terminating societies, these organizations (as the name suggests) did not have a limited lifespan, nor a restricted membership size. Instead, they operated on the principle that investors (i.e. those looking for somewhere safe and profitable to deposit their savings) and borrowers (i.e. those looking for mortgages to purchase homes) should be treated as two distinct groups.[14] This meant that they could, in theory, enrol new savers at any time, and in any number. It also meant that they could be much more flexible in terms of how and when they lent their money to prospective borrowers.[15]

Thanks predominantly to this increased flexibility and potential for growth, permanent building societies slowly emerged as the dominant organizational form in the UK building society sector, and by 1936, terminating societies made up only 16 per cent of all building societies in the UK.[16]

These permanent building societies (including, by this time, most of the subsequent 'big players' in the sector – Woolwich, Nationwide, Bradford, etc.) were also aided by the passing of the Building Societies Act of 1874, which helped further consolidate their position by providing clear guidelines as to what a building society's primary role was (i.e. to accept savings from the public and provide housing loans on the security of land) and by recognizing them as legal entities, distinct and separate from other financial organizations.[17] Despite some subsequent adjustments in later years, the basic principles underlying this legislative framework remained essentially the same up until the 1970s.

The Halifax Building Society

The origins of the Halifax Building Society can be traced back to 1852 when a group of local men affiliated to the town's Loyal Georgian Society met in the Old Cock Inn, Halifax, to discuss the possibility of setting up an investment and loan company for the mutual benefit of local workers. By 1853, they had garnered enough support to make their idea viable and by the winter of that year the Halifax Permanent Building and Investment Society, as it was then known, had been officially established.[18] The society's first secretary was Jonas Dearnley Taylor, who oversaw the organization's operations from its founding right up until his death in 1902. Under his stewardship the society rapidly expanded, and branch offices were soon opened in neighbouring working-class districts around Halifax – then a major industrial town with thriving wool and cotton manufacturing sectors.[19]

Like most other UK building societies of this era, the Halifax was an organization in which strong emphasis was placed on the virtues of thrift and self-help.[20] Indeed, at the society's first annual meeting in 1854 it was publicly noted that the guiding principle of the organization should be to encourage 'independence, enterprise, liberality and patriotism' among the region's 'labouring classes'.[21] Adopting the methods employed by most other building societies at this time, the Halifax operated on a cooperative basis whereby members of the society collectively contributed, through the purchase of subscription shares, to a central pot of money from which each individual member could, in a staggered fashion, borrow money to fund house purchases.[22] Public shares in the Halifax worth £120 were initially offered at the rate of 2s 6d per week, while borrowers could receive an 'advance share' of £60 on which they paid interest at 5 per cent over a thirteen-year period.[23] In a bid to make more funds available to those looking to borrow, the Halifax also began offering paid-up shares with an annual interest rate of 3.5 per cent from 1888 onwards, both to former members of the society who had already paid off their original subscriptions and to members of the general public who were simply looking for a secure place to deposit their savings. This in turn enabled the Halifax to dramatically expand its customer base, and by 1913 it had established itself as the biggest building society in the United Kingdom, with assets of over £3 million.[24]

In terms of its management, the Halifax was, like most other nineteenth-century building societies, very much an organization that favoured continuity and tradition over innovation and dynamism.[25] For instance, after Taylor's death in 1902, the board of directors took the decision to appoint Enoch Hill, then secretary of the Leek United Permanent Building Society, as the Halifax's new secretary, a role that he held until 1938. Similarly, every effort was made to keep staff salaries at a constant level, with the result that many of those who worked at the Halifax during the nineteenth century remained on the same level of pay throughout their time at the organization.[26]

Following the upheavals caused by the First World War, however, the Halifax – now under the stewardship of Enoch Hill – began to embark upon a much more concerted policy of branch expansion. In 1924 it opened its first London office and by 1928 it had over one hundred branches throughout the United Kingdom.[27] Its position as the market leader was further reinforced in 1928 thanks to the decision to amalgamate with the Halifax Equitable Building Society, the second largest building society in the United Kingdom at this time. This merger resulted in the establishment of the rebranded Halifax Building Society, which, with assets of nearly £47 million, was over five times larger than its nearest rival.[28] Such dominance enabled the Halifax to weather the depressed economic conditions of the 1930s and the disruptions brought about by the Second World War, and by 1967 its assets had passed the £1 billion mark.

Structural Changes

For the UK building society industry as a whole, the 1970s was very much a decade of growth and expansion. Indeed, by the end of the decade it was estimated that 48 per cent of the UK adult population held a building society account (up from 17 per cent in 1970).[29] Geographically, the building society industry also expanded rapidly during this period, with the number of branches nationwide rising from 1,662 in 1968 to 5,716 by 1980.[30] Driving this growth was a rapid rise in real incomes, which led to an unprecedented surge in demand for mortgages.[31] Also significant in this respect was the gradual withdrawal of the state from the housing market and the legislative restrictions in place at this time that prohibited the British from providing mortgages to prospective homeowners.[32]

As the undisputed industry leader, the Halifax Building Society was uniquely placed to exploit these opportunities.[33] Over a hundred new branches were opened between 1970 and 1980, and by the end of the decade the Halifax had a nationwide network of just under four hundred branches and thirteen hundred agencies.[34] Thanks in part to this expansion, the assets of the Halifax Building Society increased dramatically, growing to over £8,943 million by 1980.

Alongside this rapid commercial and geographic expansion, the 1970s was also a hugely significant decade for the Halifax Building Society in that it saw the opening of a brand new head office in the centre of Halifax at a cost of some £10 million. Officially opened by the Queen on 13 November 1974, the new building absorbed all the administrative and clerical functions that had previously been housed in the society's old Commercial Street premises, the Halifax's head office since 1921.[35] The site itself, which had previously been home to a brewery and covered an area of some 54,000 sq. ft., was also adjoined to the society's recently constructed computer centre, and thus enabled greater levels of integration between administrative and technical staff.[36] In total, the new building housed just over a thousand employees, approximately one-tenth of the society's entire workforce.[37] On top of this, the new head office featured a specially constructed sub-basement which provided over a million cubic feet of space for the safe storage of the vast numbers of property deeds held by the society.[38]

However, it was not just the size and scale of the society's new head office that was significant; it was also the extent to which the new building seemed to physically embody a new, more forward-thinking and dynamic approach to the business of money lending and deposit taking. Bold, angular, and unashamedly modern, it was both a reflection of the Halifax's dominant status and a statement about its future ambitions. Indeed, as the Halifax's chairman, Ian Maclean, informed those in attendance at the 121st Annual General Meeting on 20 May 1974, it was thanks to the 'advanced design' of the new building that the society could confidently 'meet the demands of the present and future'.[39] Furthermore, the open-plan internal layout of the new head office, influenced heavily by the 'Open Office' or '*Burolandschaft*' principles of office design that were coming into fashion at this time, also reflected the extent to which the society's management sought to encourage more flexible and integrated working habits within the organization.[40]

Alongside these improvements to the society's central administrative facilities, efforts were also made to reorganize the Halifax's internal operating procedures along more streamlined and efficient lines. Particular attention was devoted to the issue of how to maintain control over the society's ever-increasing number of branches and agencies. After much internal discussion, a decision was taken on 19 January 1977 to divide the Halifax's branch network into twelve separate regions, each with its own regional manager.[41] The most significant aspect of this new regional structure was that it devolved many of the less important clerical and administrative duties to the local management level, greatly reducing the workload of the head office and allowing for far more efficient communication between different regions. Again, the Halifax was very much an industry leader in this area, with societies such as Nationwide, Anglia, Bradford and Bingley, and the Abbey National all subsequently implementing similar structural reforms.[42] Further administrative changes also occurred within the Halifax in 1978 when it was decided that the society's board of directors would meet just once a month (as opposed to the weekly meetings that had taken place previously).[43] Again, this decision reflected a desire on the part of the society's central management to pass on more of the day-to-day management decisions to the clerical and administrative staff. Administratively, these structural changes were particularly significant in that they represented a marked attempt to introduce more streamlined and efficient approaches to the running and supervision of the Halifax Building Society, demonstrating, above all else, just how fast in this period the society was moving away from its mutual, cooperative roots and towards a more commercially oriented outlook.

Technological Innovations

Apart from the opening of the society's new head office in 1974, the most discernible structural transformations that took place within the Halifax during the 1970s were all linked to advances in computer technology. Interest had first been shown in the potential benefits of computerized systems in the early 1960s, and in 1964 a new twelve-strong task force was established to begin preparing for the installation of the new computer.[44] The machine itself – an IBM System 360 costing £300,000 – was subsequently installed in a new purpose-built eight-storey computer centre on Trinity Road, Halifax, in September 1967.[45] Initially, its function was limited solely to the computerization and centralized storage of all of the society's investors' accounts, a conversion process that was eventually completed in the autumn of 1969.[46] However, such was the success of this experiment that the society's management quickly began making plans to introduce computerized technology into other areas of the Halifax's business, and in February 1968 it was decided to install a new 'staff online system' at a cost of £21,000. It eventually became operational in early 1971, housing all of the staff records, previously locally held, on a new IBM 2740 terminal in the society's central computer centre.[47]

From an administrative perspective, the practical benefits of these new computerized data storage systems were considerable. Not only did they ensure that all of the Halifax's account data were formatted along standardized lines, but they also enabled the society's management to more easily collate information on daily returns from all the branches, and thus to better comprehend the overall business picture. Indeed, as one of the computer centre's new members of staff proudly informed one local Halifax newspaper, the 'ultra-modern' IBM system was so efficient that it was 'capable of handling workloads that would [otherwise] keep an army of clerks occupied'.[48] On top of this, the fact that all of the society's records were held on a central computer also helped to ensure that the process of 'switching over' to a decimalized currency, which took place across the United Kingdom on 15 February 1971, proceeded much more smoothly than might otherwise have been the case.[49]

Nevertheless, these initial attempts at computerization were still very limited in that they continued to operate on a rudimentary 'batch processing' system, whereby details of branch transactions were physically posted through to the computer centre in daily batches and then, subsequently, entered onto the society's central computer system. This process was not only extremely time consuming, it was also very inefficient, as it meant that individual branches did not themselves have direct access to investors' accounts.[50] As a result, the Halifax's management remained keen to introduce more efficient automating technology into the organization. The first phase of upgrading began in August 1971, and by November 1972 the Halifax's new IBM 3980 Bank Teleprocessing System was fully operational.[51] The main difference with this system was that, unlike with the previous model, account data were entered directly by branch employees into individual terminals located in branch offices, and then transmitted electronically to the central computer centre. This not only sped-up the data processing time, but also enabled branch managers to directly access information about any individual account.[52] On top of this, because the 3980 Teleprocessing System was also used by most other clearing banks in the United Kingdom at this time, tracking and recording individual money transactions was also made considerably easier.[53]

Further technological innovation continued throughout the decade. In 1974 a research team was commissioned to look into the practicalities of rewriting the society's entire accounting system to make it more computer-friendly; this eventually led to the introduction of the new Revised Accounting System (RAS) in early 1977.[54] A new automated document retrieval system called 'Conserv-a-trieve' was also installed in 1974 in the basement of the society's new Trinity Road Head Office, which had the capacity to handle up to three thousand references per hour.[55] Even more significant was the installation of the first ATM machine in July 1978. Again, this development not only enabled the Halifax to carry out transactions more effectively and speedily, it also allowed for further business expansion and product diversification, principally by enabling the society to compete more effectively for a share of the current account market.[56] Indeed, as this last example so aptly demonstrates, one of the main reasons why the technological advances made during the 1970s were so historically significant was the fact that they helped to lay the structural groundwork on which the Halifax's subsequent entry into the retail financial services industry in the late 1980s and early 1990s was based.

Organizational Culture

Like most other UK building societies, the Halifax had a well-established tradition of employing locally and promoting from within.[57] Similarly, the whole recruitment culture of the society was very much based upon the concept of lifetime employment, the expectation being that employees would progress gradually through the ranks of the company from school-leaving age onwards.[58] From the early 1970s, however, this informal recruitment and training culture increasingly began to be challenged. Greater importance began to be given to educational qualifications and, by the end of the decade, it was expected that all new recruits would possess at least six GCE 'O Levels' (including English and Maths) and two 'A Levels' (the standard exams taken by all school leavers in the United Kingdom at that time).[59] Likewise, the recruitment of experts from outside the society also increased. For instance, in the initial phase of recruitment for the new computer centre, the society's management actively sought to bring in outsiders who had previous experience of working with IBM systems, rather than just relying on internal promotion.[60]

Alongside this enhanced interest in staff training and professional development, the Halifax also began to place greater emphasis on the development of leadership qualities among its managerial staff. New training courses in 'action-centred leadership' and 'pre-manager development' were introduced, and the number of seminars and one-day training courses devoted to leadership skills also increased.[61] On top of this, the rapid expansion in higher education facilities across the United Kingdom in the post-war period, along with the increasing availability of part-time and distance-learning courses, also enabled the Halifax to begin nominating members of staff to attend specialist business training courses run by the Ashridge Management Centre and the London Business School.[62] Moreover, managerial responsibilities also began to be subdivided into separate technical, social and administrative roles as more emphasis began to be placed on the creation of individual 'management teams'.[63] Again, these trends reflected developments across the building society sector as a whole, with the ratio of management expenses to mean assets increasing throughout the industry from 0.65 in 1969 to 1.30 by 1982.[64]

Discursively, the phrases and ideas expressed in the Halifax's training manuals and assessment sheets also began to change during the 1970s as more and more terms and concepts from the burgeoning disciplines of business and management studies began to enter the society's lexicon. Specialist 'sales teams' were established in many branches, while branch managers were increasingly encouraged to 'network' at business symposiums and to implement 'manpower planning strategies' to better determine future 'business needs'.[65] On a practical level, this increased interest in management theory and organizational behaviour also had some fairly major effects upon the organizational culture within the Halifax. Of particular note was the extent to which interdepartmental communication and the sharing out of administrative responsibilities began to be actively promoted as means of improving branch efficiency.[66] Likewise, far greater emphasis began to be placed on the value of statistical and quantitative analysis, with branch managers encouraged to utilize market segmentation data and to make decisions 'on the basis of objective rather than subjective "facts"'.[67]

Another significant organizational transformation in this period was the growth in importance of the society's advertising and marketing departments. One factor behind this development was the increased competition among different building societies in the opening of new branches across the United Kingdom, which, in turn, meant that greater priority had to be attached to the targeting of new consumer groups.[68] Indeed, as the Halifax's advertising manager, Ted Cooke, stressed to the society's employees at the start of the decade: 'We cannot afford *not* to advertise. More than ever these days, with intense and increasing competition in the financial field, we dare not be smug and complacent'.[69] Full-page colour advertisements began to appear in publications such as the *Radio Times* and the *Observer* magazine, and in 1973 the Halifax started advertising in the banner space below the Royal Box at Wembley Stadium.[70]

Furthermore, it was not just the amount of money spent on advertising that increased in this period; greater attention also began to be devoted to engaging with and ascertaining the specific needs of different consumer groups. Cooke, in particular, was insistent on this point, repeatedly stressing the importance of detailed market research and of ensuring that the society was serving 'the needs of the market as they actually exist'.[71] Furthermore, branch managers were also encouraged to be more proactive in raising the profile of their branches and 'selling' the services of the society to prospective customers.[72] Professional groups and individuals who, by virtue of their profession or standing in the community, were in a position to advise and influence others on their investment strategies (notably, solicitors, bankers, accountants, estate agents and brokers) were specifically targeted, while efforts were also made to generate more business from the public authorities and armed forces. Again, from both a cultural and an organizational perspective, this increased emphasis on proactive marketing and customer relations signified a major change in attitude and priorities for the Halifax, demonstrating not only the extent to which commercial expansion was coming to be seen as a necessity for survival, but also the speed with which the society was moving away from its mutual, cooperative roots towards a more consumer-oriented footing.

Conclusion

As this chapter has emphasized, the 1970s was a decade of considerable change and upheaval for both the Halifax and the UK building society movement more generally. First, both the size of the movement and the range of services that its members provided increased substantially. As the industry leader, the Halifax was very much at the forefront of this expansion, increasing its branch network considerably and almost quadrupling its assets in the space of ten years. From a structural perspective, this rapid expansion was especially significant as it helped to establish the movement as a major player in the UK financial sector.[73] Another significant development in this period was the increasing prominence of computerized technology in the day-to-day operations of the building society movement. This not only enabled organizations like the Halifax to carry out complex financial transactions more efficiently and accurately; it also allowed for improved data collection and storage, which, in turn, made it possible to produce more accurate business forecasts.[74] Finally, accompanying (and, in some sense, facilitating) these major structural and technological changes was a more general cultural transformation within the building society movement, particularly in terms of staff attitudes, management practices and business expectations.[75] In this case of the Halifax, this was reflected most clearly in the increasing attention that came to be devoted to staff training and development, and the emergence of marketing and advertising as key aspects in corporate planning.

From a historical perspective, these organizational and structural changes are of particular significance for two main reasons. First, they reflect the extent to which profit maximization and commercial expansion began to emerge as key strategic business goals for the Halifax Building Society, and the UK building society movement as a whole, during the course of the 1970s. Such a shift in emphasis was all the more remarkable given that the UK building society industry had a reputation for being somewhat staid and conservative, and for privileging social objectives and the fostering of good relations with local communities above commercial gain.[76] Second, the fact that these organizational changes took place in the 1970s is also of particular historical significance given the extent to which previous historical accounts of the movement's commercial development and structural modernization have tended to focus on developments in the late 1980s and early 1990s. By contrast, this chapter has emphasized that, in the case of the Halifax Building Society at least, the transition towards a more market-oriented outlook, and subsequent full-scale privatization, was actually a fairly gradual and deep-rooted process that was, in many respects, founded upon the intellectual debates, organizational changes and technological innovations of the 1970s.

Matthew Hollow is a lecturer in Strategic Management at the University of York. His research focuses on three key areas: the management and mismanagement of financial institutions; the role of networks in business; and the history of financial crime and corporate wrongdoing. His work has been published in various journals, including: *Business History, Management & Organizational History, Journal of Management History, Journal of Consumer Culture* and *International Journal of Cultural Studies*.

Notes

1. Martin Boddy, *The Building Societies* (London, 1980), 79–93; J.N. Marshall et al., 'The Transformation of the British Building Society Movement: Managerial Divisions and Corporate Reorganization, 1986–1997', *Geoforum* 28(3–4) (1997): 271–88.

2. Donal McKillop and Charles Ferguson, *Building Societies: Structure, Performance and Change* (London, 1993), 213–20.

3. R. Macey and D. Wells, 'New Legislation Accelerates Change in Building Society Culture', *Management Accounting* (July/August 1987): 34–36.

4. Chris Hamnett, 'Restructuring Housing Finance and the Housing Market', in *Money, Power, Space*, ed. Stuart Corbridge, Ron Martin and Nigel Thrift (Oxford, 1994), 281–308; Michael Ball, *Under One Roof: The International Financial Revolution and Mortgage Finance* (Hemel Hempstead, 1990); Desmond King and Stewart Wood, 'The Political Economy of Neoliberalism: Britain and the United States in the 1980s', in *Continuity and Change in Contemporary Capitalism*, ed. Herbert Kitschelt et al. (Cambridge, 1999), 371–97.

5. Macey and Wells, 'New Legislation'; Mark Boleat, *The Building Society Industry*, 2nd edn (London, 1986), 198–203.

6. L. Drake, *The Building Societies in Transition* (London, 1989); McKillop and Ferguson, *Building Societies*, 12–22.

7. Herbert Ashworth, *The Building Society Story* (London, 1980), 1–3.

8. Eric Hopkins, *Working-Class Self Help in Nineteenth-Century England* (London, 1995), 16–19.

9. Ashworth, *Building Society Story*, 2.

10. In most cases, lots were drawn amongst members to decide the order in which they would each be allocated their new house (although some societies did carry out auctions to determine the allocation order instead).

11. Naturally, all the society's members (including those who had been housed early) continued to pay fees right up until the disbandment of the society.

12. Boleat, *Building Society Industry*, 1.

13. Ashworth, *Building Society Story*, 6–8.

14. McKillop and Ferguson, *Building Societies*, 6–7.

15. Ashworth, *Building Society Story*, 9–10.

16. McKillop and Ferguson, *Building Societies*, 6.

17. Ashworth, *Building Society Story*, 28–33.

18. Oscar R. Hobson, *A Hundred Years of the Halifax: The History of the Halifax Building Society, 1853–1953* (London, 1953), 11–22.

19. Sue Bamford, *The Halifax Building Society* (Hove, 1983), 29.

20. Hopkins, *Working-Class Self Help*, 20–21.

21. 'Information Card 4: The Halifax Story' (1978), Halifax Building Society (HBS) Collection, ACC.2006.3.10, Lloyds Banking Group Archives (LBGA), Edinburgh.

22. Esmond J. Cleary, *The Building Society Movement* (London, 1965), 75–99.

23. 'Information Card 4: The Halifax Story', HBS Collection.

24. Bamford, *Halifax Building Society*, 31.

25. Cleary, *Building Society Movement*, 78–80.

26. 'Information Card 4: The Halifax Story', HBS Collection.

27. Hobson, *Hundred Years*, 86–88.

28. 'Information Card 4: The Halifax Story', HBS Collection.

29. Boleat, *Building Society Industry*, 22.

30. Ibid., 11.

31. Boddy, *Building Societies*, 106–7.

32. McKillop and Ferguson, *Building Societies*, 9–10.

33. At the start of the decade, the Halifax's assets made up approximately 15 per cent of the building society movement's total. Richard Barrow, *Fifty More Years of the Halifax, 1953–2003* (Cleckheaton, 2006), 83.

34. 'Information Card 9: The Spread of Branches' (1978), HBS Collection, ACC.2006.3.10, LBGA.

35. E.N. Cooke, 'Our New Head Office', *Round the Table: The Staff Magazine of the Halifax Building Society*, Autumn 1973, 4.

36. Dennis Fisher, 'Your New Head Office', *Round the Table: The Staff Magazine of the Halifax Building Society*, September 1970, 2.

37. Bamford, *Halifax Building Society*, 34.

38. 'Information Card 6: The Head Office' (1978), HBS Collection, ACC.2006.3.10, LBGA.

39. 'Halifax Building Society 1974 Annual General Meeting', *The Times*, 21 May 1974, 23.

40. Cooke, 'Our New Head Office', 4.

41. 'The Introduction of a Regional Structure', Minutes of the Board of Directors, vol. 45 (1977), HBS Collection, ACC.45.266-8, LBGA.

42. C.J.S. Gentle, J.N. Marshall and M.G. Coombes, 'Business Reorganisation and Regional Development: The Case of the British Building Societies Movement', *Environment and Planning* 23 (1991): 1770–71.

43. Barrow, *Fifty More Years of the Halifax*, 77.

44. 'The Machine that Can Outwork an Army of Clerks', *Halifax Weekly Courier & Guardian*, 12 March 1965, 3.

45. M. Macaskill, 'Computer Progress and Plans', *Round the Table: The Staff Magazine of the Halifax Building Society*, September 1968, 5.

46. 'Computer Systems & Services' (1979), 1, HBS Collection, ACC.2003.170.4, LBGA.

47. Barrow, *Fifty More Years*, 61.

48. 'The Machine that can Outwork an Army of Clerks', 3.

49. 'Computer Systems and Services', 3–5, HBS Collection.

50. At this time, branch managers had to make direct requests for information on individual accounts to be posted out from the head office, a process that could take up to five working days. 'Computer Systems & Services', 2, HBS Collection.

51. Barrow, *Fifty More Years*, 80.

52. 'Computer Systems and Services', 3, HBS Collection.

53. W.S. Smith, 'Computer Users and Banking Services', *Business Societies Quarterly* (April 1974): 58.

54. Barrow, *Fifty More Years*, 72.

55. 'Information Card 6: The Head Office', 4, HBS Collection.

56. By 1991, the Halifax had over 1,500 ATM machines nationwide. McKillop and Ferguson, *Building Societies*, 94.

57. McKillop and Ferguson, *Building Societies*, 154–56.

58. Barrow, *Fifty More Years*, 64.

59. Bamford, *Halifax Building Society*, 11.

60. 'Computer Staff Notes', *Round the Table: The Staff Magazine of the Halifax Building Society*, August 1965, 20.

61. 'Staff Matters: Report on Training Activities,' Minutes of the Board of Directors, vol. 36 (1972), HBS Collection, ACC.2004.13.109, LBGA.

62. 'Staff Matters: Report on Training Activities', HBS Collection; Stephen W. Town, 'On Staff Recruitment', *Building Societies Quarterly* 25(99) (1971): 133–36.

63. 'Supervision and Control: A Course Summary' (1976), HBS Collection, ACC.2006.3.9, LBGA.

64. Boleat, *Building Society Industry*, 64.

65. 'Business Development for Managers' (1976), 4–7, HBS Collection, ACC.2006.3.12, LBGA; G.M. Law, 'Manpower Planning: Uses to Building Societies', *Building Societies Quarterly* 27(105) (1971): 9–13; Bernard Taylor, 'Corporate Planning: Its Concept and Use', *Building Societies Quarterly* 27(105) (1971): 21–24.

66. 'Supervision and Control', 4–5, HBS Collection.

67. Ted Cooke, 'Marketing the Building Society Service' (1978), 8, HBS Collection, ACC.2006.3.11, LBGA.

68. Deryk V. Weyer, 'The Marketing of Financial Services', *Building Societies Quarterly* 27(106) (1973): 87–89.

69. Ted Cooke, 'Why Advertise?', *Round the Table: The Staff Magazine of the Halifax Building Society*, January 1973, 3.

70. Ibid., 2.

71. Cooke, 'Marketing the Building Society Service', 12, HBS Collection.

72. 'Business Development for Managers', 6–9, HBS Collection.

73. Ashworth, *Building Society Story*, 227–41.

74. Roberta Capello, John Taylor and Howard Williams, 'Computer Networks and Competitive Advantage in Building Societies', *International Journal of Information Management* 10 (1990): 54–56.

75. Joseph Nellis and Terry Lockhart, 'The Impact of Deregulation on the UK Building Society Branch Network in the 1990s', *International Journal of Bank Marketing* 13(4) (1995): 7–8.

76. Ibid., 8.

Bibliography

Ashworth, Herbert, *The Building Society Story* (London, 1980).

Ball, Michael, *Under One Roof: The International Financial Revolution and Mortgage Finance* (Hemel Hempstead, 1990).

Bamford, Sue, *The Halifax Building Society* (Hove, 1983).

Barrow, Richard, *Fifty More Years of the Halifax, 1953–2003* (Cleckheaton, 2006).

Boddy, Martin, *The Building Societies* (London, 1980)

Boleat, Mark, *The Building Society Industry*, 2nd edn (London, 1986), 198–203.

Capello, Roberta, John Taylor and Howard Williams, 'Computer Networks and Competitive Advantage in Building Societies', *International Journal of Information Management* 10 (1990): 54–56.

Cleary, Esmond J., *The Building Society Movement* (London, 1965).

Drake, L., *The Building Societies in Transition* (London, 1989).

Gentle, C.J.S., J.N. Marshall and M.G. Coombes, 'Business Reorganisation and Regional Development: The Case of the British Building Societies Movement', *Environment and Planning* 23 (1991): 1770–71.

Hamnett, Chris, 'Restructuring Housing Finance and the Housing Market', in *Money, Power, Space*, ed. Stuart Corbridge, Ron Martin and Nigel Thrift (Oxford, 1994), 281–308.

Hobson, Oscar R., *A Hundred Years of the Halifax: The History of the Halifax Building Society, 1853–1953* (London, 1953).

Hopkins, Eric, *Working-Class Self Help in Nineteenth-Century England* (London, 1995).

King, Desmond, and Stewart Wood, 'The Political Economy of Neoliberalism: Britain and the United States in the 1980s', in *Continuity and Change in Contemporary Capitalism*, ed. Herbert Kitschelt et al. (Cambridge, 1999), 371–97.

Macey, R., and D. Wells, 'New Legislation Accelerates Change in Building Society Culture', *Management Accounting* (July/August 1987): 34–36.

Marshall, J.N., et al., 'The Transformation of the British Building Society Movement: Managerial Divisions and Corporate Reorganization, 1986–1997', *Geoforum* 28(3–4) (1997): 271–88.

McKillop, Donal, and Charles Ferguson, *Building Societies: Structure, Performance and Change* (London, 1993).

Nellis, Joseph, and Terry Lockhart, 'The Impact of Deregulation on the UK Building Society Branch Network in the 1990s', *International Journal of Bank Marketing* 13(4) (1995): 7–8.

Index

MAKING SENSE OF HISTORY
Studies in Historical Cultures
General Editor: Stefan Berger
Founding Editor: Jörn Rüsen

Bridging the gap between historical theory and the study of historical memory, this series crosses the boundaries between both academic disciplines and cultural, social, political and historical contexts. In an age of rapid globalization, which tends to manifest itself on an economic and political level, locating the cultural practices involved in generating its underlying historical sense is an increasingly urgent task.